Whitman & Dickinson

THE IOWA WHITMAN SERIES | Ed Folsom, *series editor*

Whitman & Dickinson

A Colloquy

EDITED BY

Éric Athenot and Cristanne Miller

UNIVERSITY OF IOWA PRESS | IOWA CITY

University of Iowa Press, Iowa City 52242
Copyright © 2017 by the University of Iowa Press
www.uipress.uiowa.edu
Printed in the United States of America
Design by Sara T. Sauers

The University of Iowa Press is a member of Green Press
Initiative and is committed to preserving natural resources.
Printed on acid-free paper

Library of Congress Cataloging-in-Publication Data
Names: Athenot, Éric, editor. | Miller, Cristanne, editor.
Title: Whitman & Dickinson : a colloquy / edited by Éric
Athenot and Cristanne Miller.
Other titles: Whitman and Dickinson
Description: Iowa City : University of Iowa Press, [2018] |
Series: The Iowa Whitman series | Includes index.
Identifiers: LCCN 2017010803 | ISBN 978-1-60938-531-6
(paperback : acid-free paper) | ISBN 978-1-60938-532-3 (e-book)
Subjects: LCSH: Whitman, Walt, 1819-1892—Criticism and
interpretation. | Dickinson, Emily, 1830-1886—Criticism and
interpretation. | American poetry—19th century—History and
criticism. | BISAC: LITERARY CRITICISM / American / General.
Classification: LCC PS3238 .W4 2018 | DDC 811/.3—dc23
LC record available at https://lccn.loc.gov/2017010803

Contents

Acknowledgments and Abbreviations

OUR INITIAL TRANSATLANTIC ENCOUNTER WAS ENABLED BY A
Fulbright Foundation fellowship that appointed Cristanne Miller as the
Tocqueville Distinguished Chair at University of Paris 7, Diderot, under the
sponsorship of Professor Antoine Cazé. We would therefore like to begin
by thanking the Fulbright Foundation (in particular, the Franco-American
Fulbright Commission), the University of Paris, Diderot, and Antoine Cazé.
The conference "colloquy" was hosted by the Université Paris-Est Créteil,
to which we are deeply grateful for enabling us to gather a prestigious and
lively group of North American and European scholars—including many
who are not represented here. We thank all participants in the conference
for their stimulating presentations and astutely challenging conversation.
The University Paris-Est Créteil "colloquy" was primarily organized by
Éric Athenot—who deserves special mention for this labor. We would also
like to thank IMAGER (Institut des Mondes Anglophone, Germanique et
Roman) at the University Paris-Est Créteil for co-funding the conference.
Additionally, Cristanne Miller is grateful to the American Council of
Learned Societies for fellowship support during the period of the conference
and the initial work preparing this volume, and to the State University of
New York at Buffalo for its ongoing support of her research. Although we
regard our use of all Dickinson and Whitman texts in this edition as falling
under the category of fair use (and many of the primary texts are already in
the public domain), we would also like to thank the editors of the online
Emily Dickinson and Walt Whitman archives for making manuscripts and

editions of these poets' poems so broadly and simply available to all scholars. Throughout this book we refer to either of two editions for both Dickinson's and Whitman's poems. For Dickinson, contributors refer either to Miller's *Emily Dickinson's Poems: As She Preserved Them*—published in 2016, a full year after the conference initiating this volume (and using poem numbers assigned by R. W. Franklin, parenthetically)—or to Franklin's *The Poems of Emily Dickinson* (1998). All references to Dickinson's letters are to Thomas H. Johnson's and Theodora Ward's *The Letters of Emily Dickinson* (1958), and are referred to by the letter number assigned and preceded by *L*. For Whitman, contributors refer to Justin Kaplan's 1986 edition of *Whitman: Poetry and Prose* and, for specific editions of *Leaves of Grass* not included in Kaplan's Library of America edition, to the *Walt Whitman Archive*, edited by Ed Folsom and Kenneth M. Price. References to other Dickinson or Whitman editions and texts occur in some essays, as appropriate for the particular work of that essay. Abbreviations for this volume's standard references are consistent throughout the volume, as indicated below.

EDP   *Emily Dickinson's Poems: As She Preserved Them*. Ed. Cristanne Miller. Cambridge, MA: Harvard University, Belknap Press, 2016.

L   *The Letters of Emily Dickinson*. Ed. Thomas H. Johnson and Theodora Ward. Cambridge, MA: Harvard University, Belknap Press, 1958.

Fr   *The Poems of Emily Dickinson*. Ed. Ralph W. Franklin. 3 vols. Cambridge, MA: Harvard University, Belknap Press, 1998.

WPP   *Whitman: Poetry and Prose*. 1982. Ed. Justin Kaplan. Revised and expanded edition. New York: Library of America, 1986.

WPP 1855   *Whitman: Poetry and Prose*. 1986. The 1855 edition of *Leaves of Grass*.

WWA   *Walt Whitman Archive*. Ed. Ed Folsom and Kenneth M. Price. http://www.whitmanarchive.org/.

Introduction: Transatlantic Convergences and New Directions

ÉRIC ATHENOT AND CRISTANNE MILLER

IN 2015 IT HAD BEEN 150 YEARS SINCE BOTH WALT WHITMAN AND Emily Dickinson had produced the better part of their poetic output. This collection of essays stems from a "colloquy" that brought scholars together to discuss these poets explicitly in relation to each other for the first time in all those 150 years. As any bibliographical search will confirm, Whitman and Dickinson have frequently inspired fruitful and exciting scholarship when analyzed comparatively—as they have been in several essays, especially from the 1960s on. Naturally, they also have figured alongside each other in nineteenth-century U.S. literature survey courses around the world. Yet, apart from Agnieszka Salska's *Whitman and Dickinson: Poetry of the Central Consciousness* (1985) and Christine Gerhardt's *A Place for Humility: Whitman, Dickinson, and the Natural World* (2014), books solely devoted to examining the works of these two poets in relation to each other have been notably absent.[1] Similarly, to our knowledge, there has been no conference dedicated equally to both poets until our "colloquy" in March 2015. This collection brings together original essays by European and North American scholars directly linking the work of Whitman and Dickinson in exciting ways across several fields of study. These essays reexamine well-established topics in new perspectives, open new areas of investigation, and provide new information about the intersections of Whitman's and Dickinson's lives, work, and reception.

 Whitman & Dickinson: A Colloquy will, we hope, prove to be a crucial resource for teachers of American poetry, scholars of both Whitman and Dickinson, and more generally scholars of nineteenth-century American poetry and culture. This book profoundly ponders these extraordinary poets' writing within discussions of mentorship, religion, the Civil War, philosophy, the environment, humor, poetic structures of language, and their twentieth- and twenty-first-century reception. Moreover, we hope this book will spur continuing exploration and research on topics bringing both these poets and the critics of these poets into ongoing dialogue.

The transatlantic basis of this collection is no more incidental than its broad range of topics. The historical lack of book-length considerations of the two poets together would seem to confirm the all-too-frequent acceptance by academics around the world that either the poets' differences are unbridgeable, or that Whitman and Dickinson criticism has become so polarized that it discourages all not equally versed in the poetry and criticism of both poets from entering the field. Judging only from the forms of the poems and limiting one's attention to their subject matter, one might be forgiven for thinking that these poets share no more than a vague geographical and chronological proximity—and even there one could argue that, in the nineteenth century, New York and Massachusetts were culturally worlds apart, and that Whitman's birth in 1819 made him a different generation from Dickinson, who was born in 1830. It was Dickinson herself, after all, who, in her famous disparaging comment to Thomas Wentworth Higginson —"You speak of Mr Whitman – I never read his Book – but was told that he was disgraceful"—first suggested such a separation.[2] Yet the rich intersection of interests, concerns, and radical reconceptions of poetic form, political positions, and even figures of grammar as analyzed here demonstrates how much remains to be discovered and gained by bringing these two poets into direct conversation with each other in their and our times. The discoveries of this volume were first shared in an international "colloquy" in Créteil, a few minutes outside Paris, in 2015—a place and a moment when the necessity to step outside one's established comfort zones, and to cherish international community, was being felt with particular intensity.

In 2015, when France faced brutally tragic social, political, and cultural challenges, holding "Walt Whitman and Emily Dickinson: A Colloquy" in a university located in an ethnically diverse suburb outside Paris was a reassertion of the lasting power of poetry in times of unrest and disarray, and of poetry's unparalleled ability both to bring solace and instill courage.[3]

"Resist much, obey little," Whitman cautioned the divided United States in 1860.[4] Once the Civil War was well underway, Dickinson asserted that "To be alive – is Power" (*EDP* 398, Fr 876). It may come as a surprise that such an important conference was held in a small French suburban university rather than at a prestigious American institution. The idea for this conference was developed in true transatlantic fashion by a French Whitman scholar and translator and an American Dickinson scholar and editor in Paris as part of their colloquy, and the conference setting encouraged both ongoing international and political elements of exchange. Evidence that Whitman and Dickinson themselves favored the inclusion of many voices and heteroglossia over strict monolingualism comes from both the general manner and extent of their writing and from their frequent use of cosmopolitan idiom and foreign words and place names. The analysis of such heterogloassia could fill many pages—as might each poet's relation to the French language in particular. The subtitle of the 2015 Créteil conference and of this volume, "A Colloquy," puns on the French word *colloque* (conference), driving home the association between this conversation about these two poetic giants and its location in a French town rich in cultures and idioms from many parts of the world. Such cultural diversity, involving different academic traditions, resonates in the various critical approaches and multivoiced conversation that is carried out in the following pages and that we hope will be continued outside these pages.

Although the essays collected here began as presentations at "Walt Whitman and Emily Dickinson: A Colloquy," each has been extended and revised for this volume.[5] They are attuned to differences and intersections of language, poetic form, syntax, beliefs, and ideas across cultures and time, and they stem from a range of authors, including both those with long experience teaching or writing on both poets and relative newcomers to the field. The essays also range from discussions of the poets in relation to rich nineteenth-century biographical, cultural, or intellectual contexts; to precise analyses of the two poets' language; to reflections on their legacies among twentieth- and twenty-first-century critics and poets.

In "Rethinking the (Non)Convergence of Dickinson and Whitman: The Origins of American Poetry as We Know It," Ed Folsom ponders the importance of two mentors to these poets—Ralph Waldo Emerson and

Thomas Wentworth Higginson—and presents both new information and penetrating speculation about ways these poets would or might have encountered each other in print in the 1860s and 1880s. Among other possibilities of convergence, Folsom documents that Whitman was invited to publish in *A Masque of Poets*, the collection of anonymous poems in which a Dickinson poem first appeared in a book; Whitman declined the invitation. Folsom also explores ways that the two poets both learned from and resisted their respective mentors.

In "'Sickly Abstractions' and the Poetic Concrete: Whitman's and Dickinson's Battlefields of War," Cécile Roudeau focuses on Whitman's and Dickinson's responses to the Civil War. Looking at modes of definition and naming, Roudeau parses the ways that "civil war . . . is not so much a stable concept as a deictic pointing in two directions—toward the object it waveringly designates and the situation of the subject speaker who uses it"; both poets, she argues, conceive of the war's related abstractions, such as "nation" or "liberty," in similarly unstable ways. "In wartime," Roudeau writes, "poetry was forced to its crisis as language was brought face to face with the prospect of its concrete undoing; language itself was unsettled when exposed to the Real that is beyond formalization."

Shira Wolosky's "Dickinson/Whitman: Figural Mirrors in Biblical Traditions" continues this attention to the Civil War through a focus on the way these poets shared a differently inflected foundation in biblical typology and also on how each illuminates an increased sense of the other's complexities. Read together, Whitman appears more interestingly figural and Dickinson more culturally engaged than is often recognized. Using the Civil War as a background for her exploration, Wolosky demonstrates ways that generations of critics have flattened or overlooked elements in both poets' writing.

Jennifer Leader extends Wolosky's concerns with biblical typology and religious crisis. In "'No Man Saw Awe' / 'In the Talk of . . . God . . . He Is Silent': (Not) Seeing and (Not) Saying the Numinous in Dickinson and Whitman," Leader explores ways that each poet conceives of poetry, and of the poet, in relation to the divine. In particular, both poets repeatedly render moments of contact with a wholly irreducible Other in ways that religious scholars identify as constructions of the numinous, or presence of divinity. Whitman's encounters with silence and Dickinson's encounters with facelessness lead them to understand the poet as an intermediary between the known world and mystery, circumference, or other manifestations of the nondenominational sacred.

Marianne Noble's "Phenomenological Approaches to Human Contact in Whitman and Dickinson" instead focuses on ways that both poets anticipate twentieth-century phenomenological philosophers in their understanding of the importance of physical contact and in their resistance to the powerful Emersonian articulation of a yearning for human contact that transcends individuality. Instead, Whitman and Dickinson more often indicate that such an ideal is both impossible and undesirable. Like Leader, Noble stresses the extent to which Whitman and Dickinson find the divine or spiritual in the material: as she puts it, "Both poets observe that the real necessarily includes the bodies and materials through which spirit has its only being. . . . [They] explore the idea that the self does not antedate the act of writing but instead is created in it," and that through the intersubjectivity of non-transcendent selves, selves that exist only in relation to others, comes the possibility for genuine human contact.

Christine Gerhardt's essay, "'We Must Travel Abreast with Nature, if We Want to Understand Her': Place and Mobility in Dickinson's and Whitman's Environmental Poetry," looks at nineteenth-century understandings of the environment through the context of contemporary ecocritical readings of these poets. In contrast to green readings of Whitman and Dickinson as place-oriented with emphasis on particular localities, Gerhardt demonstrates that both poets also engage with environments and creatures that are restless, mobile, on the move. They were as interested in dynamic human and nonhuman environments and relationships as in the characteristics of the local. Moreover, Gerhardt finds that issues of environmental mobility in Whitman and Dickinson "include intersections between race and ethnicity and mobile perspectives of the larger-than-human world, and explorations of collective rather than individual movements, such as westward expansion and colonial explorations."

The last of the essays in this volume that is grounded in nineteenth-century culture is Andrew Dorkin and Cristanne Miller's "Hyperbole and Humor in Whitman and Dickinson," which moves quickly beyond obviously comic elements of exaggeration in these poets' work to explore ways that each uses hyperbole to disorient and then radically reorient the reader in relation to scales of value and modes of cognition. Both comparing Whitman's and Dickinson's humorous modes to contemporary comic writing and turning to twenty-first-century scholarship on hyperbole, Dorkin and Miller argue that for both poets "humor was not a genre or style of writing but an integral part of thought and experience, of the life of language, and of the world," and that hyperbole is a figure used both as a tool of humor and to extend other features of their work that defamiliarize and disorient readers in making them think again.

Betsy Erkkila's "Radical Imaginaries: Crossing Over with Whitman and Dickinson" adopts an occasionally playful manner to rehearse the multiple fields in which these poets may be seen both as radically different from each other and as intersecting in their engagements with cultural frames often misleadingly separated as public and private. Erkkila reads Whitman and Dickinson "as poets whose unsettled and unsettling *interiors* existed *inside* rather than *outside* the political and social struggles of their times," thereby eschewing categories that have restricted understandings of their work in the past.

In "Queer Contingencies of Canonicity: Dickinson, Whitman, Jewett, Matthiessen," Jay Grossman also begins with a kind of radical imagining—in part picking up on Ed Folsom's question of contingencies that might have changed what Folsom calls "the Origins of American Poetry as We Know It." Grossman unearths significant reflections that F. O. Matthiessen makes on Dickinson's poetry, arguing that these passages suggest that Dickinson might have been an even more important precursor poet, or at least post-Emersonian poet, than Whitman for this twentieth-century canon-maker. Although Whitman is unquestionably the crucial figure moving from an Emersonian philosophy and poetics into modernism in Matthiessen's *American Renaissance*, Grossman argues that Matthiessen's praise of Dickinson (in relation to Sarah Orne Jewett and to Emerson) suggests that he was more open to female literary genius, to Dickinson's particular achievements, and even to what her life might have to say to him personally than we have known.

Grossman ends his essay by turning to one of Matthiessen's most famous students, Adrienne Rich. The final two essays of this volume turn distinctly to mid- and late-twentieth-century poets in relation to Dickinson. Vincent Dussol explores "Whitman, Dickinson, and Their Legacy of Lists and 'It's'" to argue that characteristic language features of both poets' work are shared more than has been acknowledged and have become touchstones for the work of late twentieth-century and twenty-first-century avant-garde poets in the United States and France. Whitman is well known for his poetic catalogs, and Dickinson for her indeterminate and fluid deployment of the indefinite pronoun "it." Dickinson, however, is also a poet of lists (a figure Dussol associates with epic poetry), and Whitman sometimes uses "it" in ways almost as open and undecidable as Dickinson. Other poets Dussol traces in this "heritage" range from the French rock group Christine and the Queens to H. D., Wallace Stevens, Rachel Blau DuPlessis, Lew Welch, Ann Lauterbach, Trace Peterson, and Sam Truitt.

Marina Camboni, in contrast, focuses on ways that Adrienne Rich understands the transhistorical possibilities developed by Whitman and Dickinson as "the space of the world, and not only inherently American but inherently life-saving, political, and hence human." Tracing the different paths Dickinson and Whitman provide Rich in her own life journey of poetic aspiration and politics, Camboni concludes that for Rich (as, implicitly, for Whitman and Dickinson) the "beginner" is the one who "through his/her body of work begins a truth procedure" and thereby ushers in the possibility of reorienting historical/cultural time and space. Such poetry is always in the process of beginning.

This volume, we hope, will also constitute a new "beginning" of conversation about the potential and real convergences of these two extraordinarily innovative and influential poets, leading to new international colloquies about traditions and developments in contemporary poetry. Among other results, these essays indicate to us both that Whitman and Dickinson are still very much at the forefront of conversations about poetry and that much remains to be explored, discovered, and shared.

ÉRIC ATHENOT AND CRISTANNE MILLER

IMAGER (Institut des Mondes Anglophone, Germanique
et Roman) at the University Paris-Est Créteil, France
University at Buffalo, State University of New York, U.S.A.

Rethinking the (Non)Convergence of Dickinson and Whitman

The Origins of American Poetry as We Know It

ED FOLSOM

WE ARE NOW AT THE END OF A FULL CENTURY, IN THE CASE OF Walt Whitman, and well over a half century, in the case of Emily Dickinson, of serious critical investigation of the two poets that virtually everyone now agrees mark the beginnings of a unique American poetic tradition—a dynamic, two-pronged tradition of radical innovation. American poetry, as we conceive of it today, truly is the product of an unbelievable convergence— two contemporaneous poets, one female, one male, one a New Englander to the core, one a New Yorker through and through, both working to name an intense new affectional relationship with same-sex companions, both living outside the conventions and institutions of marriage and parenting yet endlessly fascinated by them, both testing new and innovative (yet dramatically different) forms of poetic expression, both intensely local and yet wildly cosmopolitan. I want to think a bit more about why and how this convergence occurred, and why it happened in such a way that may help explain the odd barriers most of us still feel between the critical worlds of Dickinson studies and Whitman studies, even for those of us who have written about and taught both poets. If these two poets magically converged to create a distinctive American poetic tradition, they did so in such a way that they seemed oblivious to each other, enacting a weird non-convergence at the very originary heart of our poetry.

My thinking on this began when I was asked to write the essay on "Transcendental Poetics" for *The Oxford Handbook on Transcendentalism*. In tracking the now nearly forgotten category of Transcendental poetry, I began to discern a tension that, when teased out, might offer a kind of historical explanation as to why the American poetic tradition generated—and eventually was generated by—the amazing convergence and *di*vergence of Dickinson and Whitman.[1]

I'm struck, when I look at an 1870 anthology of American poetry like William Michael Rossetti's *American Poems*, how in many ways it doesn't project an American poetry all that different from what we have today, one that begins with Bradstreet, gives significant space to Bryant and Emerson, offers up Whittier and Poe and Lowell, and devotes the greatest attention to Whitman.[2] What *is* different is the absence, of course, of Dickinson, and the inclusion of many poets who have vanished from our poetic history. But clearly the effort and aim for Christina Rossetti's brother is to find a tradition of women poets in America. After Bradstreet, Rossetti includes sixteen women poets (including Caroline Gilman, Margaret Fuller, Harriet Beecher Stowe, Frances Sargent Osgood, Anne Charlotte Lynch, Maria Lowell, Alice Carey, Phoebe Carey, Adah Isaacs Menken, Elizabeth Ellet, Sarah Helen Whitman, Elizabeth Oakes Smith, Emily Judson, Sarah J. Clarke, Alice Bradley Neal), and he devotes nearly twenty pages to Lucy Larcom, who seems to be the closest thing he can find as a substitute for the Dickinson figure he yearned for but had yet to discover, someone who could rival the power and originality of Whitman, who occupies nearly ninety pages of this anthology, far more than any other poet.

The strange—*very* strange—thing about our current sense of the American poetic tradition, then, is this tense pairing of Whitman and Dickinson, absent in the nineteenth century and only gradually apparent in the twentieth, and not taking a firm hold until the 1950s, when Dickinson's poetry seemed to fully emerge in the Thomas Johnson edition, finally allowing what Adrienne Rich has memorably called this "strange, uncoupled couple, . . . a wild woman and a wild man" who formed the genesis of our national poetic arc:

Both took on North America as extremists. She, from her vantage point: female, New England, eccentric within her world, not the spinster servicing the community, but a violently ambitious spirit married to the privacy of her art. He from his vantage point: male within a spectrum that required some males to be, like Dickinson's father, stiff-collared wardens of society, while allowing others to hanker, ramble on open roads.

Whatever braids we now make of the American poetic tradition, there are virtually always two main strands—"reclusive, compressed Emily and all-hailing, instinctual Walt"—that get woven in.[3]

It's oddly easier, I think, to trace the braiding from Whitman and Dickinson forward to the poets of the twentieth and twenty-first centuries than it is to braid the wild couple into their own poetic time. That's why I've become fascinated with the ways that two important Transcendental writers, Ralph Waldo Emerson and Thomas Wentworth Higginson, in fact form what is otherwise a missing link between Whitman and Dickinson, and each one's endorsement of one of these two great innovative poets of the nineteenth century initiates something of a struggle over which of the "strange, uncoupled couple" would ultimately be sanctioned to transmit Transcendental poetry and Transcendental values into the twentieth century. Emerson and Higginson—Waldo and Wentworth, as they were known to their friends—were two of the most formidable of the first two generations of American Transcendentalists. Both wrote a substantial amount of poetry, but both—like most Transcendental poets—were much better known for their essays. Like Emerson, Higginson wrote an influential essay about poetry and the future of poetry in America ("Letter to a Young Contributor"),[4] an essay that had as direct and powerful an impact on Dickinson as Emerson's "The Poet" had on Whitman. These essays separately inspired and helped form Whitman and Dickinson as poets and prompted each of them, at early stages of their careers, to send his or her poems to one of these towering Transcendentalists. Emerson and Higginson both recognized the power and innovation in the poetry of the then-unknown poet that found its way into their hands, but both were also nonplussed by it, unsure just what it was they were reading, uncertain in fact whether they were encountering something that would redefine poetry as they knew it or whether they were confronting promising half-formed work that called out for their critical shaping in order for it to become viable as the new American poetry for which both Transcendentalists were on the lookout. They expressed their initial dazed reactions to the poetry of their unsolicited protégés in remarkably similar fashion: Emerson, upon getting his copy of *Leaves of Grass*, said "I rubbed my eyes a little to see if this sunbeam were no illusion; but the solid sense of the book is a sober certainty,"[5] while Higginson, receiving a handful of poems from Dickinson, put it this way: "The bee himself did not evade the schoolboy more than she evaded me, and even at this day I still stand somewhat bewildered, like the boy."[6] Ultimately, each of these men would come to be associated with the discovery and distribution of one of the two now-recognized founders of a distinctive American poetry. The real flowering of American Transcendental poetry came, then, not with poetry written by Transcendentalists but rather with poetry recognized and nurtured by Transcendentalists.[7]

It is important to realize the analogous ways that Whitman and Dickinson came into the American canon, how these very different, equally radical poetic voices were nurtured by Transcendentalists who were equally intrigued and befuddled by them. These two foundational American voices struck the Transcendentalists as, at once, consonant with Transcendentalism and yet oddly anti-Transcendental. And it is important to realize how a tension within Transcendental poetry itself may well have produced the "strange uncoupled couple" who form the genesis of our national poetic tradition.

Emerson, of course, famously responded to Whitman's unsolicited poems in 1855, finding "incomparable things said incomparably well."[8] Higginson's initial response to Dickinson has been lost, though he later would recall how "the impression of a wholly new and original poetic genius was as distinct on my mind at the first reading of these . . . poems as it is now."[9] Both Transcendentalist mentors ended up with their names on the covers or title pages of their protégé's poetry. When Dickinson's poems first appeared as a printed book, they appeared with Higginson's name on the title page as editor and with the evidence of what Dickinson called his "surgery" all over them, from the categories he created to arrange her poems in safe Transcendental thematic clusters, to the titles he furnished for her untitled poems, to the corrected punctuation and occasionally corrected rhyme. Emerson's name appeared on the spine of Whitman's second edition of *Leaves of Grass*, in what may be the first book-cover blurb in American literary history, as Whitman, without permission, brazenly emblazoned Emerson's words from his private letter to the poet: "I greet you at the beginning of a great career. R. W. Emerson." Higginson, at least in his own mind, was able to deter Dickinson from publishing until after her death when he could try (with Mabel Loomis Todd as his accomplice) to have his way with her poetry;[10] Emerson was not so fortunate, trying to persuade Whitman to remove the sexually explicit poems from his 1860 *Leaves*, only to be rebuffed by the poet, who was then in the process of publishing his much-expanded book in Boston with young publishers who were Emerson's friends. Emerson along with several other Transcendental poets—like Henry David Thoreau and Bronson Alcott—were fascinated with Whitman's poetry and tried to salvage his book as a Transcendental text. Higginson along with a number of other Transcendental poets—like his own brother-in-law Ellery Channing—were appalled at Emerson's endorsement of *Leaves* and did their best to distance Whitman's book from Transcendentalism. Then, soon after Emerson's attempts to restrain Whitman failed, Higginson discovered in Dickinson another radical new poetic voice, and he would hold this new find in reserve until after Emerson's and just before Whitman's death, and then release her on the nation as its new poetic voice, once he had massaged her poetry into more conventional form. Meanwhile he continued to do all he could to undermine Whitman's claim—once endorsed by Emerson—to be seriously considered as not just a poet but as America's poet.

Higginson's support of Dickinson makes perfect sense, given his strong devotion both to decorum and to women's rights. His earliest squabble with Emerson, in fact, came in 1849 over the rights of women, when the matter of women's eligibility for membership in the Town and Country Club—a short-lived Transcendentalist-friendly club organized by Emerson, with Bronson Alcott as its ongoing secretary—became a matter of contention among the membership. After Higginson had insisted on bylaws specifying that "men and women" would be eligible to join, Emerson let Higginson know that his insistence on women members could be "quite fatal to the existence of our cherished club."[11] Emerson was certainly a supporter of women's rights, but his position on women's place in society was nuanced, complex, and shifting, while Higginson was from the beginning an enthusiastic and active supporter of women's political and artistic rights. For Higginson, a woman stood at the very origins of poetry—Sappho, about whom he wrote with passion and insight, and whose ancient school he compared favorably with Margaret Fuller and her classes for women.[12] While Emerson nurtured a long line of younger male poets (including Ellery Channing, Alcott, Thoreau, and Jones Very) culminating in Whitman,[13] Higginson supported just as long a line of women poets (including Harriet Prescott Spofford, Rose Terry, and Helen Hunt Jackson) culminating in Dickinson. (These culminations are what we see from our vantage point in our literary history, of course, not what Emerson and Higginson, who both regularly lost their enthusiasm for their poetic protégés, saw; and I don't want to be categorical in the judgments on Emerson and Higginson—they did share a mutual lifelong enthusiasm for Fuller, and Higginson did support some male poets, and Emerson other females beside Fuller, like Ellen Sturgis Hooper, but their gender preferences in poetry were nevertheless markedly different.)

In "Transcendental Poetics," I track in detail the Emerson-Higginson tension starting from Emerson's rejection of a Higginson poem in *The Dial* in 1843 right on through to the ends of these two men's lives. Higginson never got over that first rejection, and he never forgot Emerson's odd dismissal of women, and that has a lot to do with how American poetic history developed. But I don't want to rehash that argument now. What I want to suggest instead is one way that putting this Emerson-Higginson dynamic into play might highlight some new and very productive intersections between Whitman and Dickinson, illuminating some surprisingly early manifestations of Whitman and Dickinson crossing publishing paths.

We tend to think of Whitman having two serendipitous relationships with major Boston publishers—Thayer and Eldridge for the 1860 *Leaves of Grass* and James Osgood for the 1881—but in fact he had a third book published by a major Boston publisher. In 1871, precisely halfway between the publications by the other two Boston publishers, Whitman published a small book, *After All, Not to Create Only*, with Roberts Brothers, the eventual publishers of Dickinson's *Poems*.[14] This book reprinted the poem Whitman eventually named "Song of the Exposition," commissioned by the American Institute to be read at the opening of its fortieth Annual Exhibition in New York in September 1871. The book has usually been ignored in Whitman criticism. This conjoining of Whitman with the publisher of Louisa May

Alcott's extremely successful *Little Women* came about via the intervention of Alcott's father, Bronson, one of Emerson's chief protégés and one of his earliest emissaries to visit Whitman.[15] Alcott steered Thomas Niles, Roberts Brothers' remarkable editor, to the still controversial Whitman[16] at a time when Whitman—having just published *Leaves of Grass, Passage to India*, and *Democratic Vistas* in a matching set with the newly resurgent J. S. Redfield, before Redfield's publishing company abruptly went belly-up—was announcing that he was now done with *Leaves of Grass* and would be working toward a new book that "Passage to India" was but the first step toward.[17] With his new publisher Redfield already out of commission, and with a growing set of problems with the men he hired to distribute his books,[18] the overture from the respected and established Roberts Brothers seemed a kind of salvation. Just as he had done with Thayer and Eldridge in 1860 and would do with James Osgood in 1881, Whitman intervened with the publisher to give precise instructions about how he wanted the type set in *After All*, what kind of paper to use in it, and how the cover should be designed.[19] His new attachment to Roberts Brothers in 1871, then, presaged a longer relationship with the publisher that never materialized. The Roberts Brothers episode thus fades out of Whitman criticism as a passing and minor occurrence, though in fact Roberts Brothers remained a presence in Whitman's life to the end, contributing generously to the various fund drives on the poet's behalf, and Whitman maintained a special fondness for *After All*, which he loved as a piece of bookmaking art whose design he had overseen.[20]

Roberts Brothers and Thomas Niles have, on the other hand, been central players in the Dickinson story.[21] Not only was Roberts Brothers the publisher of the 1890 *Poems*, but Niles, just five years after publishing Whitman's book, began his famous "No Name Series," an idea that had appeal to the publicity-shy Dickinson. These No Name books were published anonymously in order to free the writers from unwanted publicity, to allow them to write in fresh and unfettered ways, and to emphasize that the quality of the work and not the author's reputation was the important thing in judging a literary work and was ultimately necessary for a truly democratic literature, where value would be shorn from the hierarchies of reputation.[22] Finally, Roberts Brothers wanted to and succeeded in creating interest by generating a kind of national guessing game about who wrote what. The No Name Series began in 1876 and lasted (through three series and thirty-seven books) over a decade (Kilgour, *Messrs. Roberts Brothers*, 172, 188, 190). Helen Hunt Jackson, Higginson's protégé, kicked off the series with *Mercy Philbrick's Choice*, and it was through her intervention that we come tantalizingly close to Dickinson's poems actually being published in a book during her lifetime. Jackson introduced Niles to Dickinson's poetry; he was impressed and carried on an amazing correspondence with Dickinson in the late 1870s and early 1880s, in which he offered at least twice to publish a "collection of your poems, that is, if you want to give them to the world through the medium of a publisher."[23] The fact that Niles could offer the "No Name" series as an inducement couldn't have hurt: if ever there was an author made for publishing in the anonymous list, it was Dickinson, and the No Name list was dominated by women writers, including Jackson and Alcott. Jackson enticed Dickinson with the "No Name" lure, arguing that Emily's main objection to publishing was obviated by Niles's innovation.[24]

And so we have a feasible scenario: had Whitman stayed with his plan of abandoning *Leaves* and going in a different direction signaled by his 1871 Roberts Brothers publication, and had he thus stayed with the new publisher, and had Dickinson followed through on Niles's offer, we can suddenly glimpse an alternative universe, where, thanks to the Emerson forces and the Higginson forces converging simultaneously on Thomas Niles and Roberts Brothers, we would, around 1880, have had two books of poetry from the same publisher—one by Dickinson, one by Whitman—and, with such a firm originary moment, the history of American poetry would today feel quite different.[25]

As it is, as far as significance for Whitman or Dickinson studies, only one of the No Name volumes is of interest, a gathering of poems called *A Masque of Poets*, which became Dickinson's only book publication of a poem during her lifetime. Niles reported to Dickinson that the most common guess for the authorship of her contribution, "Success is counted sweetest," was Emerson.[26] Dickinson scholars know all about her publication in this odd collection, edited by a young writer named George Parsons Lathrop, husband of Nathaniel Hawthorne's daughter, associate editor of the *Atlantic*, and author of a novel in the No Name series.[27]

What is not so well known, however, is that Lathrop, who at Helen

Hunt's urging first put Dickinson into a book, was himself quite a fan of Walt Whitman, visiting him a couple of times, arranging for him to lecture in Boston, and corresponding with him. In 1877 he wrote to the nature writer John Burroughs—Whitman's friend and disciple—to share with him his newfound love of Whitman:

> Ever since I first gained some fragmentary knowledge of him thro' the pruned and lopped English edition [William Michael Rossetti's 1867 *Poems by Walt Whitman*], I have not for a moment flagged in the belief that he is our greatest poet, altogether, and beyond any measurement. He threw open a wide gate for me, and I passed through it gladly—thinking to be able in my separate way to make a kind of companionship with him.

Lathrop goes on to tell Burroughs how odd it seems for him to be so enthusiastic about Whitman while being embedded in the conventional New England literary culture:

> But my circumstances have been strangely hampering. I find myself in the midst of the camp which adheres to the old and the conventional. I am an accepted servant in it, trying to pass through my bondage patiently, working year after year in a roundabout way slowly trying to secure my position, and hoping at last to be able to let out the accumulating thunder in my own way. . . . I say it also, to explain why I would like now to convey through you to Walt Whitman some message expressing the fact that I have long wished to speak a word of gratitude to him.[28]

Whitman was saddened when Burroughs shared this letter with him, because it demonstrated the extent to which young men could be thwarted by conventional culture, and he lamented how "impossible" it was "for such a man, fine as he is, fine as his letter is, to really build up and round out a capacious career" (Traubel, *With Walt Whitman*, 1:15).

Lathrop soon had his chance to approach Whitman directly, and he did so by provocatively inviting *him* to contribute a poem or two to *A Masque of Poets*. His request to Whitman is a gem: he begins by telling Whitman how much his work has meant to him but apologizes that he is "not gifted with the faculty of praising," so he "never felt it quite the time to speak to you." Then he edges toward his offer to Whitman, one that works against every instinct in Whitman's body, arguing that the anonymity of the proposed volume has "some advantages about it which may strike you," though because of the "general character of the collection"—the poems would of necessity be "of the older and prevalent fashion"—the works Whitman needed to submit "would have to conform to the more usual rhythms at least as far as 'Captain, My Captain.'"[29] The only way Whitman could stay anonymous, in other words, was for him to contribute poems unlike Whitman's and thus to appear indistinguishable from conventional poets. Looking back at the request years later, Whitman said, "Lathrop's letter is unique—good in general, silly in one particular. His suggestion that I should disguise my literary self in order to secure entrance to a volume of anonymous poetry is too good to be forgotten" (Traubel, *With Walt Whitman*, 2:304). Whitman recalled why he turned Lathrop down: "he wants me to appear in a disguise. I do not believe even disguises would disguise me. You might as well suggest that an elephant should masquerade as a fox" (Traubel, *With Walt Whitman*, 2:316). (As the cover of Whitman's Roberts book clearly indicates—a cover Whitman in fact sketched out for Niles, complete with his name arching over the northern hemisphere of the golden globe—Whitman was as dismissive of the No Name treatment as Dickinson was attracted to it.)

Whitman was asked continually to have his poems appear in collections—collections of bird poetry or war poetry, for example[30]—and he almost always consented. Had his mood that day been different, he might easily have sent Lathrop one of his more conventionally rhymed and metered poems, like "Ethiopia Saluting the Colors" (Lathrop had suggested something "patriotic"). Had Whitman done so, *A Masque* would not only be a kind of talisman in Dickinson studies, but a key harbinger of the tradition of Whitman and Dickinson that we live with today. We came that close, then, to having Whitman and Dickinson appear (both anonymously) in the same volume in 1878; had that happened, we would again have an origin point for American poetry as we know it now, as Higginson and his largely female protégés and Emerson and his largely male protégés were vying for the power to guide Transcendental poetry into the twentieth century.

The opportunity for such a convergence passed, however, and faded into the interstices of our literary history. Instead we were left with the dismaying fact that our two founding figures were apparently ignorant of each other. There is no record of Whitman having ever uttered Dickinson's name, and Dickinson—famously now—mentioned Whitman only once, in response to Higginson's having asked her, apparently (his letter to her is no longer extant), if she had been reading Whitman (perhaps because he felt her unsteady and—to his ear—poorly rhymed verses showed the undisciplined influence of the poet Higginson had already come to hate). Her response is vintage Emily Dickinson—coy, savvy, precise: "You speak of Mr Whitman—I never read his Book—but was told he was disgraceful—."[31] She does not say she never read a Whitman poem, only that she had never read his *book*, which, she was told just two years earlier in the *Springfield Daily Republican* (which she regularly read, and which was edited by her close friend Samuel Bowles, assisted by another Dickinson family friend, Josiah Gilbert Holland),[32] was in fact disgraceful. The review she might have read was entitled "*Leaves of Grass*—Smut in Them," and it compared *Leaves* to the kind of "professedly obscene book" that might be "stuck in one's face at steamboat landings by lousy scoundrels who peddle filth for a living," and counseled that "when men and women are led by their higher affinities, they will be led straight away from Walt Whitman's 'Leaves of Grass.'"[33]

More important for our understanding of just which Whitman poems Dickinson likely did read, however, the *Daily Republican* review opens with this taunting reminder: "Some weeks or months ago, we remarked upon a poem published in the *Atlantic Monthly*, from the pen of Walt Whitman—a nonsensical, whimsical scraggy performance, about as much like poetry as tearing off a rag, or paring one's corns." The poem referred to is Whitman's "Bardic Symbols," eventually titled "As I Ebb'd with the Ocean of Life." If Dickinson had not read the poem when it appeared in the *Atlantic* in April 1860, the *Daily Republican* review would likely have nudged her to go back through the family's carefully preserved collection of *Atlantic* issues and see what all the fuss was about. But even if she didn't read the poem in the *Atlantic*, she would have encountered generous excerpts of the poem in the *Daily Republican*'s dismissive review (titled "Literary Nonsense") of "Bardic Symbols": the excerpts were printed to help readers see Whitman's "string of nonsense," his "chaos of unmeaning words and a wilderness of bad grammar."[34] And the fact that Whitman had appeared in the venerable *Atlantic*, whose poetry editor was James Russell Lowell, who had little but contempt for Whitman's poetry and for Whitman the man (Lowell, along with Longfellow and Oliver Wendell Holmes, vetoed Emerson's efforts to bring Whitman to the exclusive Saturday Club when Whitman came to Boston to oversee the typesetting of his 1860 edition of *Leaves*, and he once dismissed *Leaves* as "a solemn humbug" that needed to be kept from Harvard students), had to have been confusing to Dickinson.[35] The *Atlantic*, after all, was the safe domain of Higginson, but Emerson still held sway, and he pressured Lowell to allow Whitman into the magazine (even though Lowell demanded that Whitman excise two lines of the poem that struck him as morbid).[36] The tensed battle between Higginson and Emerson, then, was playing itself out as early as 1860, and Emerson's momentary victory on Whitman's behalf likely provided Dickinson with her first dose of "disgraceful" Whitman. (And the battle was still going on nine years later, when Whitman successfully asked Emerson to intervene on his behalf to get "Proud Music of the Storm" published in the *Atlantic*, even though J. T. Fields, a Whitman antagonist and Higginson ally, was then editor.)[37]

Although we have known for many years that Dickinson had easy access to an array of Whitman's poems,[38] with few exceptions (Ruth Miller and especially Karl Keller come to mind)[39] that knowledge has not encouraged scholars to explore instances of possible influence, affinity, or impact. There is no doubt, though, that the *Atlantic*—a journal Emerson and Higginson both leaned on to help their wild protégés—was a particularly significant journal in laying the early groundwork for what has become the double-source, male/female, New York/Boston, Whitman/Dickinson origin story of American poetry. Higginson never did use his *Atlantic* connections to get a Dickinson poem published while she was alive, but as soon as she died, and just before Whitman died, he finally made his move. In 1867 Higginson had begun his public condemnation of Whitman, which would accelerate in the following decades, when he noted in his *Atlantic* essay on "Literature as an Art" that "it is no discredit to Walt Whitman that he wrote 'Leaves of Grass,' only that he did not burn it afterward and reserve himself for something better."[40] And then, in 1891, just months before Whitman's death, in celebration of the success of the first volume of his chosen wild poet's work that he had edited with Mabel Loomis Todd and that Roberts Brothers published in 1890, Higginson published a long essay in the *Atlantic*, "Emily Dickinson's Letters," in which he wrote of his relationship to the poet he had now released to the public. He described and quoted her letters, and he reprinted sixteen of her poems that she had sent him over the twenty-plus years of their correspondence. He claimed for her the status of the new American voice: "Few events in American literary history have been more curious than the sudden rise of Emily Dickinson many years since into a posthumous fame only more accentuated by the utterly recluse character of her life" (Meyer, *Magnificent Activist*, 543).[41] He proudly suggested how his "surgery" on her poems (which had suffered from what he called her "defiance of form") worked, as he tried "to lead her in the direction of rules and traditions" (Meyer, *Magnificent Activist*, 551).

Did Whitman read Higginson's essay and thus encounter Dickinson's poetry in the final year of his life? Although he was in poor health, Whitman was still actively talking about the latest literary and social news, and Horace Traubel and other friends kept him updated on the new offerings in the major magazines. Traubel was always carrying over recent copies of periodicals—*The Atlantic, Harper's Weekly, Harper's Monthly, The Century, The Critic, Current Literature*, Traubel's own *Conservator*, and a number of others—on his daily visits to Whitman's Camden house. He would leave them with the poet and retrieve them a day or two later, with Whitman often commenting on particular articles. Whitman offered Traubel a succinct explanation of why the magazines were so vital to him: "I ought to keep on the run of things. These help me to do so" (Traubel, *With Walt Whitman*, 7:30).

On a Saturday in September 1891, several weeks before Higginson's article on Dickinson appeared, Traubel showed up with a copy of *The Critic* and read one particular paragraph aloud to Whitman. It is a stunning moment, because it is the only recorded occasion where Whitman hears Emily Dickinson's name. This is the *Critic* paragraph to which Traubel drew Whitman's attention:

A young lady writes to me from Newport of "a rather good thing" a girl said there the other day. It was this: speaking of Walt Whitman, Emily Dickinson and others, whose thoughts are extremely poetical, but whose verses expressing them have little rhythm and less rhyme, she said, "I don't call such writers poets exactly, and yet they are not, literally speaking, prose writers. There ought to be some other word to describe them—one of Lewis Carroll's 'portmanteau' words. Why not call them 'proets'?" My fair correspondent feels that this vocable meets a long felt want in our much-lacking language. (Traubel, *With Walt Whitman*, 8:525)[42]

We wait for Whitman to ask, "Who is Emily Dickinson?" We wait for Traubel to comment on this surprising new name that is so casually juxtaposed to Whitman's in *The Critic*. But there is nothing. Whitman simply accepts the comparison and responds as if it is the most natural thing in the world, and he agrees with the writer's point about "proets": "Yes, and the name belongs, too, to the Bible writers—to the old Hebrews, all—to the Hindu scripturists—to many of the Greeks and so on. Almost all the earlier fellows, in fact." Soon he is talking of Pope and Dryden and Homer, and the mention of Emily Dickinson just evaporates. The first and only known mention of her in Whitman's presence creates not a ripple.[43] What is very clear, however, is that, by this time, he knew who she was.

During the last two years of Whitman's life, there were a couple of other essays on Dickinson besides Higginson's *Atlantic* piece that reprinted her poems, including a long review of her first book of poems by William Dean Howells in *Harper's New Monthly Magazine* in January 1891, where ten of her poems were reprinted.[44] Since Whitman kept abreast of articles in *Harper's*, published his poems there through the 1870s, 1880s, and 1890s, and knew and liked Howells, it is probable that this article came to his attention and perhaps introduced him to Dickinson's work nine months before Traubel read the *Critic* paragraph to him.[45] *Harper's* was very much on Whitman's mind at the time Howells's "Editor's Study" piece on Dickinson appeared, and he was very likely checking issues, because he was waiting for his poem, "Death's Valley," to appear there; he had already been paid for the poem and was frustrated that *Harper's* was taking so long to get it into print.[46]

Howells's characterization of Dickinson's poetry as rough and unformed would have prepared Whitman for the comparison that the *Critic* writer made between the two "proets"; Howells describes her poems this way:

"Occasionally, the outside of the poem, so to speak, is left so rough, so rude, that the art seems to have faltered. But there is apparent to reflection the fact that the artist meant just this harsh exterior to remain, and that no grace of smoothness could have imparted her intention as it does. It is the soul of an abrupt, exalted New England woman that speaks in such brokenness" (Blake and Wells, *Recognition of Emily Dickinson*, 23). Howells's emphasis on Dickinson's poetry emerging from "tendencies inherent in the New England, or the Puritan, spirit" (*Recognition of Emily Dickinson*, 18) probably left Whitman relieved that her work apparently occupied a realm far different from his own, even if they shared a preference for "proetic" form. Howells also mentions that Dickinson's only book publication of a poem had been in the anonymous *A Masque of Poets*, a reference that would have caught Whitman's attention, since he had only the year before been reminiscing about Lathrop's attempt to get him to submit a poem for that volume. And Howells's association of Dickinson with William Blake and Emerson (but not with Whitman) would have fascinated Whitman as well, since his work was also often compared to those two writers.

The *Harper's* article, then, written by the friendly Howells, would not have struck Whitman as threatening. But the Higginson *Atlantic* piece was an entirely different affair. By the late 1880s Whitman spoke of Higginson, with "his strict, straight notions of literary propriety," as one of his "enemies" and generally remained dismissive of him—"he amounts to nothing, any-how—is a lady's man—there an end!"[47] (Traubel, *With Walt Whitman*, 2:372; 6:95)—but he continued to keep tabs on him. And Whitman had always had a stormy relationship with the *Atlantic*, from Lowell's grudging acceptance (and expurgation) of "Bardic Symbols" in 1860, through the magazine's rejection of two of Whitman's Civil War poems,[48] to Whitman's growing conviction that the editors and power figures at the *Atlantic*—including Higginson, J. T. Fields, and even at times William Dean Howells—were his enemies, even though the magazine published "Proud Music of the Storm" in 1869, during Fields's tenure as editor (and while Howells was his assistant), albeit not without Emerson's intervention again. Whitman stopped submitting to the *Atlantic* in the 1870s, and in an anonymous article he wrote about himself for the *West Jersey Press* in 1876, he offered this cursory judgment: "The *Atlantic* will not touch him."[49] So, though he did not subscribe to the magazine, he nonetheless kept reading it. Traubel records many instances when he brought a copy over to Whitman, and he records Whitman's reactions to various articles. Whitman even coined a word—"Atlanticish"—for the stuffy, "old, familiar" tone that he picked up in piece after piece (Traubel, *With Walt Whitman*, 7:26). Any article that mentioned Whitman received the poet's very careful attention, as when Holmes mentioned him in an 1890 article: "He could not be expected to accept us," Whitman wrote; "he would rather have 'Walter' than 'Walt'. . . . It is a parlor logic, yet characteristic of the literary man of our time" (Traubel, *With Walt Whitman*, 7:86).

And in the last year of his life, Whitman became particularly fascinated with the *Atlantic* because his now-deceased friend and fervent supporter William Douglas O'Connor was having a story posthumously published there. O'Connor's widow, Ellen, had decided to issue a collection of her husband's stories and had asked Whitman to write a preface, which he did.[50] In 1891, one of the stories in that soon-to-be-published volume, "The Brazen Android," was published in two consecutive issues of the *Atlantic*. Whitman was anxious to see those issues and kept asking Traubel to bring the *Atlantic* to him, which Traubel did on April 3. Whitman scoured those issues—April and May 1891—and the June issue had a piece on Lincoln he was interested in. We know in this last year of his life, then, that he was once again devouring the *Atlantic*: when Traubel left Whitman's home one night, he said playfully that the poet was "buried (not drowned) in the Atlantic" (Traubel, *With Walt Whitman*, 8:166).

Only a few weeks after Traubel read the *Critic* paragraph to Whitman—the one that joined Whitman and Dickinson as "proets"—Higginson's Dickinson article appeared in *The Atlantic*, and it seems all the more likely that, now that we know Whitman was well aware of her, he would have taken a look. Soon after Higginson's article appeared in October, Traubel asked Whitman if he should send a review copy of the 1892 *Leaves* to Horace Scudder, the new editor at the *Atlantic*. Whitman answered, "No, hardly him—I would not send one to him" (Traubel, *With Walt Whitman*, 9:323), clearly still thinking of the magazine—perhaps particularly after he saw it lining up behind Dickinson as the new poet for the nation—as his antagonist, even though Scudder in June 1892 would publish in the *Atlantic* a long and not unkind obituary essay on Whitman's significance, praising the poet's "deliberate attempt at an adequate mode of expressing large, elemental ideas," supporting his attempts to celebrate the sensuous man, and praising the patriotism of the 1855 "Preface," even while questioning Whitman's "universality."[51]

While we lack specific evidence that Whitman read Higginson's essay on Dickinson, we can assume there is a good chance that the poet went to his deathbed having at least absorbed Higginson's opening paragraph—a kind of slant salvo against Whitman—about how this reclusive female poet, shy about any publicity and published only because of her sister's efforts, had her poetry, in utter contrast to Whitman's, "launched quietly and without any expectation of a wide audience; yet the outcome of it is that six editions of the volume have been sold within six months, a suddenness of success almost without parallel in American literature" (Meyer, *Magnificent Activist*, 543). And if Whitman read just a couple of pages further into the article, he would have come upon Higginson's one direct dig at Whitman, delivered in the words of the new wild poet he had mentored into public acclaim at long last; he quoted Dickinson's second letter to him in full, with its casual-sounding dismissal of Walt Whitman: "You speak of Mr. Whitman. I never read his book, but was told it was disgraceful" (Meyer, *Magnificent Activist*, 546).

And so began the contentious double-sourced history of American poetry as we have come to know it. It is telling that the earliest known extended published comparison of Whitman and Dickinson came as a response to Higginson's article. Arlo Bates, a poet who served as the external reader for the Roberts Brothers on the first volume of Dickinson poems, wrote a month later that Higginson's article "conspired to render the interest in this strange personality greater than ever":

I wonder that it has occurred to nobody to make a magazine essay by considering the place in American literature of Walt Whitman and Emily Dickinson together. . . . They are both instances of the development of the sentiment and of the feeling so rapidly and so highly that the acquirement of a technique becomes impossible. It is a natural result of the hot-bed system upon which the intellectual development of this country has gone on. . . . In the case of both we have the melancholy spectacle of a mind gifted with great originality and with genuine imagination missing its best fruition through the failure to handle to the best advantage the art in which it worked.[52]

Here, just months before Whitman's death, we can glimpse the first stirrings of the dynamic that would become the dominant story of American poetry in the next century, and a dynamic that seems destined to continue to operate through the twenty-first century as well.

"Sickly Abstractions" and the Poetic Concrete

Whitman's and Dickinson's Battlefields of War

CÉCILE ROUDEAU

> Perhaps indeed the efforts of the true poets, founders, religions, litera-
> tures, all ages, have been, and ever will be, our time and times to come,
> essentially the same—to bring people back from their persistent strayings
> and sickly abstractions, to the costless average, divine, original concrete.
> —Whitman, "Nature and Democracy—Morality"[1]

WHAT GOOD ARE POETS IN A TIME OF CRISIS? MORE THAN 150
years after the conflict's ending, Hölderlin's query continues to haunt
the battlefields of the U.S. Civil War.[2] While Walt Whitman visited the
wounded in the hospitals of Washington and stained his notebooks with
more than blood, Emily Dickinson saw her life unexpectedly enmeshed in
the ongoing bloodshed, and "s[ang] off charnel steps" (L 298) as the death
tolls of the battlegrounds repeatedly reached the gates of her Amherst family
home. "War feels to me an oblique place," she wrote in February 1863 to
Thomas Wentworth Higginson (L 280). But it was not war only, it was the
name of this particular war that carried its burden of obliquity at a time
when battles were also fought over definitions.

What is now known as the "Civil War," historians have shown, was a
disputed locus of wartime lexicography and politics, a slippery and "contested concept" faced with the all-too tragic evanescence and lubricity of
all objects—including the nation itself.[3] Civil War, David Armitage has
suggested, "lacks an a-priori definition; it is liable to revision in changing
circumstances. . . . Its application may depend on whether you are a ruler
or a rebel, the victor or the vanquished, an established government or an
interested third party."[4] Civil war, in other words, is not so much a stable
concept as a deictic pointing in two directions—toward the object it waver-

ingly designates and the situation of the subject speaker who uses it. Such instability was precisely what the jurist Francis Lieber meant to overcome in 1863 when, in the darkest days of the conflict, he proposed a definition of his own: "Civil war is war between two or more portions of a country or state, each contending for the mastery of the whole, and each claiming to be the legitimate government."[5] The specious neutrality of Lieber's definition hardly hides an oblique version of the conflict. Perhaps even more than usual, defining, in this instance, became a partisan act that puzzlingly took for granted the abstract "whole" that it hoped unilaterally to perform—a paradox embraced by Walt Whitman himself, who wrote in "Origins of Attempted Secession": "I CONSIDER the war of attempted secession, 1860–65, not as a struggle of two distinct and separate peoples, but a conflict (often happening, and very fierce) between the passions and paradoxes of one and the same identity—perhaps the only terms on which that identity could really become fused, homogeneous and lasting" (*WPP* 1018). Not unlike Lieber's, Whitman's definition took as its premise, and as the premise of the war, that which in fact was not yet extant but depended on the war itself to be made concrete: a (national) identity. The war, *that* war, because it was born of the fracture of "identity" itself, of a "Union" that could not be "fused, homogeneous and lasting," challenged the very possibility of a third term that might have guaranteed the commensurability of differences within a "whole" that was no more, or never had been.

Paradoxically, however, the war was fought in the *names* of these untenable abstractions—liberty, nation—whose universal definitions, as historian James MacPherson explains, the war thoroughly challenged. Quoting Lincoln from 1864, MacPherson insists on the unstable meaning of *liberty*: "We all declare for liberty; but in using the same *word* we do not all mean the same *thing*. With some the word liberty may mean for each man to do as he pleases with himself, and the product of his labor; while with others the same word may mean for some men to do as they please with other men, and the product of other men's labor. Here are two, not only different, but incompatible things, called by the same name—liberty."[6] As for nation, MacPherson notes how the word was almost an empty signifier at the start of the war and came to supersede the word "Union" (MacPherson 6)[7] The war, in that sense, contributed to making concrete what was but a name and an abstraction: the American nation. This paradox traversed politicians' speeches and complicated generals' battle plans; it also affected the poets of the times, who found the names missing that could have told of the shattering event. Knowledge and figuration were unsettled when concepts, understood etymologically as what can be captured or circumscribed, were both blatantly inadequate and vexingly mandatory, if only as a trying justification of the bloodshed. To put it differently, while the U.S. Civil War challenged abstract categories and denominations, it also was of practical and ideological necessity an instrument of categorization, of definition. The law of war, as the law of the mutual exclusion of opposites, must rely on "the partition of the sensible," even as its violence made it impossible to find "something . . . to concrete" the opposite sides, the *membra disjecta* of the former body politic—a name, or names, to wit, a stable definition.[8]

Names were a constant concern for Whitman. Their function, as is explained apropos the name of the book that would eventually bear the title *Specimen Days*, is to bind together what is disparate, a process Whitman referred to as "concreting": "Then reader dear, in conclusion, as to the point of the name for the present collection, let us be satisfied to *have* a name— something to identify and bind it together, to concrete all its vegetable, mineral, personal memoranda, abrupt raids of criticism, crude gossip of philosophy, varied sands clumps—without bothering ourselves because certain pages do not present themselves to you or me as coming under their own name with entire fitness or amiability" (*WPP* 909). "Binding together" the diversity of what-is is also what nouns do best, those many substantives whose definition wavered as the effect of the conflict. I propose in this essay that names, the possibility of naming, of yoking a noun to the shattering reality of war, and hence of apprehending and comprehending the world, bore the brunt of an event that was also an epistemic and linguistic crisis.

The Civil War, Whitman wrote, "smash'd [the Union] like a china plate."[9] It made contours untenable and circumferences murky, those very circumferences that were Emily Dickinson's "Business."[10] As such, this essay argues, war pushed poetry to its crisis. Searching for substantives when substances eluded the lexicon's grasp, looking for definitions when circumscriptions wavered, the texts of Walt Whitman and Emily Dickinson both confronted the "litter of the battlefield" and the clutter of the Real with the injunction to write in spite of the disarticulation between world and word.[11] In such times of epistemic and political crisis, Dickinson and Whitman faced the challenge of the untenability of contours, the demise of the figure, the sickliness of abstraction—language brought face to face with the possibility of its concrete undoing.

War, the U.S. Civil War, is not merely a context that literature refers to in those years of battles and despair; it is also, I want to argue, an *event* that happened to poetic language. As has been well established by critics since the 1980s, poetry was not immune to the trauma of war, and Dickinson and Whitman's poems were anything but an exception within this larger trend. "The good gray poet" was also the "political poet," to take up Betsy Erkkila's phrase, and his involvement in the war hospitals has been amply documented. As reflected in his *Notebooks* and in his *Memoranda during the War* as well as in his war poetry, Whitman's public persona was intertwined with his private experience of the dismembered body (politic).[12] And while Dickinson may still be held as a "recluse" by some, Thomas H. Johnson's pronouncement that she "did not live in history and held no view of it" has largely been superseded by the argument that war greatly impacted the form and content of her poems. She, whose voice Shira Wolosky called a "voice of war," should be read "in time" and in conversation with "the defining historical event of [her] time"—the Civil War.[13]

Two well-known poems by Emily Dickinson, "They Dropped like Flakes – " (Fr 545, 1863) and "The name – of it – is 'Autumn' – " (Fr 465, ca. 1862), have been convincingly read as poems of war, in which war is an oblique yet not so obscure referent.[14] But what happens *in* the poem is also—and above all—what happens *to* the poem, a war on poetic diction itself, the bloody demise of the symbolic and its dutiful valets—names, figures, form as representation.

> They dropped like Flakes –
> They dropped like stars –
> Like Petals from a Rose –
> When suddenly across the June
> A Wind with fingers – goes –
> (Fr 545, stanza 1)

The demise of analogy as comparison is the event that occurs in and to the first poem. True it is that the simile in the first stanza ("like Flakes"; "like stars"; "like Petals") tries to naturalize the fact of death on the battlefield, using nature as a familiar referent to tame the uncanniness of war; yet dissonances abound as the poem works against the very analogy it proposes. First, the aural regularity of the ballad quatrain goes awry, as the first line's anticipated four stresses are visually cut into two lines. One may argue that such visual cutting, if particularly fitting here, is not specific to Dickinson's war poetry; it contributes, however, to a consistent questioning of poetic techniques in the poem. The encrypted metaphor of line five, for example, all but ruins the pastoral illusion of a reassuring equation between nature and the human. War is "[the] Wind with fingers." What if *this* were what the poem tried to tell, this and not the more soothing cosmetic imagery of stars and petals? What if this poem's unnamed referent were not so much, or not only, "The Battlefield," as Higginson surmised when he chose this title in 1890, nor the U.S. Civil War rumbling in the outskirts of Amherst, but "war" itself? The Real that war is.

When the poem starts again, its second stanza takes up the conventional ballad tune, but with an explicit referent this time—"they" meaning "the soldiers"—and "concludes with a conventional piety":[15]

> They perished in the seamless Grass –
> No eye could find the place –
> But God can summon every face
> Of his Repealless – List.
>
> (Fr 545)

The conclusion is predictable; yet the snake of dissent lies in the "seamless Grass," creating a hiatus in God's decree. The hissing lisping note ("Repealless – List") undoes the semantics of ineluctability. "Repealless" harks back to "seamless," and as we listen, which we are invited to do by the last word of the poem: "List," we hear a duplicitous score. The differences between the slain bodies may well have been erased by death with its "Democratic fingers," to take up another of Dickinson's eerie metaphors, the grass, to our ear, is also *seem*-less.[16] Repealing the trope itself that it had but just

put to use, the poem denounces the simile as a meager semblance of the
Real; it cancels the locus of consensus, those comparisons that should be
intelligible to all, and exposes the imaginary commonplace as no longer
able to fulfill the task of representation.

In that sense, however hard the poem tries to adjust to its referent (war),
it never quite succeeds in making its common measure fit the horror of the
Real. War never really gets into the poem. What remains is a suffix: "-less,"
and an uncanny metaphor, "A Wind with fingers," which, I would argue,
points to poetic diction even more than to the flamboyant absentee: war.
"I tried to match it – Seam by Seam – / But could not make them fit" says
another poem ("I Felt a Cleaving in my Mind – ," Fr 867). The seams/
seems are left open here as well. Analogy as comparison cannot cure nor
even relieve the pain or horror, it does not even come close to the Real, yet
it makes it tangible as what undoes the seam/*seem*. The efficacy of analogy,
then, is not so much to serve as an epistemic tool that would allow "us"
to understand and permit "us" to stand as a community. War has put an
end to any general agreement. The trope—understood as what "we" could
have agreed on—stands as contingent and ultimately vain. The Real, then,
may be said to put generality, the common measure and common trope
and common agreement, to the test. "We" are left with a wounded form,
the vulnerability of which, I would like to propose, is the mark of the Real.

While no name here has stood the test, which might have circumscribed
the "thing," the next poem under consideration opens with a name indeed,
as if in a manner of response:

> The name – of it – is "Autumn" –
> The hue – of it – is Blood –
> An Artery – opon the Hill –
> A Vein – along the Road –
>
> Great Globules – in the Alleys –
> And Oh, the Shower of Stain –
> When Winds – upset the Basin –
> And spill the scarlet Rain –
> (Fr 465, stanzas 1–2)

This poem is yet another case of the struggle of poetic diction with the defection of the symbolic; this time, metaphor is put to the test as what might have predicatively performed some communal agreement on what-is. Nature—more accurately, "Autumn" here—is again the supposedly common referent that will lend its attributes ("hue"; "Shower"; "Winds"; "Rain") to "it." But "Autumn," singled out within its quotation marks, is a deceptive label, and the undertaking soon verges on the "comically grotesque" (Miller, *Reading in Time*, 160). To the aforementioned series that unfolds the concrete physiognomy of "Autumn" corresponds another: "Artery," "Vein," "Globules," "Stain," "Basin," which the poem dutifully clips onto the first. To adapt another of Dickinson's striking phrases to this instance, we might say that the "staples, in the song" show, and painfully, or rather pathetically, expose the artificiality of the thought experiment.[17] The poem eventually eddies away "upon Vermilion Wheels" that carry with them the mawkish performance. Not only is the simile dismissed ("like a Rose" sounds irrelevant to describe the passing of war itself), but the whole naming process majestically fails: we are left with a name—"Autumn"—that does not quite fit the gory imagery of the poem and whose ultimate elusion, or disappearance, enhances what remains an "it"—ever unadjusted to poetic language.[18]

Renouncing the name is a piercing virtue in Dickinson's poetry. It is vain to try to draw a line around *that* which cannot be circumscribed, let alone conceived. "It" is all there is, and writing under constraint of the Real involves specific poetic restraints as well. The noun, if used, must come under erasure—hauntingly so, as famously staged in:

> It was not Death, for I stood up,
> And all the Dead, lie down –
> It was not Night, for all the Bells
> Put out their Tongues, for Noon.
> (Fr 355, 1862, stanza 1)

The poem is a form that cannot "justify"—a verb used in its last line—nor be adjusted to what it strives to tell. The pronoun that comes in lieu of the absentee anaphorically defies the poem's epistemic function. What it is *is*

what it is not. Such is the poem's strange equation. Stranger still, the sum
of its negatives is ultimately the only concrete thing there is. "And yet, it
tasted, like them all." As often in Dickinson, "all" is as close to "naught"
as to a full substantial totality; but nothingness is strangely material, and
while the sum of negatives fails to give us access to the Real, it has pictured
"it" as supplement. "One does not know what it is . . . if that exists, if it
responds to a name or corresponds to an essence," Derrida writes apropos of
the specter in Shakespeare's *Hamlet*. "Here is—or rather there is over there,
an unnameable or almost unnameable thing."[19] Death is "an unnameable
or almost unnameable thing" in Dickinson's poem. As suggested by the
adverbial supplement ("And 'twas like Midnight, some"), something cannot
be "shaven" to fit the name, the figure, nor the poem. The archaic ending
("shaven") testifies to this rest—shavings—just as the adverb "some" hang-
ing at the end of the line flaunts its presence in excess of it, like a "sum,"
that cannot quite be included in the transactions of the poem. Standing in
excess of the name, "some" both points to the default of the figure and the
surplus that is the Real—death, war.

In Dickinson's poetical arithmetic, something does not add up. The Real
does not add up—can it ever? "It" is always in excess of figuration. But the
burial of the "figures" (understood metapoetically and arithmetically in
stanza 3) is only a Dickinsonian sleight of hand.[20] The Real is made palpable
by the wounded face of the poem. In that sense, the nameless Real (here,
"Death") is not figure-less. The form, the contours, of the poem, its mangled
figure that emerges negatively from the blank page, are the condition of the
emergence of the Real just as the Real is the condition of the emergence
of the poem, no matter how the Real is, to quote Lacan's aphorism, the
impasse of formalization.[21]

In order to hold together the poem as form, the Real as an impasse,
and Dickinsonian arithmetic at its plainest, let us circuitously revert to
Alain Badiou's essay entitled "À la recherche du réel perdu" ("In Search of
the Lost Real"), in which he takes the example of arithmetic to illustrate
Lacan's aforementioned aphorism. Adding up two numbers, Badiou explains, is a simple enough operation, yet the easy process of addition can
only be valid when indexed on the concept of the infinite, a concept that
will, however, never add up arithmetically. In other words, manipulating

the finite numbers of arithmetic requires that one posit the existence of an infinite that eludes arithmetic formalization. The condition of formalization is what eludes formalization, just as, in the case of a photographic frame, an example that will bring us closer to aesthetics, the Real is what cannot be but off camera—both the condition of existence of the frame and what the frame will never be able to integrate. "As if my life were shaven / And fitted to a frame," says the poetic voice. Translated onto the realm of poetry, what is "off poem"—off the poem as *frame*, to take Dickinson at her word—is similarly both the condition of existence of the poem as form and what the form of the poem cannot contain. The Real, in that sense, is always in exile, some; it is in exile of form, yet predicated on it, just as form itself is predicated on the infinite Real that it fails to attain.

Dickinson's war poems, therefore, do not so much try to confine and define the Real as withstand its pressure and proudly bear the stigmata of such Jacobean wrestling. It is when the poem displays its notches or parades as a farce or verges on silence that it best tells *about* the Real. Only *then* is the Real enhanced, revealed, yet peripherally so, at the periphery of the poem as form. In other words, the Real "happens" as what is made palpable in the concrete bitings of the poem's own flesh, in its wounded vulnerable form. The poem's *concrete* finitude is where the infinite of the Real is being made sensible as well as being put to the test.

Being made sensible in and by the poem, the Real (war, in this case), is no longer an abstraction. It is, I would like to suggest, what happens to language when language expresses what we *feel* in front of a traumatic or ecstatic event—love, or death, or war. But those very names are deceptive, as Dickinson's poetry recurrently demonstrates. As general categories they are bound to betray what can only be *felt*, however, in language. Reminiscent thereby of her metaphysical forebears, Dickinson's poetry nevertheless refuses to give up on language; rather, her poems turn language into the place of the becoming concrete of the Real. Not unlike John Donne, in his *Devotions upon Emergent Occasions*, Dickinson never fears the violent conflagration between the abstract and the concrete, those poetic events, or "categorial disturbances," to use Julie Neveux's phrase, through which, at a time of crisis, feeling is allowed to emerge in language.[22] Examples of such conflagration are many: "The Soul has Bandaged moments – " (Fr 360);

"'Hope' is the thing with feathers – " (Fr 314), and there are many more. What is at stake in Dickinson's war poems, however, is not so much, or not only the becoming concrete of abstraction, since abstraction is precisely what the war ceaselessly, if ambivalently, questions; rather, I would propose that her war poems are the loci of the becoming concrete of the Real (that war is); they testify to the infinite of the Real when it painstakingly, ever imperfectly, takes form.

There is no dialectics at stake here, no dialectical resolution or sublation, but what we may call after Badiou a diagonal between the concrete of form and the infinite of the Real.[23] Not only is the poem a deictic of the trauma of the Real, a gesture toward what is beyond attainment; it is also, and more to the point, the inchoate manifestation of the Real, or, put differently, the ever-unachieved achievement of form. Borrowing one of Dickinson's grammatical disturbances, we might say that through her poems, the Real is made "possibler" and more potent.[24] The Real, to conclude provisionally, is not so much off poem, off frame, as it is visibly manifested in the poem's wounded circumference, in the minute or grotesquely huge categorial disturbances (metaphors, comparisons) that help make tangible the singular encounter of the speaker with the unspeakable.

The Real is also what "happened to" Whitman's poetry, the *event* that unsettled Whitman's Emersonian trust in the expansive capacity of poetic form ever to circumscribe the turgescence of what-is within its shaggy lines.

LOOK down fair moon and bathe this scene,
Pour softly down night's nimbus floods, on faces ghastly,
  swollen, purple,
On the dead, on their backs, with their arms toss'd wide,
Pour down your unstinted nimbus, sacred moon.

(*WPP* 453)[25]

Notwithstanding the conventional address to the moon that frames this quatrain, published in *Drum-Taps* in 1865, night's nimbus fails to contain the Real within its orb. The first line's iambic tetrameter, which calls on the moon to bathe the scene in a seemingly serene Romantic light, finds no counterpart in the last line of the quatrain, awkwardly burdened with five stresses and eleven syllables, as if to reject the moon itself as the undue ornament and vain prop of poetic diction. The initial lilt is deceptive; the initially regular prosodic pattern seems to burst out of its limits; there is no circumscribing the horror of the Real from a transcendent viewpoint, even that of Nature itself.

And yet, the moon persists in Whitman's war prose; it is the poet's in-termittent companion, along the streets of wartime Washington or on the battlefields of Chancellorsville, where it serves once again as a serene point of view "over all," and weaves an improbable thread between the perfume of the woods and the acrid odor of smoke and blood.

> Such is the camp of the wounded—such a fragment, a reflection afar off of the bloody scene—while over all the clear, large *moon* comes out at times softly, quietly shining. Amid the woods, that scene of flitting souls—amid the crack and crash and yelling sounds—the impalpable perfume of the woods—and yet the pungent, stifling smoke—*the radiance of the moon*, looking from heaven at intervals so placid—.
>
> ("A Night Battle, Over a Week Since," *WPP* 747, my emphasis)

The moon "staples" together, to take up once again Dickinson's striking image, what cannot otherwise be conceived *"ensemble"* nor recollected into some sort of generality.[26] *"Ensemble"* is one of Whitman's beloved French borrowings. It also appears, fittingly so, both in his "Chants Democratic" (*Leaves of Grass*, 1860–61), where the poet claims that "There shall be no subject but it shall be treated with reference to the *ensemble* of the world, and the compact truth of the world,"[27] and later in his "Song of the Universal" (1874), in which he prays for the capacity and capaciousness of encompassing all the world in his verse:

> Give me O God to sing that thought,
> Give me, give him or her I love this quenchless faith,
> In Thy *ensemble*, whatever else withheld withhold not from us,
> Belief in plan of Thee enclosed in Time and Space,
> Health, peace, salvation universal.
>
> ("Song of the Universal," *WPP* 371; my emphasis)

In his reminiscence of the battlefields of the Civil War, as in this later poem, Whitman pursues the dream of a poetic universal embrace of what-is and enacts this dream via the repetition of "moon," in this reminiscence of the battlefields of the Civil War—as if, when seen from above, from the universal point of view of nature's eye, the potency of disunion dwindled—as it should. "If beheld from a point of view sufficiently compr'hensive," Whitman wrote in his somewhat prophetic conclusion to his *Memoranda*, in 1876, "the development of a Nation—of the American Republic, ... would doubtless exhibit the same regularity of order and exactness ... as the crops in the ground, or the rising and setting of the stars."[28] In 1876, the war was over and the poet would no longer have to do with fragments, limbs, dismembered bodies; in 1876, the "Americans" had recovered a comprehensive name (Nation, Republic, common "race") indexed on the regular cycles of nature and astronomy. Chancellorsville was but a memory, apropos of which the speaker once exclaimed: "is this indeed *humanity*— these butchers' shambles? ... O well is it their mothers, their sisters cannot see them—cannot conceive, and never conceiv'd, these things" ("A Night Battle, Over a Week Still," *WPP* 746–47).

To conceive: the verb means both to understand conceptually, in its generality and to give birth to. But which "book" (hear Whitman's famous line) could tell of the Real, when the Real precisely defied any ability to grasp, when war, that war in particular, challenged both abstract circumscription (that of the name "Union," "America") and the concrete form (of bodies no longer extant, of a country whose borders no longer made up a nation)?[29] Dickinson, when confronted with the same issues, manifested the Real visually as the concrete biting at poetic substance and form, and repealed abstraction if unmarked, untainted, by the flesh and the feel of her poems; each of her poems became the trace of a *singular* encounter with "it." Whitman, who also encountered the Real as a poetic and formal disturbance, opened the flesh of his poems and prose to its galling presence as well; however, the agency of the Real, in Whitman's war writings, manifested itself less as the textual event of the singular concrete than as the assertion of what I would call the *general* concrete. Possibly because generality was the backbone of the nation that his nationalism could not do without, Whitman, I would propose, found it much harder to let go of generality. The challenge of his war writings, I suggest, was to save generality from abstraction, to *conceive* generality anew.

"IF I were ask'd *persona* to specify the one point of America's people on which I mainly rely, I should say the final average or bulk quality of the whole" ("America's Bulk Average," *WPP* 1323). These words of a dying Whitman echo an ongoing concern of the poet's oeuvre: the fleshing out of mathematical abstraction, the concreting of disseminated singularities into a sentient whole. Another favorite word of Whitman's is "bulk." In his letter to Emerson of January 17, 1863, Whitman already referred to his journal of war as growing "bulky" "as [he] took temporary memoranda of names, items, &c of one thing and another."[30] These discrete items, not yet aggregated into a whole, became bigger and bigger every day, he said, not unlike what he would later call, once the war was over, "the bulk of the average American People." But one of the effects of the war was precisely to deplete that bulk that Whitman so cherished, thereby rendering impossible the equation between mathematical abstraction ("final average") and the bodily bulky substance that his book undertook to represent, if not to be. The event of the war left the speaker/visitor in front of fragments that would not easily aggregate, let alone "concrete" into a whole—a book, a poem, or even a name. At issue was indeed, once again, the capacity *of* the name and the capacity *to* name. When the expansive capaciousness of names was no longer an option, when what was left of the beloved Union was but a "sickly abstraction," what, then, could poets do?

The capaciousness of one name in particular is put to the test by the event of the war: "grass"—not any name in Whitman's corpus. "A child said, What is the grass?" has been part of all the editions *of Leaves of Grass*. Yet, interpretation wavers when the poem is read on either side of the divide of the Civil War. In between the 1855 and 1867 editions, war happened—to the poem and to the name it celebrates. In 1855 the name, staked on the infinite turgescence of poetic diction, was capacious enough to simultaneously refer to flag, self, God, child, text.

A child said *What is the grass?* fetching it to me with full hands;
How could I answer the child? I do not know what it is any more
 than he.

I guess it must be the flag of my disposition, out of hopeful green
stuff woven.
Or I guess it is the handkerchief of the Lord,
A scented gift and remembrancer designedly dropt,
Bearing the owner's name someway in the corners, that we may see
and remark, and say *Whose?*
Or I guess the grass is itself a child, the produced babe of the
vegetation.
Or I guess it is a uniform hieroglyphic.

(*WWA* 1867, 28)

Grass has encompassed all that is (from God to the "I" itself) and knit the
different parts together, or even fused them through the syntax of equiv-
alence. When the poem was republished in 1867, these lines remained
identical, except for punctuation and italics. However, the Real, I would
contend, had caught up with the figure. War had happened and troubled
the hopeful weaving of the world into one word, one embrace. It had
unsettled both the poetic statement of hope—"The smallest sprout shows
there is really no death"—and the gothic metaphor of the "uncut hair of
graves" "transpir[ing] from the breasts of young men" (*WWA* 1867, 29, 28). A
grimmer referent now stood in the way of any further creative expansiveness.
"All goes onward and outward, nothing collapses, / And to die is different
from what any one supposed, and luckier" (*WWA* 1867, 29).[31] The bodies
slain, the fragments of war, the unnatural deaths of the battlefields could
no longer be mustered under the once-encompassing noun (and book):
grass. The prosodic supplement—"and luckier"—no longer pointed to a
smiling beyond; it looked like a grin on the face of fate.

The war had raised a poetic problem that had political echoes: how to
trust the name that said the whole? How to aggregate, how to concrete what
had indeed collapsed? Whitman's prose of war, his *Memoranda*, addressed
this question of names by dutifully, systematically, turning fragments into
specimens, into "samples" that gestured toward an abstract totality, now
missing, toward a whole that they represented metonymically, or at least
intended to. In the *Memoranda*, the failing balm of metaphor yielded to
the *pharmakon* of systemic categorization. When faced with the horror of

the Real that eludes figuration, the text appealed to arithmetical figures and nosological cases.

> Interesting cases in ward I; Charles Miller, bed 19, company D, 53d Pennsylvania, is only sixteen years of age, very bright, courageous boy, left leg amputated below the knee; next bed to him, another young lad very sick; gave each appropriate gifts. In the bed above, also, amputation of the left leg; gave him a little jar of raspberries.
>
> ("Back to Washington," *WPP* 738)

Cases keep melancholy away; they cover the scandal of the death of one with the mantle of generality. Abstraction here is what soothes, what relieves the pain of the Real. The nosological category sublates the various singularities of amputated bodies that are in exile of representation. A case, dictionaries tell us, is both the patient and the wound; but it is also a compartment, a category that allows singularity, once reduced to a symptom, to find its place in the haven of classification. Some hermeneutic order is thereby reestablished in and by a text that is strewn with numbers, statistics, estimates, not unlike the reports required by the modern state apparatus, born of the war, which increasingly took it as its duty to count and classify, to compile and aggregate.

From 1864 on, statistical tables were indeed part of the routine of the war hospital.[32] Using the lever of generality, data compilation imposed a conceptual grid upon the clutter of the Real. Words such as "mean," "average," or even "aggregate average" recur in tables and captions in an uncanny echo to Whitman's prose of war.[33] In fact, the speaker in the *Memoranda*, a text written in part when Whitman himself served as clerk in the federal government,[34] never recoiled from the efficacy of arithmetical figures, to wit: the entry entitled "The Million Dead, Too, Summ'd Up."

> The dead in this war—there they lie, strewing the fields and woods and valleys and battle-fields of the south— . . . the varieties of the *strayed* dead, (the estimate of the War department is 25,000 national soldiers kill'd in battle and never buried at all, 5,000 drown'd—15,000 inhumed by strangers, or on the march in haste, in hitherto unfound

localities—2,000 graves cover'd by sand and mud by Mississippi freshets, 3,000 carried away by caving-in of banks, &c.).

(*WPP* 800)

Figures here take on an iconic value; they are endowed with a strange materiality reminiscent of the statistical mise-en-scène of the driest hospital reports, which, unexpectedly perhaps, also pretended to "embody" the facts of war, as they routinely collected the singular deaths under "heads" that were supposed to comprehend what was scattered; or provided "consolidations," a word that obliquely tells of the body injured and cured. Not unlike these reports, Whitman's prose makes tangible the materiality of the general. But this is not yet what makes it concrete. The becoming concrete of generality surfaces, I would suggest, when the figure is ripped open, not so much canceled as displayed in its vulnerability.

Ampersands repeatedly puncture the prose of Whitman's *Memoranda*, as a tragic reminder of the failure of circumscription, as a herald, also, of the impossibility of totalization. The sum that the previous entry braggartly advertises will never materialize for the reader. In fact, the very word that tells of totalization ("sum'd") ominously stands gaping in the title of this vignette. Numbers, here and elsewhere in the *Memoranda*, are missing or, rather, they come up under erasure: "number-less," "count-less," and when they resurface, the text denounces them as deceptive approximations ("hundreds, thousands"; "dozens, scores"; "thousands, aye tens of thousands"). What remains is a convulsive, obsessive repetition: "—the dead, the dead, the dead—*our* dead—or South or North, ours all (all, all, all, finally dear to me)—" (*WPP* 801), reminiscent of yet another Whitmanian poetic iteration, that of the "low and delicious word death, / And again death, death, death, death, / Hissing melodious. . . " in "Out of the Cradle Endlessly Rocking" (*WPP* 393). But if, in the latter, the melancholy chant whispered by the sea brings the comfort of a "rustling" name to the poet's ear, the solace of the noun that tells of the thing is forever missing in the former. In the *Memoranda*, the finality of the dental consonant ("dead") has replaced the whispering melody of "Death." The rustling beauty of the universal (death) is no more. "The dead—*our* dead" has turned the far evanescence of Death into the scandalous oxymoron of a touching, intimate, generality.

In Whitman's *Memoranda*, therefore, not a figure, not even a noun, abides but as a melancholy remainder pointing toward a generality that can only be made concrete by its predication on the self, on the experience of having seen, yet still not grasped, the Real. The Real that war is does not add up; it can only be surmised, somewhere in between "the general million" and "the infinite dead."

Here, as in Dickinson's poetry, the Real defies the contours of the name, of the figures(s). To take up Badiou's logic, "the infinite dead," or, shall we say, the infinite Real in Whitman's *Memoranda during the War*, is not to be formalized in and as the statistical abstracts of the war or the lists of numbers droned out throughout the text; the Real actually becomes palpable, in the wounded word that tells of the incapacitated dream of circumscription, in the dramatic crumbling of the master figure of totalization. The Real, in Whitman also, is without a noun that would circumscribe its substance, let alone its essence; its pressure is made visible in the demise of generality *as* abstraction. Like Dickinson's poetry, Whitman's war prose immodestly displays the materiality of a wounded form that tells of the pressure of the infinite Real and manifests "it" in a text that bears the mark of the concrete. With its maimed figures and improper totalization, the text demonstrates the speaker's exposure to the traumatic encounter with what is off the symbolic, an exposure that is also what we readers experience in Dickinson's war poems. And yet, it does not quite *feel* the same.

The categorical disturbances of Dickinson's poetry bear witness to the singular encounter of the speaker with the Real that war is. If the name does not hold, if the trope cannot do its communal office, there remains what Christine Savinel has called a regime of the "common singular" (*"régime du singulier commun"*) in the sense that the singular voice of the poem is the only possible expression of a communal yet ever singular trauma.[35] The extreme singularity of experience is offered as what "we," an ever-fragile deictic, can have in common. To put it differently, the nation as community dies as abstraction the better to be born again as a commons of singular encounters with the infinite Real, the concreteness of which manifests itself as a troublesome supplement that leaves its mark on the language and form of Dickinson's poems of war. Whitman, on the other hand, who also had to come to terms poetically with the demise of the abstract generality of

43

community, entrusted his writing with the arduous task of reviving what we have "between us."[36] To do so, as I have proposed, he relied on the general concrete as a way of fleshing out a contested abstraction; but instead of adopting a regime of the common singular, I suggest that he turned to what may be called the serial singular. In this matter, once again, it is key to take him at his word and focus on that "profound, vexatious, never-explicable matter—this of names" ("Cedar-Plums—Like Names," *WPP* 909).

In lieu of nouns (the soldiers, the casualties), Whitman's *Memoranda during the War* repeatedly favors the nominalized adjective: "the wounded," "our American wounded," "the dead and wounded."[37] Nominalized adjectives, grammarians tell us, are a way of giving referential autonomy to parts of the discourse that are usually devoid of it. How true it is when the adjective is "dead" or "wounded." Whitman's book of war, I suggest, gives agency to that which is not a substance so much as a quality, not an essence so much as the experience of vulnerability. In so doing, Whitman's *Memoranda during the War* attempts to recover generality ("*our* dead"; "*our* American wounded"; my emphasis) while bypassing abstraction, yet without giving up on singularity.

Indeed, the mark of the Real as the wound of the text does not so much cancel singularity as create a seriality that diagonalizes the singular and the general. The text of the *Memoranda* often aligns a series of initials in lieu of the names of the hospitalized soldiers; the pages are interspersed with disembodied letters: "*W. H. E., Co. F., 2d N.J.*"; "J. G. lies in bed 52, ward I; is of company B, 7th Pennsylvania"; "J. T. L., of company F., 9th New Hampshire, lies in bed 37, ward I" ("Some Specimen Cases," *WPP* 749, 750). Those specters of a name, however and paradoxically, do not repeal singularity: W. H. E. likes his tea green and strong while J. G. cares for tobacco. The initials are no disembodied graphs. Unnaming the soldiers whom he loves not only allows them to be loved in secret, but also allows each reader, whoever he or she is, to love them, each of them, in both their generality and their positive yet unobtrusive singularity.

In Whitman's *Memoranda during the War* the general, therefore, does not forbid the singular, and the reverse is equally true. Serial singularity gives generality a body without threatening it as generality. It is why—and this is Whitman's tour de force—proper names can find their way back into the text without endangering its relentless ambition to rebuild the yearned-for Union. Unlike *Drum-Taps* or *Leaves of Grass,* critics have noted that the *Memoranda* is also full of proper names and, as such, reminiscent of Whitman's *Notebooks* and their famous or infamous lists standing as the epitome of sexual commodification. Instead of contrasting the clandestine list of the *Notebooks,* the lists of the lover soldiers of the *Memoranda during the War,* and the lists of common names of the poems, I would suggest they all partake of an attempt at combining, or diagonalizing, generality with the infinitely reproducible singularity of a one-to-one relation. Through this diagonal, I would argue, Whitman's *Memoranda during the War* turns the generality of the commons poetically concrete through its homage to serial singularity.

"This war for a bare idea and abstraction" was not Whitman's, nor Dickinson's for that matter.[38] Abstraction itself, I have suggested, was put to the test by a war fought for a "thing" impossible to circumscribe in the safety net of a name, a noun, let alone to "concrete" as a whole ("nation," "America" or "the United States" failed as names in those years when they all went without a common stable circumscription or referent). At stake, then, in Whitman and Dickinson's war writings was the very possibility of the concept, understood as what can be safely captured or marked off; the validity of names that never could fit the thing; and the legitimacy of tropes that could no longer be predicated on a dubious transcendence or on the unlikely consensus of a community of readers. In wartime, poetry was forced to its crisis as language was brought face to face with the prospect of its concrete undoing; language itself was unsettled when exposed to the Real that is beyond formalization.

Dickinson and Whitman's are sentient battlefields in which the feeling of the Real emerges through the violent conflagration between the abstract and the concrete—in the dented circumference of Dickinson's poems, in their "categorial disturbances" where something of the speaker's singular encounter with the infinite of the Real is made sensible; in the convulsive approximations of Whitman's war prose, where figures are ripped open, displayed in their own vulnerability. Abstraction itself is exposed, made palpable in its wounded, derelict, becoming; poetic language proves the locus of its excruciating and paradoxical embodiment.

Circuitously salvaging the "idea" of the nation by embodying what remains of the "we" within the wounded, gaping, form of poetic language, each poet found his or her own way of restoring, or performing, the commons without giving up on singularity. Dickinson's common singular and Whitman's serial singularity were born of their wild hopes to maintain some communality that could withstand the pressure of the infinite Real, but the commons their texts conjured up was no abstraction; it endured as an uncanny generality embodied in an "original concrete," the poem or the text itself.

Dickinson|Whitman
Figural Mirrors in Biblical Traditions

SHIRA WOLOSKY

DESPITE THEIR PRONOUNCED DIFFERENCES, DICKINSON AND Whitman are looking-glass reflections of each other and of America; although, as in facing mirrors, each one's work is also the inverse of the other. One crux of this mutual reflection is their shared figural traditions of American culture. These originate in the biblical typologies that promised to align not only spiritual and mundane worlds, but the extensions of these into self, community, history, and God. Each practices and also tests this habit of figural alignment. The poetry of each is figurally complex, in ways often overlooked in Whitman (who can seem like the "scrapbasket" an early reviewer called him) but that reading him with Dickinson makes visible.[1] Narrative and expansive against Dickinson's miniature intensity; self-dramatizing; apparently rambling and spontaneous (which his revisions belie), Whitman emerges into figural complexity when seen from a Dickinsonian perspective. Conversely, reading Dickinson with Whitman opens paths toward seeing her engagement in culture. This engagement remains, as she wrote Higginson of the Civil War, "oblique" (February 1863, *L* 280). Nonetheless, cultural experience such as history, economy, religion, and gender enter into her work no less than into his, but where Whitman's texts seem to gather up all diversity in waves of correlated energy, in Dickinson's these diverse areas visibly strain against each other, often failing to fulfill the analogical and combinatory promises apparently offered. In each, figural complexity representing these diverse areas at once draws on American traditions and tests and contests them, probing not only their claims but their grounds. For both authors, furthermore, such figural construction was put under severe pressure by the Civil War period, in the context of the many social, historical, and religious transmutations erupting in and through nineteenth-century America.

Self, community, history, and God: these are the strands that traditional biblical hermeneutics attempted to bind together, although with different priorities, emphases, and structural distributions at different times. The earliest typologies matched Old Testament "literal" history with New Testament "figural" eternal pattern. This in turn was interiorized into the inner spiritual life of each Christian in conformity with the pattern of Christ's life in suffering, death, and resurrection; the so-called tropological level. Lastly, there were Last Things, individually in each person's death and judgment and historically in the Apocalypse that would finally end world and time altogether.[2]

This figural system pledged above all to connect time to eternity, events to integrated pattern, and self to immortality. In the turn the American Puritans then gave to it, these correlations were extended further from inner self to outer self, with "calling" both a spiritual and mundane path in the world, inscribing each self into historical community in contemporary history.[3] Pattern was no longer only eternal, but concrete and immediate in American history itself. On one level, the structure is theodicean: events are incorporated into a redemptive pattern in which suffering is justified. Indeed, the two are intrinsically linked: suffering is necessary to redemption. As John Brown later proclaimed, "without the shedding of blood there is no remission of sin." American typology incorporated not just discrete and personal events, but communal historical ones into this traditional structure of theodicy. The course of history, seen by Augustine as merely fallen and to be transcended in a vision of the City of God, now also takes its place in a redemptive pattern seen as progressive. Earthly sacrifice is bound to eternal meaning in ways that incorporate both inward self and historical community, which is to say America itself. Biblical history becomes American history, while the figural correlations of biblical hermeneutics transform into the figural elaborations of poets such as Dickinson and Whitman. Yet, where there is pattern there is also imposition. Manifest destiny claimed to fulfil biblical figural practices.[4] Dickinson and Whitman reflect in their figuration the patterns that claim to render experience coherent and meaningful, but also their failure to account for experience as well as the dangers and possible violence of incorporation and appropriation.

Just how the Civil War drew upon these biblical traditions remains a background for both Dickinson and Whitman, who write in its shadow in ways that show both the force of figural claims and also their failure to render history coherent or redeem it.[5] Dickinson's poem "A Tooth upon Our Peace" manifests these counter-forces.

> A Tooth upon Our Peace
> The Peace cannot deface –
> Then Wherefore be the Tooth?
> To vitalize the Grace –
>
> The Heaven hath a Hell –
> Itself to signalize –
> And every sign before the Place –
> Is Gilt with Sacrifice –
>   (*EDP* 336 [Fr 694], 1863)

Written during the Civil War in 1863, the poem speaks not of war but of "Peace." Yet "Peace" here is elusive, threatened, corroded. "Hell" is commonly associated with war, as in Tennyson's well-known "Charge of the Light Brigade," whose (doomed) soldiers ride "boldly into the mouth of Hell." If Tennyson in the poem then asks "When can their glory fade?" Dickinson does not. Instead she questions any such justification. The gnawing as well as the pain of tooth imagery registers the rupture of pattern by event. Rather than a design absorbing suffering into a larger meaning—as part into whole, loss into gain, test into confirmation, trial into strength, perplexity into understanding, error into resolution—in Dickinson, anomaly, pain, loss, intrusion threaten to unravel the patterns supposed to contain, place, and give them meaning.

The centrality of interpretive work in this project of justification, as the means through which patterns of meaning are revealed or imposed, is named in this poem in terms of interpretation: "signalize" and "sign." Their

49

theological echoes emerge through the term "grace." Sacraments are defined by Augustine as visible signs of invisible grace.[6] And "Sacrifice" is perhaps the most significant of key terms in war as in Christic paradigms, crucial to the attempt to make sense of and justify death and bloodshed. In sacrifice, the religious and the political intersect. American civil religion, come to extreme urgency in the Civil War, was impelled by the state's claiming meanings that had hitherto been the domain of religion. As Drew Faust sums up, "sacrifice and state became inextricably intertwined" in the Civil War. The "domain of sacrifice" shifted from religion to patriotism as the "claim of ultimate meaning for the individual citizen."[7] Alice Fahs similarly sees the major form of consolation in mid-nineteenth-century American Protestantism to be the "promise of salvation through suffering," via themes of "sacrifice, suffering and redemption" expressed in sentimental writings: "The dead bodies of soldiers became vehicles for a new sentimentalism that fused patriotism and Christianity," and through the appeal to sacrifice "suffering tied them to the nation."[8]

Neither the religious nor the patriotic claims really stand up under Dickinsonian scrutiny. "A Tooth upon Our Peace" poses the traditional structure in which suffering is understood "to vitalize the grace." Grace presumably delivers the self from hell to heaven. In this poem it becomes difficult to distinguish between them. One serves "to signalize" the other; but this makes heaven the image or "sign" of hell rather than its rescue.[9] In the poem's final line, the "gilt" of sacrifice puns both on guilt as the supposed reason for suffering taken as punishment, as well as economic display and hypocritical concealment.

This poem does not point to any specific biblical text or historical or personal event. As so often in Dickinson, experiences of suffering remain unspecified. And yet they are linked to the public sphere, showing how the most personal confrontation is also a historical, publicly hermeneutical one. Here, words that seem private connect to surrounding discourses, including those of war: peace and sacrifice, grace and hell. The principles the text invokes of suffering, atonement, and grace, of sacramental signs, are those that claim to deliver redemptive patterns, summoned to explain and justify both personal and historical anguish. As Dickinson wrote to her Norcross cousins in 1862: "I wish 'twas plainer, Loo, the anguish in this world. I wish one could be sure the suffering had a loving side" (*L* 263). In the poem what endures is the opening question that the poem fails to answer: "Then Wherefore be the Tooth?" No response to this challenge is forthcoming, but rather, a querying of justifications at once theological, historical-political, and personal, in which the gaps between suffering and meaning, different levels of experience and their purported integration in pattern, are left painfully open.

Dickinson's terse text thus offers almost an abstract version of core paradigms for interpreting events, especially ones of suffering and trauma and war: those teeth upon our peace. Suffering, violence, conflict: these are the materials that cultural paradigms structure and explain, the signs to be interpreted through their frameworks and patterns (what makes them signs at all). Dickinson makes these paradigms visible in her contest with them, a contest that crosses through the diverse levels of experience that it is her art to assemble, interweave, and counterweave.

Dickinson thus continues to assume, and also to invoke paradigm expectations, the disappointment of which causes her acute distress. Her poems enact this appeal to/denial of paradigms. In aesthetic terms, Dickinson's poems register a crisis between addresser and responder, where shared frameworks are vulnerable and fragile under the pressure of war. Claiming to fulfill religious patterns in political and social terms, the Civil War seemed to her instead a dreadful challenge to them, violently betraying the promised redemption. These tensions structure her compositional practices of interference in syntax, meter, punctuation (can her dashes echo the new telegraphic communication that was conducted during the war?) as well as her use/disruption of hymnal forms. The destabilization of meaning itself converges in the apparent question "Wherefore be the Tooth" and what amounts to a retractive (non)answer. In the final gilt/guilt pun, the promised reward of value is intimately tied to a guilt that may be a problematic appeal to sacrifice, and/or may be mere glitter. This and other formal, compositional elements cannot be separated from the history and ideology the poem addresses, with the aesthetic exactly the inextricability of their interplay.

A second example, "That after Horror," is dated 1862. Although this particular poem has not been a focus of discussion as a war poem, the ever-widening field of commentary on Dickinson and war provides a frame for reading this and many other texts in the context of the Civil War. The historicist turn of criticism in the 1990s strongly impacted Dickinson studies. Research has explored a variety of Civil War contexts for Dickinson's work culturally, historically, technologically, politically, and in relation to gender.[10] A series of articles have thus linked Dickinson's texts to contemporary communication technologies such as photography, telegraph, aerial balloons, railroads, journalism, and the mass of other Civil War poetry circulating within this nexus of transformed communication. Cristanne Miller explores Dickinson's poetry alongside the mass publication of other Civil War poetry.[11] Eliza Richards speaks of a "network" of communications and the imagery and rhetoric these generated. Her discussions of photography, for example, explore how the frozen moment of the text reflects the dead photographic image as it in turn affects and deadens the viewer.[12] These studies balance historicist information with textual analysis in terms of genres, metaphoric structures, and also, notably by Faith Barrett, problems of lyric address and lyric status compared to pastoral and elegy, very interestingly in relation to Walt Whitman.[13] All the discussions underscore a crisis between public and private spheres, which Dickinson particularly exposes but which extends to all Americans experiencing the Civil War.[14]

Yet oddly, this criticism at times verges into just this split of public and private, now on the side of the public. Dickinson emerges as an instance of contemporary communications, largely eliding the interiority that had been the mainstay of earlier Dickinson criticism. Placing Dickinson into contemporary cultural, historical, rhetorical, popular, and gendered contexts is imperative. Keeping these in balance with the phenomenological and aesthetic dimensions of Dickinson remains a challenge and also a necessity. This is precisely what multidimensional figural theory can offer: a view of how these different levels of address, trope, reference, and structure invoke each other, with or without correlation.

There are specific discussions of "That after Horror" in the earlier, more phenomenological Dickinson criticism, where interior, privatized interpretation occludes further cultural or historical reference:

That after Horror – that 'twas *us* –
That passed the mouldering Pier –
Just as the Granite crumb let go –
Our Savior, by a Hair –

A second more, had dropped too deep
For Fisherman to plumb –
The very profile of the Thought
Puts Recollection numb –

The possibility – to pass
Without a moment's Bell –
Into Conjecture's presence –
Is like a Face of Steel –
That suddenly looks into ours
With a metallic grin –
The Cordiality of Death –
Who drills his Welcome in –
(*EDP* 129 [Fr 243B])

Phenomenological discussions of this poem focus on the effects on consciousness of facing an unknown and terrifying event. According to Sharon
Cameron, the speaker "documents the experience of near death" and its
assault on consciousness, leaving "gaps in thought that attest to the terror
of fragmentary comprehension."[15] In Helen Vendler's reading, the poem
registers a moment when "without warning a dreadful possibility confronts
us," as for example "a dreadful diagnosis or a hair's breadth escape from
death," leaving "two forms of post-traumatic response: after horror, numb
recollection."[16]

These phenomenological readings are also New Critical: the text as a
tableau of consciousness, caught in a formal moment whose elements cut
time into lyric stasis. The lyric itself is temporal interruption, catching consciousness in its self-reflection. Neither is situated in terms outside of the
text. Even consciousness is a process of textual encounter, mainly cognitive

and mainly about cognitive possibility: how to grasp time as sequence, how to compose it into coherent wholes, what happens when such composition is resisted: lyric interruption. Domhnall Mitchell, citing Jerome McGann's dictum that Dickinson's manuscripts "urge us to treat all scriptural forms as potentially significant," turns from formal discussion of the poem to include manuscript structure.[17] He too then sees the manuscript formation of cut-off words and lines in "That after Horror" as acting to "delay the encounter between the speaker and Death—heightening the sense of dreadful anticiptation—and perhaps also performs the desire to postpone that final meeting"; although warning that it is hard to prove specific intentions, since "almost any feature of Dickinson's manuscript can be interpreted to suggest a proleptic concern with the semantic potential of the poem's visual properties."[18]

These readings leave the text unembedded in cultural or historical context, with Dickinson herself an almost pure interiority engaged in self-reflection, almost like the skull that Vendler sees in the poem's image of the "Face of Steel" and "metallic grin"—"confronting a skull—not a corruptible skull but an immortal Platonic Form of face made of steel."[19] And yet, this very image could point decisively outward from Dickinson's interior consciousness. In 1862, a "face of steel" that "drills" death's welcome could refer to the guns of war, with "drill" itself a military term. The "Bell" image could also have historical reference: church bells were rung to mark military engagements, alarms, and victories.[20] The incursions into and fragmentation of consciousness here could thus have an exterior and historical reference if not direct cause, a phenomenology of war with wide implications and not only ones idiosyncratic to Dickinson's poetic or vulnerable consciousness.[21]

The poem thus inter- and counter-weaves both phenomenology and history, requiring a method and an aesthetics that acknowledges both. There are other dimensions as well. Characteristic of Dickinson, as also evident here, is a religious dimension, proposed in the poem's first two stanzas:

> That after Horror – that 'twas us –
> That passed the mouldering Pier –
> Just as the Granite crumb let go –
> Our Savior, by a Hair –

A second more, had dropped too deep
For Fisherman to plumb –
The very profile of the Thought
Puts Recollection numb –

The term "Savior" resonates religiously. "Fisherman" in this context could also evoke Christ the fisherman of men, here unable to save.[22] "Pier" recalls Dickinson's wavering poem "Faith – is the Pierless Bridge," which, as so often in Dickinson, at once declares faith to be and not to be a bridge that can sustain her (*EDP* 451 [Fr 978]).[23] "Pierless" is multiply resonant: a pun on "peerless," affirming faith's unique and eminent status; yet also denying the "Pier" that would anchor the bridge of faith to experience. In "That after Horror" the pier is "mouldering," with the speaker veering over its edge into a drowning depth no "Fisherman" can "plumb."

The phenomenological fracturing this poem enacts extends beyond consciousness; and indeed, demonstrates how consciousness is itself embedded in patterns of understanding whose crises this poem registers. The very fragmentation of interiority this poem performs is also a fragmentation of patterns on which consciousness relies. "The very profile of the Thought / Puts Recollection numb –" is an extraordinary summation of how recollection and thought both rely on "profile," the outline that places things. Around and in this text, such "profile," paradigm, pattern, placement has been assaulted: in the poem's second half by the rupture of death. Death here seems to be set in the 1863 context of war guns' "face of steel" and "metallic grin" in military "drill"—as one extreme way of death in its unpredictable incursion at any time in any manner. Death has always been a challenge to human consciousness. What has changed here is the collapse of pattern that placed death in some order with meaning. That order had been, up until Dickinson's time, religious. To her this has begun to collapse, becoming a "mouldering pier" that does not bridge this world and the next, experience and meaning. The war itself with its particular schisms, including in the American churches, subverted religious certainty in writers like Dickinson and Melville. It, with other contexts of skepticism such as biblical criticism, science, and the technological, social, and demographic revolutions of the nineteenth century in America, are registered here as a fragmentation of consciousness. That fragmentation, which Dickinson's formal practices so powerfully render, reaches into consciousness as it loses its scaffolding of patterned meanings, which are cultural. In the poem, in fact, "Conjecture" is cited as threat, to which the suddenness of (war) death is compared. The conjecture is questioning itself, Dickinson's doubts as to the patterns that bound together past present and future, not least through Christic centering. Christ is the crux through which all things and times pass and in which they are bound. This is the pattern Dickinson inherited, underwriting the relationships between events and experiences, internal and external, cognitive and historical. This poem, like so many in Dickinson, shows the effects of these integrating correlations as they come apart, under pressures outside no less than inside her. This does not, however, in my view, make Dickinson's a position that "held every position"; nor one "testing out opposing ideologies"; nor does it indicate that in Dickinson's war (or other) writing there is no "personal feeling but carefully crafted response to other poems."[24] Such arguments, while embedded in historical and cultural context, propose Dickinson as ultimately a detached spectator almost disembodied in experimenting or even registering different possible responses. Yet I by no means argue that Dickinson offers any single unified synthesis or position encompassing or reconciling divergent views, as if this were the only alternative to open experiment. Instead, I see the multiple perspectives, possible configurations, and contradictory positions that Dickinson deploys not as detachment but as contest and disputation. Powerfully and crucially caught in the contradictions of her cultures, history, religious beliefs and doctrines, and gendered and personal experiences, Dickinson's work shows the fraying of paradigms of cultural understanding as these were deeply and profoundly at stake for her. Breaks among and juxtapositions of different worlds especially explode in war, which shatters norms and challenges cultural paradigms of interpretation. This is what Dickinson exposes and engages.[25] Caught between paradigms, attempting now one, now another approach and account, Dickinson's work is, I feel, that of an engaged but contested person displaying the increasingly disparate and inconsistent claims that she and her world could offer. It is in the context of just such a contested, multiple textuality of contending levels of experience and their interpretation that Dickinson's resources in hermeneutic figural traditions are visible. Alicia Ostriker points in this direction when she sees scripture as generating a plurality of interpretations, as does Dickinson, although I think that Ostriker, as a contemporary writer, feels more at ease with such pluralities than did Dickinson.[26]

Whitman's "I Sing the Body Electric" appeared as one of the sequences in the 1855 edition of *Leaves of Grass*; and then with significant revisions in the 1856 edition, revised again in 1860, until reaching its final form in 1867, when this title first appeared. As Betsy Erkkila has explored, this poem is focused not simply on the body and sexuality as is often claimed, but is directed through the human body to the body politic, specifically attacking American racism, which emerges dramatically in the slave auction scene of section 7.[27] Sexuality makes up only one layer of a many-layered figuralism in which no one level, sexuality included, is the only, or ultimate, or determinative meaning. Indeed, in Whitman's figural poetics no single level of meaning commandeers significance in ways that dominate all others. Each level enters in its own integrity and force; yet it is the core of Whitman's art, energy, and also visionary hope that each can extend into others, in a multidimensionality of experience that nevertheless remains mutually supportive in ways that are rarely recognized or explored. His poems, that is, no less than Dickinson's, although in ways less noticed, explore a variety of spheres, each of which is a figure for the other. The challenge is how these levels do or do not together represent an American culture that Whitman yearns to believe can sustain this very diversity.

Physical eroticism thus takes its place among other figures orchestrating various relations to each other across multiple levels of meaning. Sexuality, however, does have a signal significance for Whitman, in that he refuses its reduction in dualist terms. From its 1856 version forward, "I Sing the Body Electric" opens with a challenge to dualist divisions: "And if the body were not the Soul, what is the Soul?" (*WPP* 250). Whitman is not reversing dualist axiology to privilege the material body, or to make it his primary subject. What he does is resist the dualisms that have governed Western tradition and the hierarchies, oppositions, and enmities these institute. Whitman refuses such dualist splits or hierarchies, as between mind and body, spirit and matter, or man and woman to which these have been correlated. Wittgenstein said: "the human body is the best picture of the human soul."[28] In Whitman, the body is a picture that he means to reflect and expand upon others, replacing reductions with expansions and multiplications.[29] This is hinted in the word "electric" of the poem's title, beginning in 1867: "electric" itself is one of Whitman's characteristic figures for just such figural connections, as a term at once scientific, sexual, visual, and poetic, energizing, coordinating, impelling, as the material of his song.

One level of experience decisively incorporated into "I Sing the Body Electric" is that of the polity, which in section 7 is invoked as "the start of populous states and rich republics." Here both national and economic prosperity are indicated—economy being for Whitman, in his best moods, also a possibility of expansion and invention. Science, too, is brought in through the human evolutionary miracle which Whitman embraced first via Lamarck and later Darwin: "For it the globe lay preparing quintillions of years" (WPP 255). To Whitman, evolution is as equalizing as his anti-hierarchical and anti-dualist mind/body integration, confirming the value and parity of each person: "Limbs, red, black, or white" all incarnate the "all-baffling brain; In it and below it, the makings of heroes," by which Whitman means leaders and poets, indeed each individual creative and contributing. There is no lower physical nature to be renounced in the name of some higher one. The human is embodied selfhood, all from the same genealogies, in an evolutionary rephrasing of the equal creation of humankind.

"I Sing the Body Electric" thus brings different levels of experience into interplay in a visionary oratory that recalls biblical traditions, transformed in significant ways but underwriting this very figural multiplicity itself. Indeed, I propose the poem to be a commentary on Genesis 1:27: "So God created mankind in his own image, in the image of God he created them; male and female he created them." This of course is the proof-text of the entire discourse of the human as created in the image of God, today a fundamental element in discussions of human rights. It is a text central to both abolitionist and feminist discourses, which cited this account of equal creation as against the second story of female secondarity in Genesis 2, where, as Elizabeth Cady Stanton protested, woman is fantastically born of men.[30]

Whitman's "I Sing the Body Electric" invokes this most central of biblical texts at its own core. Section 5 refers to the "divine nimbus" that "exhales" from the "female form . . . from head to foot" (man and woman were inspired or "exhale[d]" to life in Genesis by the divine breath). Section 6 specifies that this sacrality includes the body: "The man's body is sacred, and the woman's body is sacred / No matter who it is, it is sacred" (*WPP* 254). Section 8 insists again: "If any thing is sacred, the human body is sacred" (*WPP* 256). On the one hand, this focus on the body as the sacred site is a challenge to the tradition. On the other, it also carries forward elements from earlier Puritan typologies that incorporated exteriority in the forms of the historical and the mundane, as well as national polity and prosperity.

And yet Whitman, like Dickinson, is painfully aware that these correlations and expansions have been far from fulfilled. In his earliest version of this poem, in 1855, his attempts to correlate between religious, civic, and economic equalities register the failure to fulfil such mutual reflections:

> Is it a slave? Is it one of the dull-faced immigrants just landed on
>   the wharf?
> Each belongs here or anywhere, just as much as the well-off—
>   just as much as you.
>
> (WPP 1855, 122)

The very inclusion of "slave" in this declaration of equality (later omitted from the poem) contradicts the political, social, and economic reality in which Whitman writes, whose inequalities are registered in the very terms "slave" and "dull-faced."

These vistas—physical, sacral, political, gendered, conceived in egalitarian and democratic ways—are stretched across what opens in the poem as a terrible breach. The prosperity of "rich republics" at this moment of 1855 includes an economy in which persons are not sacred, but instead reduced to owned objects. The biblical "sacred" body then becomes the auctioned body of the slave, where, in a dramatic rhetorical inversion, Whitman takes the very scene of reduction of the human to property and makes it a declaration of the inestimable value of each person, gainsaying the auctioneer by outdoing him. "I help the auctioneer. . . . the sloven [this is surely a wordplay on "slave," now referring to the auctioneer] does not half know his business" (*WPP* 1855, 123). The word "business," like other economic terms in Whitman, is lifted out of its reductive monetary sense to wider meanings. Here it transforms sales-pitch into revelation. The body presented as object is unveiled as "wonder," a miracle of divine image. Converting the very language of economic assessment, the poet turns it to a value beyond measure: "Whatever the bids of the bidders they cannot be high enough for him" (*WPP* 1855, 123). Earlier in the poem Whitman insisted: "The expression of the body of man or woman balks account, / The male is perfect and that of the female is perfect" (*WPP* 1855, 118). "Account" itself is converted from calculation to narrative and testimony, as the poet translates (to use another key Whitmanian term for figuration) economy from reductive price to marvelous appreciation.

Whitman in this scene at once protests and registers how far America is from his own transformed senses of economy, as if these can express and be in harmony with democratic social and political life. He shows how property of persons ruptures and betrays America's multiple promises. In the America that this poem represents and addresses, the reduction of the human to slave is a chiasmic wound that threatens Whitman's art of figural extension. Even as he celebrates America he dissents from the given social economic order of America as it now, in 1855, exists; although he remains as well fundamentally within his cultural horizons that limit his dissent and urge justification.

To claim that Whitman is weaving biblical reference as one layer of his text (as he himself hinted in a notebook, where he called his work "The Great Construction of the New Bible")[31] and to claim that he is recalling and reworking the multiple levels of biblical hermeneutic, is not to say that he does not depart from and significantly revise these traditions. Strikingly he eliminates Last Things (whereas these can threaten to consume all else in Dickinson). Whitman is rarely eschatological. For him, as he writes,

Each has his or her place in the procession.

All is a procession,
The universe is a procession with measured and beautiful motion.
(*WPP* 1855, 122)

Whitman pledges this ongoing figural extension even over the abyss of slavery, which is to say against a history that ruptures and threatens his visionary procession. This is a measure of his transfigurative courage. Whitman, although acutely, painfully aware how fragile are inherited paradigms and correspondences and radically critical of them, gathers up with force the parts and pieces to weave them into hopeful, unfinished, unfurling energies. Thus in "Song of Myself" section 6, he figures himself as the grass, "the flag of my disposition, out of hopeful green stuff woven" (*WWA* 33). The imagery is at once public "flag" and personal "disposition," interior and political; while, as he goes on to say, the grass is also the "handkerchief of the Lord," a figure and sign for him to read and himself to weave.

"Song of Myself" section 3 presents a curious case of almost a specific rewriting of biblical passages, especially Romans 1. As usual in Whitman, the cadences of parallel repetitions recall biblical verse form.

> I have heard what the talkers were talking, the talk of the beginning
>   and the end,
> But I do not talk of the beginning or the end.
>
> There was never any more inception than there is now,
>   Nor any more youth or age than there is now,
>   And will never be any more perfection than there is now,
>   Nor any more heaven or hell than there is now.
>
> Urge and urge and urge,
>   Always the procreant urge of the world. . .
>
> Clear and sweet is my soul, and clear and sweet is all that is not
>   my soul.
>
> (*WWA* 30–31)

The "talkers" who "talk of beginning and the end" are biblical ones. "I am Alpha and Omega, the beginning and the ending," prophesies John in Revelations 1:8, "which is, and which was, and which is to come, the Almighty." But it is just this revelation of an eternity collapsing time which, in absorbing all time into itself consumes it, that Whitman rejects. His re-written Bible is a Bible of time in the world, not of eternity above, outside, and over it: "But I do not talk of the beginning or the end." In the next stanza, "inception" internally rhymes with "perfection," making what is traditionally oppositional into something matching. This gives the world of time, body, the investment that traditional metaphysics divests from it.

Whitman dismisses all metaphysics. He erases the other worlds of heaven and hell for this one here and now, writing "Nor any more heaven or hell than there is now," whereas in Romans 1:17–18, Paul writes, "For therein is the righteousness of God revealed from faith to faith: as it is written, The just shall live by faith. For the wrath of God is revealed from heaven against all ungodliness and unrighteousness of men, who hold the truth in unrighteousness." The "unrighteousness" that unleashes the wrath of God from heaven to hell is idolatry, specified by Paul as taking "the glory of the uncorruptible God into an image made like to corruptible man, and to birds, and fourfooted beasts, and creeping things" (Romans 1:23). For this, as he writes, is to substitute the visible for the invisible, the seen for the unseen: "For the invisible things of him from the creation of the world are clearly seen, being understood by the things that are made, even his eternal power and Godhead; so that they are without excuse." Whitman counters:

> Clear and sweet is my soul, and clear and sweet is all that is
>   not my soul.

> Lack one lacks both, and the unseen is proved by the seen,
> Till that becomes unseen and receives proof in its turn. . .
>   (WWA 31)

Whitman takes up the Pauline language of the seen and the unseen, not to direct from the visible world to "invisible things" beyond it, nor from the "things that are made" to an "eternal power," but instead emphatically to affirm the ongoing world "that becomes." Here as often in Whitman a specific philosophical vocabulary can be glimpsed, of Platonist Being against Becoming, and of "proof."[32] These are formulae Whitman would confute. In Whitman there is no hierarchy between the seen and unseen, soul and not soul. Each generates the other in an ongoing procession, a chain of becoming, not of being. And both seen and unseen are necessary and valuable: "Lacks one lacks both."

In Romans 1, Paul has a specific sin in mind, in which body betrays soul, a sin that Whitman might want particularly to contest.

[24] Wherefore God also gave them up to uncleanness through the lusts of their own hearts, to dishonour their own bodies between themselves: [25] Who changed the truth of God into a lie, and worshipped and served the creature more than the Creator, who is blessed for ever. Amen. [26] For this cause God gave them up unto vile affections: for even their women did change the natural use into that which is against nature: [27] And likewise also the men, leaving the natural use of the woman, burned in their lust one toward another; men with men working that which is unseemly, and receiving in themselves that recompense of their error which was meet.

The "recompense" of the sin of "vile affections" is hell, an ultimate case for Paul of serving the creature more than the Creator, where these two are in tension if not opposition; the lust of "men with men working that which is unseemly." But Whitman in section 3 celebrates "the hugging and loving bed-fellow [who] sleeps at my side through the night, and withdraws at the peep of the day with stealthy tread." Although this could be any "bed-fellow," "fellow" points to a male gendering. And Whitman does not condemn, but explicitly elevates physical embrace: "I am satisfied—I see, dance, laugh, sing," a singing he performs in this very Song.

> That they turn from gazing after and down the road,
> And forthwith cipher and show me to a cent,
> Exactly the value of one and exactly the value of two, and which
>   is ahead?
>
> (*WWA* 31)

Whitman's gaze is "after and down the road," forward into future time, moment following moment, giving value exactly to what Paul condemns, "Who knowing the judgment of God, that they which commit such things are worthy of death, not only do the same, but have pleasure in them that do them" (Romans 1:32).

63

Whitman's commitment to transfiguration in time and the world re-weaves the terms of traditional biblical prophecy and typology from vertical hierarchies, tensions, and opposition to horizontal unfolding, where the various terms interchange and interact in ongoing creativity. It is his own faith (and like any faith, it exceeds evidence) that these varieties of transfor-mation can propel each other in generative directions, "Leaving me baskets cover'd with white towels swelling the house with their plenty." He, like Dickinson, registers a profound crisis in cultural habits of interpretation, correlating unseen and seen, soul and body, past, present, and future, in meaningful patterns.

For both Whitman and Dickinson, the certainties of metaphysics have become conjecture, leaving gaps between the terms that prophecy, typol-ogy, and metaphysics itself had promised to bind. Dickinson's work most powerfully registers these gaps themselves, as refracted through her strained poetic ruptures. Whitman reweaves them into an ongoing production whose terms have changed from static to temporal meanings, undertaken in his verse's rhythmic correlations. Dickinson retains, even as she rigor-ously and painfully critiques, the older yearning for some general pattern in nature. In "A Tooth upon Our Peace" she asks "Then wherefore be the Tooth," echoing questions she poses elsewhere, as when in the poem "Four Trees" she demands "What Deed is Theirs unto the General Nature – / What Plan," but this is a question she can only answer with "Unknown – " (*EDP* 382 [Fr 778]). Her work is a record of paradigms that do not, enough, account for her world. Her figuration is an image of this failure, but also of her effort and desire for correlation. Whitman works in a counter-direction. Both poets weave texts out of multiple figural strands, whose very corre-spondences are at stake. Yet both work within an inherited supposition of multidimensional reference, itself biblically based, where the formal extends into the many levels of experience, at once historical and private, affirmative and skeptical, embodiment and its limits, pattern and its constant clash with the unformulation of the changeable and unknown.

"No Man Saw Awe" / "In the Talk of … God … He Is Silent"
(Not) Seeing and (Not) Saying the Numinous in Dickinson and Whitman

JENNIFER LEADER

ONE MIGHT IMAGINE THAT FOR ALL HER ADMIRATION OF RALPH
Waldo Emerson, Emily Dickinson would secretly have agreed with Walt
Whitman's sideswipe at that oracle on the occasion of Emerson's birthday;
in an 1880 essay in the *Boston Literary World*, Whitman wrote: "At times
it has been doubtful to me if Emerson really knows or feels what Poetry is
at its highest, as in the Bible, for instance, or Homer or Shakspere. . . . Of
power he seems to have a gentleman's admiration—but in his inmost heart
the grandest attribute of God and Poets is always subordinate to the octaves,
conceits, polite kinds, and verbs" (*WPP* 1054). Indeed, despite their many
differences, Whitman and Dickinson both claim audacious, near divine
powers for poets. Whitman's poet is the great namer of the unity behind
all things; he is a Christ-like figure whose flesh becomes the poem, who
"indicates the path between reality" and our "souls," and whose messianic
call is to liberate camerados to become their own poets and priests (*WPP*
1855, 10). Dickinson's poet is creator and destroyer who through reverie
and philology makes prairies and suns, who with one hand gives sensory
experience and dazzling revelation, only to use the other hand to "Pluck
up" her linguistic "stakes, and disappear," leaving "just the miles of Stare – "
(*EDP* 126, Fr 257). Further, despite their substantial powers, Whitman's
poet as transubstantiator of the quotidian and Dickinson's poet as rival
to Jehovah both occasionally deploy the concept of God as a kind of rhetorical absolute zero that serves to curtail their poetic scopes. The wholly
and irreducibly Other appears in these moments not as another trope for

what poetry can and should do but as the functional edge of a divine Ur-power that, by suggesting limits, oppositely sets the poets' own prowess and projects in relief.

For although the differences between Whitman's and Dickinson's poetic projects are manifold, both had keen, startlingly original, religious imaginations and were explicit in their insistence on the spiritual components of their visions, despite a heterodox inventiveness that was (in Whitman's case), or would have been (in Dickinson's), offensive to a majority of the Christian reading public. While there has been a respectable amount of scholarly attention given over the past century to elements of spirituality and belief in Whitman and Dickinson's work, much of this focus has been directed toward aspects of their thinking that can be specifically identified with particular religions or theologies. Less attention, on the other hand, has been given to what the philosopher and scholar of comparative religion Mircea Eliade deems "the existential dimensions of religious man," a phenomenon he believes that modern "desacralization" has made "increasingly difficult" for contemporary audiences to "rediscover" in the art of previous centuries.[1] Where Whitman and Dickinson gesture toward nonrational experiences of a non-anthropomorphized, divine impingement upon the natural world, the lenses of religious phenomenologists such as Eliade and his predecessor, Rudolf Otto, offer critical insight.[2] Whitman's trope of mystical silence and Dickinson's trope of faceless awe, in fact, are both among the several cultural representations these scholars have identified as ancient and universal ways of attempting to render the numinous in art. Concomitantly, both poets employ transformative encounters with what Eliade has termed "hierophany," "the act of manifestation of the sacred," to vividly dramatize concepts central to their beliefs about what poets and poetry should accomplish.[3] Whitman's ideal poet uses wordless silence as the place to turn back from pondering mystery to the embrace of language that is embodied in the here and now, for "the attributes of the poets of the kosmos concentre in the real body and soul and in the pleasure of things they possess."[4] Dickinson's poet returns from harrowing encounters with facelessness to find, like the prophet Moses, that the poet's calling is to become the intermediary between the known world and the circumference of awe, "Myself – the Term between – " as she puts it in "Behind me dips Eternity" (EDP373, Fr 743).

To utilize the discourse of religious phenomenology, of course, does not imply that the poets were aloof from their own cultural, religious contexts. Indeed, elements of influence in each poet's early religious experience suggest possibilities for how the conceits of silence and facelessness came to signal hierophany in their writings. By his own account, chief among Whitman's literary and spiritual influences were the Old and New Testaments, works whose "divine and primal poetic structure" he considered to be the twin "fountain heads of song," foundational to all civilization (*WPP* 1166–67).[5] Additionally, while the spiritual proclivities in Whitman's earliest poetry bear the marks of his initial embrace of Emerson's Transcendentalism, scholars have also long mentioned the imprint of Quaker spirituality on Whitman's thinking.[6] Christina Davey, for instance, has examined familial influences on the poet, noting that Whitman's maternal grandmother, with whom he had a close relationship until her death when he was seven, was a practicing Quaker, and that his mother most likely passed on aspects of the Quaker ethic to him, as well.[7] In "Seeds of Quakerism at the Roots of Leaves of Grass," Susan Dean compares Whitman's vision of democracy with similar and contrasting philosophies in Quakerism; she claims "especially in the 'Calamus' poems, Whitman is trying to win for the gay minority in nineteenth-century America what the Quaker minority had won in England in the seventeenth."[8] Whitman himself gladly acknowledged the long duration of the Quaker influence in his life. As he joked about writing at an advanced age in a late interview with biographer Horace Traubel, "I have to go slow, and only work on days when the spirit moves me; for you know I am half Quaker and go a little on the light within."[9] The poet's most direct articulation of the importance of Quakerism to his spiritual and artistic development is in his late essay "Elias Hicks." Hicks was a farmer from Long Island and an itinerant Quaker speaker and leader of such renown that his teachings had precipitated the 1827–28 split of the Friends into the Orthodox and Hicksite groups.[10] Recording his deep impressions of the Brooklyn meeting where he had heard Hicks speak nearly sixty years before (the essay first appeared in the 1888 *November Boughs*), Whitman recalls that Hicks "was very mystical and radical, and had much to say of 'the light within.' Very likely this same *inner light* . . . is perhaps only another name for the religious conscience" (*WPP* 1258–59). Whitman goes on to stress that being awakened to one's individual "religious conscience," that is, to the "inward Deity-planted law of the emotional soul," provides the "antiseptic," "the moral power and ethic sanity" Americans need to resist the corrupt social and political "inflammation[s]" of their day (*WPP* 1259).

Along with the Friends' belief in the Inner Light as the guide to individual and authentic spirituality, their practice of worshipful silence also seems to have had a profound impact on the young Whitman, who later remarks upon "the perfect stillness" of the Quaker meeting three times in his recollection of the evening with Elias Hicks (*WPP* 1257). In fact, by the time he wrote "Elias Hicks" Whitman had already linked the Quaker emphasis on silent contemplation with the development of a distinctively American, democratic spirit in several of his important essays. In the 1871 "Democratic Vistas," for instance, Whitman holds up "Conscience" and "Religion" as the necessary incubators for the developed soul that "emerges" from a practice of silence: "Alone, and silent thought and awe, and aspiration—and then the interior consciousness . . . beams out its wondrous lines to the sense. Bibles may convey, and priests expound, but it is exclusively for the noiseless operation of one's isolated Self, to enter the pure ether of veneration, reach the divine levels, and commune with the unutterable" (*WPP* 989). Earlier still, in his "Preface, 1855," Whitman had implied this principle when he enjoined future poets to "argue not concerning God" (*WPP* 1855, 11).[11] The new race of poet priest "shall not deign to defend immortality or God or the perfection of things or liberty or the exquisite beauty and reality of the soul" (*WPP* 1855, 25). In short, "in the talk on the soul and eternity and God off of his equal plane he is silent" (*WPP* 1855, 9). Consequently, the poet's work is to encourage his audience toward developing their own abilities to "reach the divine levels, and commune with the unutterable," and so to embrace the spiritual life for themselves (*WPP* 965). For one who is fully alive to his or her potential, as he explains in "Democratic Vistas," "Religion" becomes "a part of the identified soul, which, when greatest, knows not bibles in the old way, but in new ways" (*WPP* 989). The spiritual affinities between the Hicksites' practice of silent worship as openness to the Inner Light (defined by one religious historian as "the direct personal experience of the spirit of God within oneself") and Whitman's own cry of "Divine am I inside and out" are conspicuous, at least in terms of shared emphasis on an interior, mystical union (*WPP* 211).[12] Whitman had in fact collected a large amount of material concerning Elias Hicks in the hopes of writing an entire book about him. That he failed to achieve this ambition, Lawrence Templin has posited, is attributable to the fact that Whitman was unable to reconcile Hicks's larger Quaker belief system involving the denial of personal desire and the acknowledgment of individual sin with his own embrace of the self in its entirety, including its "forbidden voices," "the flesh and the appetites" (*WPP* 211).[13]

Yet Whitman would make good on his assertion in "Preface, 1855" that "in the talk on the soul and eternity and God off of his equal plane" the poet "is silent," leaving signposts throughout his oeuvre that reiterated the need for his readers to discover the spirituality of silence for themselves (*WPP* 1855, 9). For instance, in "A Song of the Rolling Earth," Whitman's early nod to Emerson's Transcendentalist vision of nature as symbol of the spirit, he declares that "the substantial words are in the ground and sea" (*WPP* 363) and that "all merges toward the presentation of the unspoken meanings of the earth," for "what is better than the best" is "always to leave the best untold" (*WPP* 367). Likewise, in the late poem "A Riddle Song," the poet constructs a puzzle out of "that which eludes this verse and any verse, / Unheard by sharpest ear, unform'd in clearest eye or cunningest mind" (*WPP* 587). Calling Whitman's silences "strategic," David Kuebrich asserts that the poet "would not have demanded so much of his readers if he had not subscribed to the notion that perfect sanctification was possible and that the future religious democracies of America and the world demanded a new race of spiritual athletes who would strive for perfection."[14] By leaving room for the mystical, contends Kuebrich, Whitman intends for his reader "to have a religious experience that will enable him or her to realize the unstated spiritual truth that resolves the poem."[15]

Whitman's refusal to finally delineate the "unutterable," along with his oft-repeated admonitions throughout his work that "Not I, not any one else can travel that road for you, / You must travel it for yourself," implicitly align silence with receptiveness to spiritual epiphany (*WPP* 241). In this associative sense, silence becomes a metaphysical placeholder both for the numinous and for a concomitant rejection of analytical and theological interpretations of religious experience, foci that the poet believes to be distractions from loving attention to hearing, seeing, and finding in the here and the now. In section 48 of "Song of Myself," for instance, the poet advises, "Be not curious about God / For I who am curious about each am not curious about God"; and "I hear and behold God in every object, yet understand God not in the least" (*WPP* 244). "I hear," "I see," "I find," the poet repeats in this section, yet he does not claim to "understand." Instead of doctrine, the poet characteristically offers himself as one whose spiritual longings are fulfilled by acceding to the experience of embodied immanence: "Why should I wish to see God better than this day? . . . / In the faces of men and women I see God, and in my own face in the glass" (*WPP* 244–45). With typical cadences reminiscent of the authority and grandeur of the King James Bible, Whitman ends the section: "I find letters from God dropt in the street, and every one is sign'd by God's name / And I leave them where they are, for I know that wheresoe'er I go, / Others will punctually come for ever and ever" (*WPP* 245). In "leav[ing] them where they are" the poet recalls to his readers the highly familiar Exodus narrative of the ancient Hebrews who received manna from Heaven as they wandered in the wilderness during their sojourn from Egypt. Instructed by God to gather and eat the manna each day and not to try to store it overnight (except before the Sabbath), the Hebrews who disobeyed were shocked to discover that their hoarded manna had turned to maggots. Setting himself in contrast with their faithlessness, Whitman's poet refuses attempts at greedy autonomy from the numinous, offering instead a spirituality of trust and play, supremely confident in the source of all things that the dropped "sign'd"/ signs/sign of divinity needn't be suspiciously nor graspingly held, for they "will punctually come for ever and ever."

Whitman's resistance to subject-object opposition, to boundaries between the me and the not-me, makes instances of encounter with the truly Other in his poetry rare. Indeed, in his study of the influences of Vedantic mysticism on Whitman, V. K. Chari asserts that the poet vastly favors nondual, intuitive, "knowing by being" to oppositional, Hegelian dialectic.[16] Yet in those moments where Whitman does attempt to limn the numinous as a force originating from outside the self, he foregrounds the poet's affective and sometimes harrowed responses to an awe-inspiring silence that seems particularly akin to the powerful stillness of a Quaker meeting. In these instances, the poet's encounter with mystery and power most closely approach what Eliade has deemed the hierophanic moment when something "shows itself as wholly different from the profane [i.e., from the natural world]."[17] In "Passage to India," for example, while celebrating the culmination of the poet-priest's lyrical powers at their most divine, Whitman's poet is momentarily overawed by the silent, "shapeless vastness of space" (*WPP* 538). In this paean to the future unity of all things, technological advances have prophetically heralded the moment when "Finally shall come the poet worthy that name": when "All these separations and gaps shall be taken up and hook'd and link'd together, / . . . Trinitas divine shall be gloriously accomplish'd and compacted by the true son of God, the poet" (*WPP* 534–35). Near the end of the poem, however, this messianic figure finds his powers to say and to know curtailed by a meeting with the "Nameless," the "fibre and the breath, / Light of the light, shedding forth universes" at the far reaches of his spiritual quest (*WPP* 538). Reaching the periphery of the conceivable, the poet recoils: "Swiftly I shrivel at the thought of God, / At Nature and its wonders, Time and Space and Death" (*WPP* 538).

The pattern for recovery from the momentary curtailing of his powers is already knitted into the fiber of the poem, however, for the poet has forewarned readers about the inevitable encounter with the "Thou transcendent" on his journeying (*WPP* 538). Earlier in the section Whitman has rejected the compunctions of those Christian penitents who "deprecate" or "weep for sin, remorse, humiliation" (*WPP* 537). Their self-belittling resistance to the normal frailties of human embodiment is the very attitude the poet wishes to refute. For the true poet, the only purpose of limits is to restore him to himself: "Ah more than any priest O soul we too believe in God, / But with the mystery of God we dare not dally," he answers back to the self-deprecators. Thus, the intrusive silence of the hierophanic "Nameless" at the end of the soul's "passage" is the signal to the poet that he has reached the profitable limits of his pondering and must return to the language of an embodied, yet divinized self. Whitman responds to the silent moment of awe: "How should I think, how breathe a single breath, how speak, if, out of myself, / I could not launch, to those, superior universes?" (*WPP* 538). Serving as the outermost limit of the poet's powers of Adamic naming and linguistic unification, "the mystery of God" remains

71

unsayable, thus throwing the reunified ego back on itself to develop its own godlike faculties. It is from "out of myself" that the poet and his soul can "launch, to those, superior universes," universes that are ultimately interior realms rendered visible by the allusion to an exterior cosmos. Juxtaposed against this backdrop of the sense of the infinite, the soul on its inward seafaring voyage may always "farther, farther, farther sail!" (*WPP* 540); as Mary Arensberg has pointed out, in its "endless paths of circumnavigation toward a primal scene of language," it is the poem's "failure to reach beyond the shores of writing that keeps . . . [this text] afloat."[18]

It is in another oceanic poem, "As I Ebb'd with the Ocean of Life," that Whitman sets out his most dramatic encounter with hierophany. Here the poet responds to a dark revelation of the universal human conditions of suffering, failure, and death with allusion to the rebuked silence of Job, the eponymous hero of a book of the Old Testament that Whitman particularly associated with "the sense of Deity."[19] Walking along the shores of Long Island, "fascinated" by the flotsam and jetsam on the flowing tide, the poet is suddenly "seiz'd by the spirit that trails in the lines underfoot, / The rim, the sediment that stands for all the water and all the land of the globe" (*WPP* 394). Overwhelmed by the disparity between the enormity and indifference of nature and the slightness of his own "arrogant poems," the sound of the waves becomes a "dirge" of "the voices of men and women wreck'd," and the poet realizes, "I too but signify at the utmost a little wash'd-up drift, / A few sands and dead leaves to gather, / Gather, and merge myself as part of the sands and drift" (*WPP* 394–95).

Unlike in "Passage to India," the effect of this moment of hierophanic darkness leaves the poet utterly defeated and without recourse to body/ soul-sufficiency. "O baffled, balk'd, bent to the very earth, / Oppress'd with myself that I have dared to open my mouth," Whitman writes in echo of Job's cry, "Behold, I am vile; what shall I answer thee? I will lay mine hand upon my mouth" (*WPP* 395; Job 40:4).[20] In the biblical text, subjected to terrible personal suffering, Job dares to complain to God about the injustice of his trials and is rejoined with a barrage of unanswerable questions and visions of the mysterious wonders of natural world ("Hast thou perceived the breadth of the earth? declare if thou knowest it all," God challenges him) (Job 38:18). Job concedes at the end of his interview with God—before

God restores his health and fortunes—"Therefore have I uttered that I understood not; things too wonderful for me, which I knew not" (Job 42:3b). In a similar manner, Whitman's poet comes to an awareness of his own diminutive stature, admitting, "I perceive that I have not really understood any thing, not a single object, and that no man ever can" (*WPP* 395). It is not the ancient God of the Judeo-Christian scriptures with whom the Whitmanian poet must contend, however, but the divinized "real Me" who "stands yet untouch'd, untold, altogether unreach'd, / Withdrawn far," who is "mocking . . . with peals of ironical laughter at every word I have written, / Pointing in silence to these songs, and to the sand beneath" (*WPP* 395).

One of the patterns of encounter with the numinous that Rudolf Otto analyzes in his classic study *The Idea of the Holy* involves a protagonist making a chastised renunciation of language that, in turn, serves to precipitate revelation. The ancient figure of Job experiences "an inward relaxing of his soul's anguish" even though he is never given an explanation for his suffering, Otto writes, because he is shown mystery itself, natural and supernatural wonders "presented in . . . pure non-rational form," rather than logical explanations that would satisfy his reason.[21] Finding a universal principle in Job's acceptance of awe as answer for his suffering, Otto concludes that "this very negation of purpose becomes a thing of baffling significance"; Job finds there is "*intrinsic value*" in the "incomprehensible character of the creative power" of God and his ongoing maintenance of the universe.[22] Likewise, Whitman's poet, intent to find the universe's "secret," contends with his inner and outer deity after the fashion of Jacob wrestling with the Angel ("I throw myself upon your breast my father, / I cling to you so that you cannot unloose me, / I hold you so firm till you answer me something"); however, the darkness of the vision prevails, and he must admit, "I too am but a trail of drift and debris" (*WPP* 396, 395).[23]

From "out of fathomless workings fermented and thrown," then, the Whitmanian poet visualizes the inevitability of his physical decay, picturing the "Me and mine, loose windrows, little corpses" "ooz[ing]" "froth . . . from my dead lips" (*WPP* 396). Yet, strangely assuaged by yielding control of the outcomes of his "song," the poet presses forward to discover meaning in the thought of personal annihilation. Acquiescing to "merge myself as a part of the drift," he is somehow assured that in exchanging his individuated "Me" for the greater cosmic currents of "We," his message will be carried forward in wordless, tactile connection to future readers. "We, capricious, brought hither we know not whence, spread out before you, / You up there walking or sitting, / Whoever you are, we too lie in drifts at your feet," he concludes. If, as one critic has plausibly suggested, "As I Ebb'd with the Ocean of Life" puts readers "in the midst of a poem about the formation of poetry," then the verse enacts the creative, tidal oscillation between the poet's ideal visions of unity and his despair at the limits of what words alone might "signify" (*WPP* 395).[24] The poet resolves this dilemma by receiving the hierophanic "silence" as a harbinger of the cosmic self beyond language; in that realm even a "little wash'd-up drift" touches every shore and is folded into eternity, to ebb and flow with the endlessly recycled tides.

Like Whitman, Emily Dickinson also invokes a non-anthropomorphic and numinous Other as a limit to set her own poetic acumen in relief. Yet raised in a more hierarchical Christian denomination than the Quakers, Dickinson's spiritual and poetic universe is far less democratic than Whitman's. Here we find no gracious and guiding Inner Light freely available to all but, in keeping with her Reformed tradition, the understanding that divinity speaks from outside of and beyond the self, even if this speaking is only directed to a chosen few, and even if it may only be inferred from a "certain Slant of light" (*EDP* 153, Fr 320). Dickinson's poet doesn't trouble herself to be an egalitarian "true Son of God" as does Whitman's, but wishes to confront directly the only other Being endowed with her destructive and creative powers. As she puts it in one poem with reference to the pillar of cloud that led the ancient Hebrews in Exodus: "My Business – with the Cloud, / If any Power behind it, be" (*EDP* 137, Fr 292). In fact, Dickinson makes at least twelve references in her poetry to the book of Exodus and is particularly taken with the Old Testament prophet Moses. It is the trope of the unseeable face of God—inspired by Moses's experiences with YHWH—rather than Whitman's unsayable mystery that comes to stand as the maximum value of the poet's range.[25] Moreover, her distance from the "House," or "Face," of "awe" as she phrases it in "My period had come for Prayer" (*EDP* 289, Fr 525), creates a power differential she feels more keenly than Whitman. Thus for Dickinson more so than Whitman, the unseen serves as a boundary that paradoxically invites transgression, not as a signal to return to an embodied or even a cosmic self. Concomitantly, Moses and his daring colloquies with YHWH become for Dickinson a metaphor for the poet herself.

Although the adult Dickinson formed her own idiosyncratic belief system that differed radically from the beliefs of most of her family and friends, there is no doubt that her religious training from her earliest years was far more consistent and thorough than Whitman's.[26] Dickinson and her family regularly attended the First Congregational Church of Amherst, Massachusetts (although the poet herself stopped attending services at some point in her late twenties or early thirties), and she obtained an intellectually rigorous, parochial education at the local Amherst Academy, followed by one year at Mount Holyoke Female Seminary. The theology espoused in Dickinson's educational and religious circles was based on the Reformed tradition, but her ministers and teachers were trained in the New Divinity (Andover and Amherst College) or New Haven (Yale) theologies—kinder, gentler versions of the formidable Calvinism of fifty years earlier. While these theologies still strongly embraced the notion of the total sovereignty of God and the absolute differentiation between Creator and creation, they moved the emphasis away from predestination and toward the individual's responsibility to listen and respond to the salvation that was preached from the pulpit and in the Bible.[27] This dual emphasis on the bounded nature of spiritual selfhood and on the individual struggle to choose against self and sin in order to receive salvation is reflected in Dickinson's refusal of Emerson's understanding of the self as benevolent, unified, and "part or particle of God."[28] As Linda Freedman puts it, Dickinson's "imagination was fundamentally of an older cast than Emerson's . . . . Where Emerson's 'priest or poet' desired illimitability, blurring the distinction between divinity and humanity, Dickinson's theological poetics exploited that distinction for its tensions."[29]

Adding to Dickinson's conception of faith as a struggle to realize and articulate the spiritual life was her religious tradition's heightened emphasis on actively using the imagination to descry the presence of an almighty and invisible God present in nature and everyday life. As William Dyrness elucidates in *Reformed Theology and Visual Culture: The Protestant Imagination from Calvin to Edwards*, the Reformation iconoclasm of Calvin and Luther that brought about "the external removal of divine images [also] stretched an internal canvas on which God's presence could be painted," creating a state of inward "iconopoesis" in Reformed believers in which God could be discerned in even the most mundane aspects of their lives.[30] Consequently, while Dickinson's Congregationalists did not hew to a notion of an Inner Light that put believers on an egalitarian footing with the Bible as did the Hicksite Quakers, they did acknowledge the importance of listening to the Holy Spirit for individual revelation of God's guidance. Moreover, there were numerous progressive voices within the Reformed theologies of Dickinson's day who advocated for an understanding of religious inspiration as something primarily dynamic, open-ended, poetic, and accessible to all. For example, in *Sermons on the New Life*, a book in the Dickinson household library, Congregational minister Horace Bushnell deems it "a great misfortune . . . that we have brought down the word *inspiration* to a use so narrow and technical; asserting it only of prophecy and other scripture writings, and carefully excluding from it all participation, by ourselves, in whatever sense it might be taken. . . . The result is that we are occupied almost wholly with second-hand relations to God."[31]

Sensitive to these contemporary voices, Dickinson was intensely interested in forging her own firsthand relations with a concealed yet omnipresent God, and with doing so in ways that emphasized the glorious but double-edged nature of the tools of the poet's trade. She wrote a trio of poems in which she fuses ideas of revelation, of the powers and limits of poetic calling, and of the dangerous allure of being consumed by a God whose face is hidden: "My period had come for Prayer," "No man saw awe, nor to his house," and "To pile like Thunder to it's close." Each of these poems alludes to Moses's experiences as mediator between the grumbling Hebrew people he has been called to lead out of their slavery in Egypt and an omnipotent, awe-full God.[32] In so doing, Dickinson purposely conflates elements of Moses's story for her own purposes of dramatizing the charged boundary between self and the divine Other. Exodus 3 details Moses's initial encounter with God in the form of a bush that burns but is not destroyed by the flames; in this meeting Moses learns he has been appointed by YHWH, or "I AM THAT I AM," to lead the Hebrews. Later, Exodus 33 and 34 detail some of the frequent conversations Moses has with God during the long course of receiving the Ten Commandments (twice) and leading the children of Israel through the wilderness toward the Promised Land. It is in these passages where we are told that Moses conversed familiarly with I AM; the relationship is delineated idiomatically as "face to face, as a man speaketh unto his friend" (Ex. 33:11). I AM's dictum to Moses that "thou canst not see my face: for there shall no man see me, and live" comes several verses later in response to Moses's request to physically see God: "I beseech thee, shew me thy glory" (Ex. 33:18 and 20). I AM covers Moses with his "hand" and reveals aspects of his character but not his essence. While these chapters certainly display the expected and frequently reiterated austere and terrifying holiness of God, they are also very much marked by the intimate tone of Moses's friendship with YHWH. Moses is not merely awestruck, but he also argues, demands, and adores.

It is the unrealized desire for intimacy with the Wholly Other that fuels the tension in Dickinson's "My period had come for Prayer – ," a poem as much about the art of writing poetry as it is about spiritual seeking. Here Dickinson meditates on what she terms the "Art" of "Prayer," dismissing premeditated "Tactics" and instead turning toward the *via negativa* where "His House was not – no sign had He – " (*EDP* 289, Fr 525). The movement in the poem from a position of naïveté and faux mastery in the first half to being overmastered by awe in the second is a frequent route Dickinson traverses in her writing to undercut the well-worn tropes of a sentimentalized Christianity she characteristically resists and to re-sacralize the idea that the truly numinous is still close at hand for those who pay attention. The speaker begins by absurdly literalizing the notion of God in a Heaven somewhere physically over our heads by reasoning "God grows above – so those who pray / Horizons – must ascend – ." Yet at the top of this vista, there is no anthropomorphic "Curious Friend" "To see." In fact, there is "no sign," no "Chimney" nor "Door" from which to "infer his Residence." Instead, "Vast Prairies of Air // Unbroken by a Settler – / Were all that I could see – ." Such immense reaches of open space, as Rudolf Otto has explained in *The Idea of the Holy*, are frequently experienced as signifiers of an encroachment of the numinous into the realm of natural existence. Characteristically, however, Dickinson's speaker does not shy away from this incursion of the supra-natural, but echoing Moses, asks "Infinitude

– Had'st Thou no Face / That I might look on Thee?" In response, "The Silence condescended – / Creation stopped – for me – / But awed beyond my errand – / I worshipped – did not 'pray' – ." Having upended the "Tactics" that "missed a rudiment" at the start of the speaker's quest, the numinous from beyond nature brings the speaker to a state of being "awed beyond" her "errand" at the poem's conclusion.

As in the "miles of Stare" Dickinson depicts in her poem "I've known a Heaven, like a Tent – " (*EDP* 126, Fr 257), "My period had come for Prayer – " turns on the metaphor of repeatedly vexed physical sight taking the place of spiritual vision. Michelle Kohler has examined Dickinson's propensity for such frustrated visual metaphors at length, noting how the poet refuses to equate clear seeing with the poet's imagination in the way Emerson does with his trope of the transcendental eyeball.[33] Instead Dickinson purposely incorporates metaphors of limited human vision into her poetry to overturn the habitual substitution of seeing for spiritual knowing. As Kohler notes, in moments where readers would anticipate resolution, often "expectation of revelation is countered by the speaker's idiosyncratic metaphors, which cannot quite signify or reveal their subjects."[34] Correspondingly in this poem, like the response Moses receives, the poet's request to "look on" the "Face" of "Infinitude" is not answered with a metaphor of sight. Instead darkness gives way to an awe-inducing "Silence" and stillness that transform "'prayer'" (the final word of the poem set in ironic quotes) into the self-abandonment of "worship," tactics into art. Hence the moment of hierophany calls forth the deeper work from the poet; to create art one must brave the uncanny and faceless "Infinitude" of the mind, the universe, and the blankness of the page—the un-"settled" "Vast Prairies of Air," places where calculated "Tactics" are liable to fail.

In "No man saw awe, nor to his house" (*EDP* 661, Fr 1342; 1874) and "To pile like Thunder to its close" (*EDP* 713, Fr 1353; 1875), poems dated approximately eleven years after "My period had come for Prayer," Dickinson returns to the Exodus story, this time delving into the mysterious relationships between love and divinity and creation and destruction. In both poems (similar enough in theme and composition date as to be considered companion pieces), Dickinson's poet simultaneously suggests and overcomes limits of poetic range. In so doing, the holiness of God becomes a figure for the poet's power, and Moses and the burning bush stand in for the poet herself. In "No man saw awe" (*EDP* 661, Fr 1342) the intrusion of the invisible I AM and his dwelling place is perceived through a near-death encounter with "awe" instead of being sought out through "worship," as in "My period had come for Prayer." Here, rational judgment is contrasted with a deeper, felt experience that is given by dint of our "human nature," whether we wish to have it or not. In the poem's first two stanzas, Dickinson constructs a parallel between the looming but unrecognized certainty of one's own death and the omnipresent but veiled proximity of "his awful residence" and "his dread abode." The speaker did not "dee[m]" or regard the human condition as such until "laboring to flee / A grasp on comprehension laid / Detained vitality." In contrast with factual knowledge, the lived experience of "comprehension" so "grasp[s]" the intuition that "vitality" itself is taken captive, and one is rendered so incapacitated that "breathing is the only work / To be enacted now."

Recovering from such an experience, "Returning," as the poet writes at the beginning of the third stanza, calls for "a different route." As Jed Deppman points out, "the poem suggests that our inability to understand the steps leading to and from a sublime experience is cognate with our inability to understand death. . . . One can neither leave the state of awe the same way one enters nor mentally reconstruct the experience."[35] At the same time, however, the image of labored gasping on a deathbed suggests more than Dickinson's Kantian understanding of the sublime. The "Spirit" and "breathing" of lines ten and eleven play on the Latin word *inspirare*, suggesting that the poem is also a depiction of the process of giving oneself over to inspiration. In this reading, the poet's response to awe is to be receptive to the spiritual, creative "work" that is "to be enacted now."

Such an interpretation prepares us for Dickinson's final stanza in a way that restricting the poem to a depiction of the Romantic sublime does not. Instead of being undone by the immolations of poetic inspiration, the poet affiliates herself with Moses, who survives his encounters with the invisible I AM, emerging from them as a prophet tasked with writing the Pentateuch: "'Am not consumed,' old Moses wrote, / 'Yet saw Him face to face' – / That very physiognomy / I am convinced was this." While Whitman insists upon the poet's realm as unbounded and available to all, Dickinson's religious imagination perceives boundaries between the me and the not-me. The difficult "work" of creativity requires the poet to make some kind of trade-off—a sacrifice of the imagination's reign against the edge where the unknowable Other begins, the loss of complete rational control over one's final artistic product. In "old Moses" Dickinson finds a model of the poet as intermediary between self and the edge of awe, one who does "Return" from conversing "face to face" with the unseen. The "very physiognomy" that Moses beheld and withstood, the poet concludes "was this"—the awe of being "consumed" by one's poetic calling yet somehow remaining oneself, neither merging with death nor the wider universe, the same way the bush retained its identity in the hierophanic moment when "the Lord appeared to him in a flame of fire out of the midst of a bush: and he looked, and, behold, the bush burned with fire, and the bush was not consumed" (Ex. 3:2).

Dickinson also meditates on the pleasures of simultaneous creation and destruction in "To pile like Thunder to its close." In this poem, she describes the poet's powers with frankly apocalyptic language that alludes to Revelation 6. That chapter (which includes another reference to the "face" of God) depicts the day of judgment as one in which kings and slaves alike will hide in caves and call on the mountains to "'fall on us, and hide us from the face of him who is seated on the throne and from the wrath of the Lamb, for the great day of his wrath has come; and who shall be able to stand?'" (Rev. 6:16–17):

> To pile like Thunder to its close
> Then crumble grand away
> While everything created hid
> This – would be Poetry –
>
> Or Love – the two coeval come –
> We both and neither prove –
> Experience either and consume –
> For none see God and live –
> (*EDP* 713, Fr 1353)

Rightly one of Dickinson's most frequently analyzed poems, "To pile like Thunder" is a masterpiece of precision and multiple referentiality that enacts the same compressed power of language that it illustrates. Many Dickinson scholars have ably elucidated the connections that the poem forges between language and power and between desire and loss. Cristanne Miller, for instance, has connected the poem's dramatization of the "impossible experience of seeing God" with Dickinson's acknowledgment that love and poetry, "like divinity, stand above human knowledge . . . one can only *believe* they exist, encouraged in the belief by epiphanic glimpses or sensations of their reality and their power" (emphasis added).[36] Sharon Cameron has read Dickinson's arrangement of "coeval" "Poetry" and "Love" as an exploration of the way "desire must suffer a conversion, whether to language or to the exigencies of other loss."[37] Considering this poem in the light of both the Exodus story and its companion "No man saw awe, nor to his house," adds another dimension to these classic interpretations—the poet's fascination with her role as liminal prophet standing between the realms of the profane and the awe-inducing, faceless invisibility of the sacred.

As in "No man saw awe," one implicit contrast that Dickinson makes in this poem is between ratiocination (as implied by the notion of judgment in the poem's allusion to the second coming of Christ and by legal and mathematical aspects of the term "prove") and felt "Experience." Ideal "Poetry" ("Or Love – " she adds, as if an afterthought, at the start of the second stanza) is identified not by theorem but through a cataclysmic impact that causes "everything created" to "hid[e]." This impulse to hide or shield oneself from the enormity of Love and Poetry is not only a future-oriented reference to the aforementioned Apocalypse, but also a gesture backward in time to Adam and Eve who, having tasted the forbidden knowledge of good and evil, hide in the garden. Hence, a second, more subtle contrast in the poem is made between time and eternity. The fact that "Poetry" and "Love" "coeval come" (instead of "coequal") underscores the importance of origins in the relationship between poetry and godlike power that Dickinson is enacting. Consequently, the poet's subjunctive "would" in line four is the axis upon which the poem turns: the word grants her the imaginative possibilities not only to fashion and then destroy the natural, "created" order, but also to be simultaneously present at the beginning and ending of time as is the God of Genesis and Revelation. Like God, truly great poetry must stand outside the bounds of one individual's life span.

Indeed, that there could be limits at all to this poet's power is a notion merely implied through the negation contained in the Exodus reference in the last line of the poem. Although Dickinson does not speak of "my soul and I" in the manner of Whitman, in "To pile like Thunder" the allusion to Moses sets up dual supposed selves working in concert. By conflating the unmaking holiness of God, the undoing sway of love, and the earth-shaking powers of immortal poetic creation, the speaker first identifies with the I AM, for to know love or poetry at the ideally apocalyptic level calls for exposure to such pure power that it would be a human self's complete undoing. Yet to "experience" and record the destruction of "everything created" in the service of poetry and love also calls for a second self, the poet as the see-er, the Moses-like exception to the rule that "none see God and live – ." This ideal poet lives in proximity to the "Thunder" of Mt. Sinai, an in-between space of "both and neither" that she "prove[s]" or testifies to by virtue of her poetry. To "Experience either" and not be "consume[d]" is to withstand the potentially annihilating forces of God, time, and desire and to emerge from that lofty cloud with "Poetry."[38]

Finally, then, the illumination that Dickinson's poet strives to bring—the "Lamps" enlarging "Circumference" through the "Age[s]," as she calls it elsewhere—initiates those willing to examine their own felt experience into moments of fleeting enlightenment (*EDP* 436, Fr 930). Indeed, Dickinson's universe is made up of a series of these bounded circumferences, the "Circumference thou Bride of Awe" she lauds in one of her late poems, that invite risky transgression and lure us with promises of fulfillment (*EDP* 648, Fr 1636). Yet, in the tension of these liminal spaces lie potential encounters with meanings so awe-filled that perhaps only the poet herself can dare to approach them on our behalf. "Too bright for our infirm Delight / The Truth's superb surprise," Dickinson cautions us (*EDP* 563, Fr 1263). The poet's art is to "ease" the "Lightning," so that when she brings the needful awe to bear, "the Truth" will "dazzle gradually / Or every man be blind." For Whitman, by contrast, drawing on his own affinities with aspects of pacific Quakerism, "whatever would put God in a poem or system of philosophy as contending against some being or influence is . . . of no account" (*WPP* 1855, 16). Instead of dazzled blindness and frustration, Whitman's moments of hierophanic stillness offer readers avenues to the "mystical," "perfect silence" of the stars overhead, suggesting that we, like the poet in "When I Heard the Learn'd Astronomer," can escape from our encumbrances by an embrace of the egalitarian, democratic, and fecund sacredness of the visual and tactile natural world (*WPP* 410). Consequently, his poet's astonishing power is to convince us that "through the divinity of *themselves* shall the kosmos and the new breed of poets be interpreters of men and women and of all events and things. They shall find their inspiration in real objects today, symptoms of the past and future" (*WPP* 1855, 25, emphasis mine).

It has been several decades now since Agnieszka Salska so ably outlined the chief differences in these two poets' "central consciousness": in Whitman she locates a purposeful "poetic quest . . . to make a discovery, a phrase that conveys well the mediating, active-passive role that becomes assigned to poetic consciousness," while in Dickinson she finds an "emphasis on the mastering function of consciousness in its confrontation with the intensity of experience."[39] Comparing the spiritual impulses at the core of each poet's vision sheds further light on their differing perceptions of the functions of poetry, yet also illuminates the ways each believes poets are called to liberate their most attuned readers. In this sense, Whitman's emphasis on immanence and a self that finds unity through growth serves to dissolve the false divisions that threaten and distort the nation's democratic impulses. In her turn, Dickinson's acknowledgment of transcendent and fundamental power differentials at the core of reality makes her a poet who reveals and troubles false pairings that in the name of unity would subsume the identity of the weaker into the stronger. In the works of both, tropes of the unseen and the unsaid demand an accounting of the soul's relation to its universe, whether that reckoning leads to inspired creation, to democratic nation-building, or to the Cloud of Unknowing itself, as one medieval mystic has termed the spiritual path.

Phenomenological Approaches to Human Contact in Whitman and Dickinson

MARIANNE NOBLE

ANTEBELLUM AMERICAN LITERATURE IS PERMEATED BY A YEARNING for human contact. Ralph Waldo Emerson, for example, despairs that relationships are superficial, indeed that all of our experiences are superficial. Our encounters with people and the things of life never satisfy our hunger for the real. In his 1844 essay "Experience," he writes:

> There are moods in which we court suffering, in the hope that here, at least, we shall find reality, sharp peaks and edges of truth. But it turns out to be scene-painting and counterfeit. The only thing grief has taught me, is to know how shallow it is. That, like all the rest, plays about the surface, and never introduces me into the reality, for contact with which, we would even pay the costly price of sons and lovers. Was it Boscovich who found out that bodies never come in contact? Well, souls never touch their objects. An innavigable sea washes with silent waves between us and the things we aim at and converse with.[1]

We do not "contact" one another, nor the world as it is, he says, using the word twice. But what does "contact" mean to him?

Tracking down his allusion to Boscovich does not answer this question, but it does at least contextualize it. Roger Joseph Boscovich, an eighteenth-century Croatian physicist and priest, posited an atomic theory of matter in 1758, almost a hundred years before Emerson wrote "Experience" (1842):

The primary elements of matter are in my opinion perfectly indivisible & non-extended points; they are so scattered in an immense vacuum that every two of them are separated from one another by a definite interval; this interval can be indefinitely increased or diminished, but can never vanish altogether without compenetration of the points themselves; for I do not admit as possible any immediate contact between them.[2]

The building blocks of matter are individual entities—non-extended—he posits. They necessarily have space between them, and were that space to be negated, the atoms would "compenetrate," and thus distinction would be dissolved. Consequently, "immediate contact between them" is impossible.

It would seem that this concept from theoretical physics functions as a metaphor for human contact for Emerson. Human contact, if we ever experienced it, would be like the contact of atoms, "compenetration." However, it would also necessarily eradicate the individuals that we are, and thus it is impossible. Hence we do not contact one another. Instead, just as atoms float in a vacuum, people float in a sea of alienated individuation. We long to experience in our relationships, as in life in general, "reality, sharp peaks and edges of truth. But it turns out to be scene-painting and counterfeit." We get only representations of some presumably real other or thing. We can hear echoes of Kant's thing itself, and of Plato's allegory of the cave, in Emerson's thinking; indeed, in the ideal of compenetration, we hear echoes of Emerson's own "I become nothing; I see all; the currents of the Universal Being circulate through me; I am part or particle of God."[3] The tone in "Experience," written six years after "Nature" (1836–42), is elegiac, the dream of transcendent vision unattainable. That said, the dream of transcendent contact—the total overlap of self with alterity—remains unchanged, but it no longer seems possible. Thus, later in the essay, he writes: "Two human beings are like globes, which can touch only in a point, and, whilst they remain in contact, all other points of each of the spheres are inert." Again, human contact is conceived as an experience of touching at all points. And such an overlap, he imagines, would open the individual into totality itself: "The universe is the bride of the soul." He laments, however, that such spiritual marriage "is impossible." "There will be the same gulf between every me and thee, as between the original and the picture. . . . All private sympathy is partial." In our relationships, we want the revelation of the totality that informs each person, he says, yet all we get is mimesis and partiality.

Emily Dickinson and Walt Whitman also engage the philosophical question of what it means to contact others, and in keeping with the Romantic thought that Emerson exemplifies, both poets initially approach human contact as an experience of perfect knowledge of the other's essence achieved by something like the fusion of two souls. Contact in its purest form would be a state of non-separation, compresence, or even non-distinction. However, as they think the issue through, Dickinson and Whitman both reject their own received metaphysical thoughts and reconceive the nature of human identity—and contact between human selves—by refusing to separate matter and spirit. In doing so, they turn away from Romantic idealism and toward twentieth-century phenomenology, as articulated by Edmund Husserl, Martin Heidegger, and Maurice Merleau-Ponty. Both of them cultivate a poetics that enables them to think beyond dualisms, one that presents human contact as possible, though different from what they had first imagined.

It is not surprising to argue that Whitman unifies body and soul, but it is less conventional to contextualize that unity in twentieth-century phenomenology. Most major studies of Whitman interpret this major theme; Roger Asselineau's *The Evolution of Walt Whitman,* Stephen John Mack's *Whitman and Pragmatism,* and Vincent Bertolini's "'Hinting' and 'Reminding': The Rhetoric of Performative Embodiment in *Leaves of Grass*" are particularly insightful.[4] But the phenomenological context offers a new point of view on this theme and a vocabulary that streamlines our understanding of exactly what it does and does not mean to claim that body and soul are one. When David Daiches writes that Whitman's theme is "how to escape the prison of the self" by "projecting oneself into the identity of others," he frames the issue of human contact as one of escaping from one monad and penetrating another one.[5] With the assistance of phenomenological terms, I hope to show instead that Whitman comes to understand contact not as a projection of self into the other but instead as an awareness of the self as always already in contact with the other. If selfhood is embodied and intersubjective, then the self is not in prison after all. Contact does not go somewhere else; it reconceives what already is.

It might seem more surprising to argue for the unity of body and soul in Dickinson, whose poetry frequently invokes the radical division of body and soul in the Calvinist and Transcendentalist cultures that influenced her. In *Touching Liberty* (1993), Karen Sanchez-Eppler challenged this view, high-lighting Dickinson's anti-dualist emphasis on embodied selfhood.[6] In 2008, Jed Deppman continued that trend in the context of his broader argument that Dickinson's writing is "an early, intense response to the fragmenting epistemological conditions . . . attending the weakening of authoritative Western narratives of history, God, nature, the self."[7] Many of the essays in the recently published *Emily Dickinson and Philosophy* also present an anti-metaphysical thinker, affiliating her with Nietzsche, Dewey, Levinas, Heidegger, Derrida, and Merleau-Ponty, as opposed to Kant or Calvin.[8] This essay's exploration of the implications for human contact of her erosion of the subject-object divide is part of this trend, revealing Dickinson to be a thinker anticipating some of our own theories of selfhood and contact.

In the 1855 version of the poem later titled "Song for Occupations," Whitman implores:

> Come closer to me,
> Push close my lovers and take the best I possess,
> Yield closer and closer and give me the best you possess.
>
> This is unfinish'd business with me . . . . how is it with you?
> I was chilled with the cold types and cylinder and wet paper between us.
>
> I pass so poorly with paper and types . . . . I must pass with the contact of bodies and souls.
>
> (*WPP* 1855, 89)

Here Whitman voices the conventional conception of "contact" as a merge, a perfect overlap of self and other. He suggests that to contact another would be to eradicate all barriers between self and other, such as clothing or—in this case—paper and types. Pressing past these would bring selves into contact with "the best" in one another, which we can understand in opposition to the "scene-painting and counterfeit" that Emerson views as the norm. In these lines, it seems that it is not only papers and types that prevent selves from "pass[ing]" into one another, but even the bodies themselves. To be sure, the lines imagine bodies as vehicles of merging, but they simultaneously imagine bodies as impediments to merging. The contact imagined here would somehow press so close that the bodies and the paper and type would disappear in a state of non-differentiation. The telos of such pressing closer is something like Boscovich's compenetration.

Dickinson also imagines transcendent human contact. In the 1862 poem "There came a Day – at Summer's full," for example, she recalls, or imagines, an experience of perfect human contact:

> The time was scarce profaned – by speech –
> The symbol of a word   [The] ~~falling · figure~~ –
> Was needless – as at Sacrament –
> The Wardrobe – of Our Lord –
>
> Each was to each – the sealed church –
> Permitted to commune – this time –
> Lest we too awkward – show –
> At "Supper of the Lamb."
>   (*EDP* 155, Fr 325)

The tone is remarkably different from Whitman's, but the passage resembles his "Press closer" lines in stressing the absence of intervening or mediating entities such as words, clothing, and symbols between the two beloveds. This poem depicts human contact as the unmediated mutual presence of beings who are spiritually naked before one another. Dickinson invokes biblical imagery to depict this ideal of total human presence: "Blessed are they which are called unto the marriage supper of the lamb" (Rev. 19:9), the chosen ones who are "sealed . . . in their foreheads" (Rev. 7:3).[9] These passages from the book of Revelation describe the marriage of Christ to the church, his bride, and Dickinson envisions an apex of human contact

89

patterned on this sacred ideal. Two lovers each represent the sealed church to one another; no longer subject and object to one another, they are instead merged and mirror images of totality for the other. Individuality is lost in this sacred, Eucharistic presence in which the beloved incarnates totality to the other. Like Emerson's spiritual marriage in which the soul weds the universe itself, this union transcends "private sympathy."

However, while such passages invoke an understanding of human contact that transcends individuality, Whitman and Dickinson both more frequently argue against such an ideal, imagining it as impossible and quite possibly pernicious. The problem in idealizing contact that gets past bodies and selves—which seem to interpose layers of seeming between supposedly deeper realities—is that it misrepresents the real. Both poets observe that the real necessarily includes the bodies and materials through which spirit has its only being. Whitman edited out of later editions the lines in which "contact" is a metaphor for penetrating to "the best."[10] Dickinson did not revise "There came a Day" along these lines, but her poetry increasingly moves away from metaphors of human contact as the marriage of the soul with totality, exploring instead forms of contact centering on a materialized spirit. Both rejected their own engrained transcendental idealism, registering again and again that it is a fool's errand to seek human contact by trying to get past contingencies in search of essences. In this, they echo the late Emerson.

Unlike Emerson, however, they do not therefore voice eulogies for the dream of human contact. All three are trying to conceive an experience in which experiences with others seem "real," as opposed to "counterfeit"; in which others are present, as opposed to pretending to be something they are not; in which souls "touch their objects," as opposed to straining toward an ever-receding telos. Whereas Emerson despairs, both Whitman and Dickinson redefine, reconfiguring contact as an experience embedded in the relationality and materiality of identity. Understanding contact in non-transcendent ways enables us both to affirm and celebrate experiences of genuine human contact.

In making this anti-metaphysical swerve, Whitman and Dickinson anticipate early twentieth-century phenomenology. Philosophers like Husserl, Heidegger, and Merleau-Ponty similarly stress that people are inconceivable apart from the material world in which they create themselves and in which they have their only true being. Consequently, these philosophers claim, anything that might be thought of as human contact will necessarily involve the materiality of everyday life. Human contact is possible, they posit, if we begin with the premise that other people are not stable and essential things—not Boscovich's "perfectly indivisible & non-extended points"—but instead dynamic beings creating themselves through worldly contingencies. In this, these philosophers echo Whitman and Dickinson.

Whitman describes his own turn toward something like a phenomenological conception of human contact in the poem "Of the Terrible Doubt of Appearance." This poem opens with an expression of skepticism over the terrible feeling that we are all merely touching life accidentally, never contacting the world as it is and the people in it as they are, encountering only appearances whose relationship to "the real" is unverifiable:

> May-be the things I perceive, the animals, plants, men, hills, shining
>   and flowing waters,
> The skies of day and night, colors, densities, forms, may-be these are
>   (as doubtless they are) only apparitions, and the real something has
>   yet to be known.
>
> *(WPP 274)*

Whitman acknowledges an agonizing, or "terrible," feeling that we do not perceive "the real something." We yearn to secure definitively that we are not seeing apparitions, that the things we are involved in really are "the real something."

The parenthetical comment "as doubtless they are" is curious, seeming to establish as obviously true the possibility he is most worried about—that the things we see are only apparitions, not "the real something." He repeats this claim a few lines later: "May-be seeming to me what they are (as doubtless they indeed but seem)." We can reconcile these confusing interjections with the general drift of the rest of the poem in various ways. Perhaps he is observing that from an imagined plane of transcendent knowledge, all of our knowledge is patently incomplete. Or perhaps he is acknowledging that things do appear to us and we do not have to associate them with pejoratives like "mere." And yet, the phrase might hint at something different too. We might read the parenthetical comments, with their repetitions of the word "doubtless"—pointing back to the same word in the title—as foregrounding the issue of doubt itself. It might hint that if we require "doubtless" knowledge of the real something, we will necessarily miss it, but if we adopt another kind of thought, we might be satisfied. Such a reading would be consistent with the rest of the poem:

> . . . [These doubts] are curiously answer'd by my lovers, my dear
> friends,
> When he whom I love travels with me or sits a long while holding me
> by the hand,
> When the subtle air, the impalpable, the sense that words and reason
> hold not, surround us and pervade us,
> Then I am charged with untold and untellable wisdom, I am silent,
> I require nothing further,
> I cannot answer the question of appearances or that of identity
> beyond the grave,
> But I walk or sit indifferent, I am satisfied,
> He ahold of my hand has completely satisfied me.
>
> (*WPP* 274–75)

In this response to the initial desire for "doubtless" knowledge, Whitman describes experiences of human "with-ness" that satisfy the spasms of skeptical doubt. When he is with lovers, traveling or sitting with them, when they hold his hand, when he feels the way he and his lovers are pervaded and surrounded by "the subtle air, the impalpable"—which is to say the way they are physically in a shared space that is also in them both—then, he says, he is no longer troubled about the reality or non-reality of things.

But why? Emerson surely held people's hands and experienced shared space many times. Why do Whitman's experiences of physical "with-ness" satisfy the pangs of skepticism, where Emerson's experiences of physical "with-ness" did not?

In part, the difference lies in the way the two writers conceive the identity of the things being contacted. Emerson famously defines the "me" in opposition to the "not-me," including within the "not-me" his own body. Whitman, by contrast, defines the self in fluid intersubjective continuity with the material world and foregrounds selfhood in the body. He understands identity as a "with" thing, not a "not-with" thing. The first half of the poem portrays a speaker increasingly flustered over questions like the nature of "identity beyond the grave." In the second half of the poem, he models an inclusive understanding of identity, and in doing so overcomes the skeptical doubt of the first half.

These lines foreground a kind of thought that he calls "holding." The word "hold" appears three times: "holding me by the hand"; "words and reason hold not"; and "He ahold of my hand has completely satisfied me." The demand for "doubtless" understanding achieved through reason and packaged into words turns out to be the problem; the answer to it is "the sense that words and reason hold not." That is to say, while "words and reason" separate things in discrete identities, a thought that promotes feelings of contact is one that "holds." When used as a metaphor for thought, "to hold" is to think in "with" ways that stress tactile connections as part of things. Holding brings things together in a way that supports and surrounds them, without possessing them or objectifying them. It is a "sense," a corporeal form of thought that is different from intellectually thinking *about* things.[11] The quest to know the reality of things in this poem is achieved by contemplating them holistically, seeing them in and through relationships with other people and things in the world. Conceiving of oneself and all of reality as relational and integrated rather than as essential yields neither truth nor knowledge, but "wisdom," a kind of understanding that is "untold" and "untellable." It refuses logocentric stabilization of the "identity" of things, refuses to understand the real as centering on transcendent matters like "identity beyond the grave." Instead, it approaches being within a context of mutual relatedness, corporeality, and affection.

In locating the answer to skeptical doubt in a relational and corporeal form of thought like "holding," Whitman anticipates similar lines of thought in the philosophy of phenomenology, as theorized first by Edmund Husserl, then by Maurice Merleau-Ponty, and more recently developed by phenomenological cognitive scientists. Among these are Shaun Gallagher and Dan Zahavi, two leaders in the field who have helpfully encapsulated its central tenets in their influential introduction to the subject, *The Phenomenological Mind*. The most basic phenomenological idea is that people exist only in the world and that all consciousness is only of things in the world. The mind considered in isolation from its objects of thoughts makes no sense; thought is about the world. Likewise, our sense of the world itself necessarily is oriented toward our own relationship to it; as neuropsychologist Chris Frith put it, the world is "a map of signs about future possibilities. And through this map of future possibilities our bodies are intimately tied to the world immediately around us. I just have to look at that mug over there and my brain starts tensing my muscles and curling my fingers in case I should want to reach for it. This is how our minds become embedded in the physical world."[12] We are not separate from the world; when we contemplate mugs, we see them as things-we-might-grasp, not things unrelated to ourselves. Alterity involves us and our bodies, and we involve alterity. We do not exist primarily in and of ourselves and then turn our integral selves outward toward a fundamentally separate world. Emerson's division of the world into the "me and the not-me," and Boscovich's "indivisible and non-extended points," could not be further from the truth, according to phenomenology.

There is no question that Whitman understands selves as intersubjective beings defined in and through relationships to things in the world:

There was a child went forth every day,
And the first object he look'd upon, that object he became
(WPP 49)
*
Was somebody asking to see the soul?
See, your own shape and countenance, persons, substances, beasts,
   the trees, the running rivers, the rocks and sands.
(WPP 183)
*
The impalpable sustenance of me from all things at all hours of
   the day
(WPP 308)
*
Is this then a touch? quivering me to a new identity,
(WPP 215)

Whitman portrays selves as unstable, constantly "quivering . . . to a new identity" as they encounter different things and selves in the world. Our souls take shape in and through worldly engagements with the trees, rivers, rocks and sand. These externalities are "dumb, beautiful ministers" that "furnish [their] parts toward the soul" (*WPP* 313). Our souls are always changing as they respond to the stuff of which we are conscious. Consequently, to experience something like contact with another person, we must take into account the worldly context of the other person; he or she exists through worldly engagements. If a child becomes what he looks upon, any effort to contact that child will necessarily involve the objects through which he creates himself, the "substances, beasts, the trees, the running rivers, the rocks and sands" around him. In suggesting as much, Whitman anticipates phenomenology, which turns away from trying to access the other person's mind and instead suggests that "a more productive focus is on the other person's world." As Merleau-Ponty puts it: "In so far as I have sensory functions . . . I am already in communication with others."[13] Gallagher and Zahavi interpret this quotation as meaning that, in trying to understand other people, "I have to pay attention to the world that I already share with them."[14] Selves are "extended" into their surroundings; consequently, contact prioritizes such extension.

Phenomenologists define the self as embodied and conclude that this being the case, at least some aspects of other minds and feelings are directly available to us. As Gallagher and Zahavi write: "Affective and emotional states are not simply qualities of subjective experience; rather, they are given *in* expressive phenomena, that is, they are expressed in bodily gestures and actions and they thereby become visible to others."[15] We do not simply feel emotions; they are inseparable from corresponding bodily actions.[16] And likewise, as onlookers, we see emotions directly on the face and on the body; we do not interpret them. As Wittgenstein says, "We *see* emotion . . . We do not see facial contortions and *make the inference* that he is feeling joy, grief, boredom. We describe a face immediately as sad, radiant, bored, even when we are unable to give any other description of the features."[17] The common belief is that emotions are interior and hidden, but phenomenologists propose the opposite. So does Whitman. When he looks at a horse driver, he sees that "His glance is calm and commanding" (*WPP* 198). He does not deduce the other's emotions from physical signs; he sees them directly.

Phenomenologists and Whitman also agree that we see thought as well as feeling in bodily expressions. As Gallagher and Zahavi write, "some of our mental states find a natural expression in bodily behavior," and consequently, "In seeing the actions and expressive movements of other persons, one already sees their meaning. No inference to a hidden set of mental states is necessary. Expressive behavior is saturated with the meaning of the mind; it reveals the mind to us."[18] Whitman anticipates such thoughts. Consistently, his poetry suggests that embodiment makes other minds at least partly present to us, inhering in the actions people do. When he looks in the street, he sees people's minds, or selves, present in their actions rather than occluded by them. As he writes in "Song of Myself":

> The butcher-boy puts off his killing-clothes, or sharpens his knife at
>   the stall in the market,
> I loiter enjoying his repartee and his shuffle and break-down.
> Blacksmiths with grimed and hairy chests environ the anvil,
> Each has his main-sledge, they are all out, there is a great heat in
>   the fire.
>
> From the cinder-strew'd threshold I follow their movements,
> The lithe sheer of their waists plays even with their massive arms,
> Overhand the hammers swing, overhand so slow, overhand so sure,
> They do not hasten, each man hits in his place.
>   (*WPP* 198)
>   *
> The boatmen and clamdiggers arose early and stopt for me,
> I tuck'd my trowser-ends in my boots and went and had a good time;
> You should have been with us that day round the chowder-kettle.
>   (*WPP* 196)

These simple perceptions disclose the real. When the butcher-boy puts off his killing-clothes, an onlooker knows that he no longer intends to perform butchery. This is not a mere appearance; the onlooker does not need to speculate. When the blacksmiths swing their hammers back, we know they intend to circle them back onto the anvil. Mind is present because thought involves intentions in the world. Contact does not require exposure of putative hidden essences ("the best you possess"). In listing human actions, Whitman rejects the Transcendentalist ideal of human contact and signals a phenomenological one. He anticipates Gallagher and Zahavi's assertion that "the proper way to respond to the sceptical challenge is . . . by abandoning the radical divide between the subject's mind and body."[19] The body is not the inferior expression of the superior thought or feeling; contact does not inhere in the correct deduction of a nuanced and separate interior state. The body's actions manifest thoughts, feelings, and intentions directly. We can experience human contact by adopting what Gallagher and Zahavi call "non-mentalizing, embodied perceptual approaches to questions of understanding others and the problem of intersubjectivity."[20]

Whitman models such non-mentalizing approaches to others by "holding" them. Another verb he uses to communicate an embodied understanding of contact is "to mind." This verb appears at the end of the famous passage in section 8 of "Song of Myself" depicting "the blab of the pave, the tires of carts, sluff of boot-soles, talk of the promenaders." Recalling these sounds, and many others, the poet writes: "I mind them or the show or resonance of them" (*WPP* 195). The verb "to mind" names the non-dualist thought he models. To "mind" is to "care," as in "Do you mind if I smoke?" It is also to "have in mind" or "remember," as in "I mind how once we lay such a transparent summer morning" (*WPP* 192). Minding is different from caring or remembering, though. If we care or feel or remember, there is a distinction between the mental organ and its action; we care with our hearts, feel with our bodies, remember with our brains. In "minding," by contrast, the agent of the mental action (the mind) and the action it performs (minding) are one and the same; the thing we are doing is one and the same with the body with which we do it. We are not separating thought from the material but foregrounding their oneness. To *think about* the blab of the pave is to imagine a mind that is separate from its objects of thought, as the presence of the preposition "about" in the phrase "think about" makes clear. There is the thinker, there is the action of thinking that she does, and there is the object she is thinking about. Rather than imagining a self thinking thoughts "about" things, Whitman imagines a self that is minding things directly. "I mind them," he writes. "To mind" things is to embrace the way that intersubjective consciousness unites the self with other things in the world; it is affiliative and affective. We might note also that what he minds is "the resonance of them," a phrase suggesting a quality of vibration, which in turn suggests a dynamism in the other that once again breaks down the distinction between identity and extension of being into the world.

Contact is not intimacy. Whitman acknowledges that people have secrets that are not visible to others, "hot wishes" and secret affinities with the "wolf, the snake, the hog" (*WPP* 311). Disclosure of these facets of hidden interiority is not the crux of contact for him, however, as it is for many people who conceive of contact as some form of total disclosure, some radically sincere psychological nakedness, or some Emersonian total overlap of one self with another. He acknowledges that he plays "the part that looks back on the actor or actress" but does not deem that such self-masking invalidates the experience of contact that inheres in the simple fact that intentions are evident in actions (*WPP* 313).[21] Nor do phenomenologists. They too acknowledge that their focus on the materialization of thought does not imply that the other's mind is totally displayed to an onlooker: "The expressive relation between mental phenomena and behaviour is stronger than that of a mere contingent causal connection, though weaker than that of identity."[22] Human actions do not simply reveal the other, neither truly (they could be lying) nor fully (there's more to a person than meets the eye). Yet the correlation between action and identity is not, therefore, contingent; a vast number of the things people do in fact correlate with the mind of the doer. A blacksmith may not have his mind on his work, but we know that it was on it to the degree that it caused him to raise the hammer and pound the iron. The butcher-boy may chafe at the performance of a racially coded dance, but at least part of his mind is attending to its steps. The reality of hidden recesses does not invalidate the fact that when people perform actions, their minds are present in that action. "In seeing the actions and expressive movements of other persons, one already sees their meaning. No inference to a hidden set of mental states is necessary. Expressive behavior . . . reveals the mind to us"—not the whole mind, but that part that is expressing itself in that behavior. And for phenomenologists, as for Whitman, realizing this presence of mind in action is the basis of human contact. Concealed thoughts do not mean that there has not been contact; rather, they mean that the other is *other*. "As Husserl points out, if I had the same access to the consciousness of the other as I have to my own, the other would have ceased being other, and instead have become a part of myself."[23]

(On this, we might recall Boscovich's understanding of the contact of two atoms as "compresence," a state that he, like Husserl, argues would destroy the separateness of the two entities.)

If contact does not require disclosure, for Whitman, then the empathy he voices is not guilty of some of the charges leveled at it. Beginning with D. H. Lawrence, a steady stream of readers has objected to Whitman's depiction of empathic identification.[24] Walter J. Slatoff, for example, objects to lines like "Agonies are one of my changes of garments, / I do not ask the wounded person how he feels, I myself become the wounded person" (*WPP* 225), adding "there is something abstract and unconvincing about the passage and glib about the 'all those I feel or am'"; he stresses "that Whitman does not, in fact, become the wounded person but remains the poet writing about himself becoming the wounded person; he is experiencing not the full ache of the wound but the exaltation of writing."[25] Whitman, he believes, assumes too much. Along similar lines, Leslie Jamison identifies "an arrogance to these demonstrations of sympathetic immersion," which "seem more like acts of imaginative innovation—breathless leaps across traditional boundaries of class and circumstance—rather than genuine articulations of the 'agony' that true identification would yield."[26] They are, she says, mere "aesthetic forays" for an "exhausted but not unhappy" speaker who is disturbingly "energized by his empathic capacities." She contrasts these lines with the superior accomplishments of *Drum-Taps*, in which acts of "true identification" lead the speakers "deep, deep" into another body, "their very boundaries dissolved by the suffering they encounter."[27]

However, the 1855 poems never claim to feel the full ache of the wound nor describe "true identification." Whitman never claims that his empathy reveals the other's full mind or emotional reality or self. When he says "I do not ask the other how he feels," from the point of view of a philosophy of "minding," we recognize that in not asking, he refuses to privilege a putative hidden self as "the true self." His thought can be better understood as anticipating Heidegger's critique of conventional views of empathy. According to Heidegger, a person who idealizes empathy "typically assumes that "the 'I' is at first in its ego-sphere and must then subsequently enter the sphere of another." Heidegger posits, however, that "the 'I' does not first break out . . . since it already is outside, nor does it break into the other, since it already encounters the other outside."[28] We may experience separation from the other, but Whitman and Heidegger find the antidote not in using empathy to break through to the inside of the other's mind but in viewing that difference as illusory. Along these lines, we can observe that Whitman's metaphor "Agonies are one of my changes of garments" does not claim an empathic understanding that reveals the other's interiority but instead claims an intersubjective unity with the wounded person. There is no flow out of self into the other, none of the fallacy of empathy as Heidegger imagines it. After all, the poet imagines wrapping the garment of the other's agony around himself, not projecting himself inside the other, as Jamison wants him to. Praising the capacity of identification to produce "boundaries dissolved by the suffering," she objects to what she describes as Whitman's "sympathize[ing] from a distance," treating agony as "yet another hypothetical costume."[29] Jamison is championing the capacity of empathy to overcome dualism. I would argue by contrast that Whitman denies that dualism altogether. The process is better understood as quivering to a new identity, now in relation to the wounded man; he is being in this way—in relation to the wounded man—now. He is holding him in mind, or minding him.

Contact is a matter of holding and minding, neither an act of listening nor a "complete collapse" achieved by "acts of identification."[30] In the 1855 and 1856 poetry, Whitman celebrates the way that contact inheres in run-of-the-mill corporealization of thought and feeling.[31] We may believe that Whitman *should* have more interest in a first-person knowledge of the other, particularly with people of a different race, class, gender, or religion. We might feel that if contact does not involve an understanding of the competing perspectives individuals have on a common culture, then contact is trivial, as though Whitman's answer to our deepest cravings is merely advice to lower the bar of care. But Whitman stresses that while the bar may indeed be lower in terms of what we might know about the other, what we get when we approach contact this way is amazing:

Beginning my studies the first step pleas'd me so much,
The mere fact consciousness, these forms, the power of motion,
The least insect or animal, the senses, eyesight, love,

The first step I say awed me and pleas'd me so much,
I have hardly gone and hardly wish'd to go any farther,
But stop and loiter all the time to sing it in ecstatic songs.

(WPP 171)

The kind of contact Whitman celebrates is only the first step, he confesses. There is, of course, more to other beings than "the mere fact" of "consciousness" visible in living forms and motions. But where others insist that that "more" is what matters, Whitman says he is so stunned by the simple yet ecstatic experience of ongoing contact with another consciousness made visible in forms and motions, that he does not need anything deeper.

Whitman's subject is not the interiority of the fellow citizens with whom he claims contact. From one perspective, this indifference can seem like a hegemonic claim to speak for all, with the violent reduction of multiple perspectives that Slatoff protests, but in his professed indifference to interiority, Whitman also frees us from the normative effects of cherishing hidden "true" interiorities. Not focusing on the nuances of interiority, Whitman is able to conceive a wildly democratic form of contact, one that affirms the consciousness of all members of the society equally, from the president to the prostitute, and including everyone in between.

Like Whitman, Emily Dickinson also imagines non-metaphysical forms of human contact. Her poem "They say that 'Time assuages'" almost reads as a direct contradiction of Emerson's claim in "Experience" that suffering never touches us, that we never experience contact:

They say that "Time assuages" –
Time never did assuage –
An actual suffering strengthens
As Sinews do, with Age –

Time is a Test of Trouble –
But not a Remedy –
If such it prove, it prove too
There was no Malady –

(EDP 395, Fr 861)

Here Dickinson reports that one can experience real suffering that actually touches one, and that this feeling remains keen for years. In fact, Dickinson's poems are full of fulfilled, not wished for, feelings of contact. Even if the feeling described is one of loss or grief, it implies that the contact was once strong or real. As suggested earlier, while in 1862 she idealizes contact, understood as an unclothed communion in which "each was to each the sealed church," increasingly, her later poems describe such an out-of-time conception of contact as both impossible and inimical to what contact is and can be. Increasingly, her poetry rejects any approach to human contact that involves transcending bodies, selves, and "private sympathy" in quest of the universe itself.

Maurice Lee similarly argues in *Uncertain Chances* that Dickinson turns away from a metaphysical understanding of things.[32] Lee and I disagree, however, over what Dickinson turned *to* when she turned away *from* metaphysical notions of contact. While I see a turn to phenomenology similar to that of Whitman, Lee claims that Dickinson turned toward skeptical empiricism, an attitude he affiliates with pragmatism like that of William James. According to his line of thought, Dickinson realizes that we will never grasp a person's true nature and so she turns to empiricism—the effort to gain a true-enough understanding through repeated experiences with them. He interprets the 1865 poem "Experiment to me" as representative of this claim:

> Experiment to Me
> Is Every One I meet
> If It contain a kernel –
> The figure of a Nut
>
> Presents upon a Tree
> Equally plausibly –
> But Meat within is requisite
> To Squirrels, and to Me
> (*EDP* 484, Fr 1081)

According to Lee, the first lines ask whether we can know that the things we see in the world are real, not mere "figure[s]," but the rest of the poem goes on to reject this familiar skeptical question, suggesting that we cannot know whether a given nut is real by looking at it; there's no point in trying to know what is inside of it by theorizing. We need to crack one after another—which is to say, engage in repeated experiences with nuts, or as he puts it, pursue "repeated experiments and probabilistic thinking within a community of inquirers."[33] Truth will have to be determined by probability, a shared sense of what is most likely true. The best way to get what we need from the world is to crack a nut, get what we can from it, and move on to the next one. Analogously, the best way to know who people are is through repeated experiments, which afford a good-enough though never definitive understanding of their nature.

Though Lee rejects the possibility of definitive knowledge of the other, contact remains an epistemological inquiry for him, one of good-enough rather than secure knowledge. In contrast, I read this poem as less focused on questions of truth than on questions of value and personal connection. The phrase "Meat within" does not suggest a true self to be known, whether through probability or deduction. It suggests some inner "value" or "substance" that nourishes the speaker. A person with "Meat within" has something "to me"; he or she feeds my soul, so to speak. This inner meat is less of a quality of true interiority—some hidden truth—than it is a quality of exteriority, a value for me. In this poem, contact is not a question of epistemology, but relationship, as the homonym "meet within" suggests (picking up on the word "meet" of the second line). A person who has meat within is a person with whom I can have a meeting. Admittedly, the idea of a "meeting within" is paradoxical, since it erodes the distinction between the space within and the exterior that enters it. But that is the point. The people who will be "Meat" to me—who will become part of me and will sustain my soul—are those with whom I can have a "meet[ing]."

The related term "kernel" also suggests an inner impetus toward externalization. A kernel is not "the thing itself" but the beginning of something. The kernel of a story is the first glimmer of it that will develop into a story. The kernel of a tree is that first glimmer, an impetus in this case toward growth and development into a tree. A kernel contains the promise of a life cycle of growth from germ into fullness in the world within a specific temporal duration. Kernels only have "being" through a lived cycle of self-actualization—a developmental arc that puts into play—in the world at large—the instinct of growth and engagement inside. We might recall the image in "Split the Lark" of music understood as "Bulb after Bulb, in silver rolled" (*EDP* 427, Fr 905). Bulbs are not the "true self" of music, nor of a flower; they are capsules of potentiality for flowering and song, which will be unleashed into the air in a finite space of time.

If we understand human contact as a relationship with a human-being-in-process in the world, then we need to rethink the way we relate to the "figure[s]" we meet in the world. Squirrels, of course, have no compunctions about tearing open shells to get to the meat within, but this poem does imply such compunctions when the matter is one of human personae. If we approach human figures as tropes or symbols—metaphorical nuts that need to be cracked—then we misunderstand the human being we are trying to contact, with potentially violent results. The previously discussed poem "There came a Day – at Summer's full," imagines such an attitude of figure-as-symbol. In fact, the word "figure" appears in that poem too, as a variant for the word "symbol." Hence, the lines previously discussed can also read:

> The time was scarce profaned – by speech –
> The figure of a word
> Was needless – as at Sacrament –
> The Wardrobe – of Our Lord –
>
> (*EDP* 155, Fr 325C)

Figures, symbols, and words all mediate between the thing and a perceiver seeking truth. This poem's representation of contact rejects all such figures, words, and symbols that would obstruct contact, as would Christ's clothing during the Eucharistic consumption of his body and blood. In this poem's imagination of contact, figures, symbols, clothing, and words are all irrelevant, because they only represent the real thing, and the speaker is in contact with the real thing itself.

However, in "Experiment to Me," the figure of a nut does not represent an inner truth. It is neither a symbol nor a form of clothing. It is more intrinsic to the thing itself than it is a mediating representation of that thing. Admittedly, if we tear the husk off a nut, we will get its meat within, but if we tear the shell off a person in search of his or her self, we will miss what we seek, for people can only actualize their inner principle of dynamism—that kernel of being—in a materialized existence. Contact, in this case, is not ripping off layers of seeming to the kernel of being inside, but instead is understanding the interplay of inner dynamism and outer materialization. A person with whom I can have a meeting is one who makes that inner dynamism more accessible than one who keeps it locked inside the hard shell of a fixed and perhaps normative persona. Our social personae, for better or for worse, are the way we manifest our being in the world, and they cannot be simply cast aside in our quest for the real.

If there is any "true self" imagined in these poems, it is closer to D. W. Winnicott's conception of the true self as a verb than it is to a good-enough knowledge of a fundamental essential interiority.[34] We encounter people all the time, but when we can perceive the dynamism behind a finite persona in a way that nourishes ourself, that is the moment of contact. A person is more than the figure she presents, but that "more" is not an essence; rather, it is a plenipotentiary possibility for self-creation in the world. Robert Weisbuch aptly describes this inner quality as "an electric reality [that] lives within us and abroad." He claims that Dickinson stresses that "a life of power depends upon its actualization."[35] If we understand the "Meat within" and the "Bulb after Bulb, in silver rolled" as something like this electric reality, then we can see that this poem reimagines contact as an experience when a person actualizes his or her electric reality in a way that nourishes the soul of another person. As Dickinson writes in 1871:

> The Bone that has no Marrow,
> What Ultimate for that?
> It is not fit for Table
> For Beggar or for Cat –
>
> A Bone has obligations –
> A Being has the same –
> A Marrowless Assembly
> Is culpabler than shame –
>   (*EDP* 505, Fr 1218, stanzas 1 and 2)

As in "Experiment to me," value in this poem is external—a bone is valuable for table, or cat, or other external "obligations." Its significance is to contribute to a just "Assembly"; if it has "no Marrow," it will still contribute to an assembly, but it will be a "culpabl[e]" assembly. "Marrow," like a "kernel," is an intrinsic quality of integrity whose value is for others—an internal drive toward exteriorization.

In presenting selfhood as something always in process in the world, Dickinson's thinking in this poem resembles the phenomenological view of selfhood that Whitman calls "quivering me to a new identity."[36] As already noted, phenomenologists stress that consciousness is contingent upon the objects of consciousness and that, consequently, Being is always intentional and therefore fluid, changing in relation to the assembly in which it finds itself at any given moment. For both poets, one of the most important intentions through which being creates itself is the work of writing—that is to say, the intentionality of consciousness takes form in poems. And thus, poems are sites of potential human contact. Rather than symbolize a true self or bridge gaps between selves through the transmission of meanings, poetry manifests selfhood directly: "The Martyr Poets – did not tell – / But wrought their Pang in syllable –" (*EDP* 315, Fr 655), Dickinson writes. Similarly, Whitman describes his writings as "act-poems of eyes, hands, hips and bosoms" (*WPP* 250). External manifestations of the inner impetus toward creation, poems are "drops of me" that "stain the page." Reading, therefore, is an encounter with that intentionality. Where Dickinson imagines the inner drive toward externalization as a kernel or marrow, Whitman compares it to a sunrise: "Something I cannot see puts upward libidinous prongs." It "provokes" him to "send sun-rise out of" him: "why don't you let it out then?" (*WPP* 212–13).

Because poetry materializes thought and soul, for both poets, writing is a site of human contact. Writing is not the production of "figures" understood as symbols that encode essential meanings but the production of "figures" understood as intentional acts of a passionate consciousness. Reading is contact not insofar as one true self makes its meaning clear to another, but because all selves are intersubjective and the act of reading causes the reader to create a dynamic self now in relationship to the poet's written thing. Writing neither symbolizes contact nor aims at it through ever-clearer expression of meanings. It directly manifests a self creating itself now in writing, and addresses a self creating itself now in reading.

The 1862 poem "Going – to – Her! / Happy letter!" is a particularly extravagant and sophisticated development of the way contact—at least one form of it—inheres in the reader-writer relationship.

> Going – to – Her!
> Happy – Letter! Tell Her –
> Tell Her – the page I never wrote!
> Tell Her, I only said – the Syntax –
> And left the Verb and the Pronoun – out!
> Tell Her just how the fingers – hurried –
> Then – how they – stammered – slow –slow –
> And then – you wished you had eyes – in your pages –
> So you could see – what moved – them – so –
>
> Tell Her – it wasn't a practised Writer –
> You guessed –
> From the way the sentence – toiled –
> You could hear the Boddice – tug – behind you –
> As if it held but the might of a Child!
> You almost pitied – it – you – it worked so –
> Tell Her – No – you may quibble – there –
> For it would split Her Heart – to know it –
> And then – you and I – were silenter!
>
> Tell Her – Day – finished – before we – finished –
> And the old Clock kept neighing – "Day"!
> And you – got sleepy –
> And begged to be ended –
> What could – it hinder so – to say?
> Tell Her – just how she sealed – you – Cautious!
> But – if she ask "where you are hid" – until the evening –
> Ah! Be bashful!
> Gesture Coquette –
> And shake your Head!

(*EDP* 529, Fr 277B)[37]

This poem invokes (in order to reject) a metaphysical notion of writing as the flawed expression of an idea that is perfectly conceived in its author's mind. The speaker would be seen to be saying: "My perfect meaning exists, but it exists only on the page I never wrote, in my head. Unpracticed writer as I am, I could not express it on the page. It's not that my meaning was incomplete nor that I suffer from unclarity; it's just that feeble me was not up to the task of communicating my true idea." The speaker toys with the idea of writing as communicating a coherent message and the idea of poetry as a struggle with language to encode it—with imperfect results.

The poem raises such ideas, however, only to replace them with a phenomenological conception of meaning and identity. The poem undermines its own metaphysical forays by concentrating its message on the fact of writing the letter. After all, the *only* message this letter contains is the author's act of writing. In writing about writing, the speaker foregrounds the "now-ness" and "this-ness" of her message, effectively saying, "I am here, writing you, and there is no more fullness to me than the way all of my being is currently occupied with *this*." Equally, the poem foregrounds the "you-ness" of the writing self. "Right now, my being is taking form in its relationship with *you*." Dickinson is depicting something like what Whitman calls quivering to a new identity. The speaker's self is contingent, inextricable from her intentions, which at this moment involve her writing and her beloved. Like Whitman, she is becoming what she looks upon, though Dickinson's treatment suggests a different way of thinking about it from his ideals of holding and minding. Consider the complex pun in the end of the first stanza, which imagines that the fingers hurried, then stammered, "And then – you wished you had eyes – in your pages – / So you could see – what moved – them – so – ." The pronoun "what" and the verb "moved" have crucially ambivalent meanings. The letter wishes it could see what moved the hands. These words invite a few equally plausible meanings. On the one hand, they seem to say, "You, letter, wish you could see the beloved, who really moved me, emotionally speaking." On the other hand, they seem to say, "You, letter, wish you could see the beloved, who inspired me to move my hands across the page, physically speaking." And the lines might also be saying "You, letter, wish you could see me, the one who is moving her hands." Who exactly was it that moved the author's hands?

The author, or the beloved? We cannot say. This is phenomenological. Actions cannot be understood apart from their objects, phenomenologists remind us. The objects cause the actions and are therefore one with them. (Experiments have shown that different neurons fire depending on which object we reach for, even if they are the same size and in the same spot. Neurologically, then, actions includes their objects. We are not Boscovich's "non-extended points.")

The poem similarly anticipates phenomenology in equating the passion that "moved" the poet with the movement of her hands. Phenomenologists stress that emotion is a bodily thing, a feeling that includes its corporeal expression. What writing can there be in the absence of a passion-to-write? None. To separate the movement of the hands from the emotion of being "moved" is to falsely separate passion from passion-to-write. It is to falsely separate emotional movement from physical movement, writing from in-spiration-to-write. Our feelings are never intrinsic; we feel and move only with regard to particular things in the world.[38] Our feelings equally are inseparable from the bodies that express them. They are passions-to-write-you or passions-to-touch-you, not pure passions expressed imperfectly in material actions. The poem develops the corporeality and intentionality of thought: "You could hear the Boddice – tug," and "it worked so," and the fingers "stammered." The self as imagined here is, as Merleau-Ponty writes, less of an "I think" than it is an "I can," an impetus to do things in the world.[39] Right now, in this poem, the poet's self is being by creating a letter; it is moving a hand across the page.

Like Whitman, Dickinson chooses forms that not only refuse to dis-tinguish self from other, but also refuse to distinguish self from poem. Whitman stresses these in long lines and lists that hold things together and mind them; Dickinson's form pursues these goals by breaking down coherent and stable referentiality. The confusion of pronouns in the line "You almost pitied – it – you – it worked so – " exemplifies this. Bear in mind: "you" is the letter, while "it" is the bodice of the author. She means that the letter almost pitied the author, she worked so. However, as written, it is difficult to keep apart the maker, the maker's body, and the thing made. If she had written, "You almost pitied her, she worked her body so hard," these entities would be distinct; by collapsing these distinctions, she presents a phenomenological understanding of identity. Consistently, Dickinson's form refuses discrete identities.

In foregrounding the presence of the writer in the act of writing, Dickinson resembles Whitman. Both poets explore the idea that the self does not antedate the act of writing but instead is created in it, as it is in other intentional acts. Both also depict intersubjective selves, selves that exist only in relations to others. Both find that our condition as intersubjective beings who exist through intentions in the world makes it necessary to develop modes of thought that dissolve distinctions between subjects and objects. Whitman pursues this goal through championing forms of thought like "holding" and "minding," which refuse the otherness of the other. Dickinson pursues it in polyvocal uses of language that splinter what purports to be the stability of things. Ultimately, both echo the yearning of their culture for genuine human contact, and they record its fulfillment in the human presence manifest in poetry, that miraculous presence that Dickinson calls the "consent of language."

"We Must Travel Abreast with Nature, if We Want to Understand Her"

Place and Mobility in Dickinson's and Whitman's Environmental Poetry

CHRISTINE GERHARDT

OVER THE PAST DECADE, ECOCRITICAL APPROACHES HAVE PRO-
foundly changed the way we read Dickinson and Whitman. In particular,
ecocritical analyses have stressed that for all the symbolic and transcendental
orientation of Dickinson's and Whitman's poetry, an abiding interest in
physical places and people's relationships to specific geographies constitutes
a defining feature of their art that has important ecological implications.
However, most of these green rereadings have put special emphasis on
Dickinson's and Whitman's rendition of local areas and people's steady
ties to their environs. In the case of Dickinson, ecocritics have argued that
she challenged patriarchal paradigms through a "located" New England
epistemology, that she shared Thomas Wentworth Higginson's fascination
with close nature observation that didn't require much travel, and that
her ecopoetics was informed by local perspectives even when it embraced
regional and global realms.[1] Similarly, environmental critics have claimed
that Whitman "is at his best as a local poet" whose responses to neighboring landscapes echo bioregionalist principles; whose "best poems, if they
don't stay close to home, return to shorelines and wetlands"; and who
shows a "growing unease with the environmental effects" of Manhattan's
urban density, which threatened "the nature he loved."[2] Looking beyond
Manhattan and Long Island, ecocritics have focused on the local as well,
arguing that Whitman's "most thorough consideration of the relationship
between humans and their nonhuman environment" can be found in the

Timber Creek sections of *Specimen Days*, that the green undertones of his Southern poems stem largely from their local situatedness, and that his regional and global perspectives remain shaped by a sense of local place.[3] That is, while ecocritical analyses have recharged Dickinson and Whitman studies in important ways, they also suggest that what is environmentally most significant about their work is its keen attention to local realms and lasting forms of place-attachment.

Dickinson's and Whitman's poetry does speak powerfully to notions of dwelling, bioregionalism, and related forms of environmental place-orientedness that emphasize local groundedness. They also, however, wrote about places characterized by remarkable degrees of mobility and engaged the world from perspectives of speakers who are themselves on the move, all in the context of an increasingly mobile American culture and transnational dynamics of travel, exploration, and colonization. From Dickinson's numerous poems in which birds and insects figure not only as symbols of resurrection but also as migrating creatures, to Whitman's ways of casting himself as a restless poet who "walk[s] New England," "cross[es] the prairies" ("Starting from Paumanok"), and "wander[s]" "round the earth" ("Facing West from California's Shores," *WPP* 185, 267), both poets were as interested in human and nonhuman forms of mobiblity as in rootedness and staying put.[4] So far, however, ecocritics have largely bracketed mobility from discussions of Dickinson.[5] In the case of Whitman they have even emphasized that mobility stands in direct opposition to his environmental outlook: M. Jimmie Killingsworth's perceptive studies, while being among the very few ecocritical analyses of Whitman that mention mobility at all, have suggested that Whitman's "bioregional intensity" was a way of defying his culture's increasing mobility, that he struggled to "retain a view of the land that suggests older tribal models, an attachment that resists the free-ranging mobility of modern times," and that many of his poems grew out of a "need for relief from the pressures of social and geographical mobility, of city life and mass communication, of homelessness in the bioregionalist sense."[6] Similarly, Lawrence Buell has found that "Crossing Brooklyn Ferry" sees urban transit as a threat to human place-connectedness, and expresses an idealizing "reinhabitory vision" of what commuting might be like in the future, a kind of mass transportation that would restore people's contact with the landscape and "retain a measure of rural healthfulness."[7] From a postcolonial perspective, George Handley, too, has emphasized the tension between Whitman's poetry of "expansion and sweeping generalizations" and his "democratic poetics of the local and the particular," while also showing how his poetry links the dynamics of (neo)colonialism to ideas about a changing universe, and "the commotions of human history" to natural particulars.[8] My own comparative study of Dickinson and Whitman, while emphasizing their shared interest in dynamic environments and human-nonhuman relationships, and in various kinds of movement within and between geographical scales, has excluded the discussion of mobility as an environmentally significant dynamic or force.[9] I would like to open a new dimension in the ecocritical debate about place-connectedness in Dickinson and Whitman here and argue that for all their interest in the local and people's lasting ties to well-known places, mobility is neither ancillary nor antithetical to Dickinson's and Whitman's place-oriented ecopoetics. An abiding interest in a mobile world, and in mobile ways of relating to such a world, forms an integral part of their environmental imagination and constitutes an important connection between their bodies of work.

With this double interest in place and mobility, Dickinson's and Whitman's poetry intersects in important ways with the environmental discourses of their day. In the mid-nineteenth-century United States, the gradual shift toward granting the nonhuman world a value of its own and seeing it in need of protection marked the beginning of a modern environmental consciousness.[10] This transitional moment was in crucial ways linked to questions of mobility. On the one hand, prominent strands of the time's proto-ecological discourses were characterized by an explicit valorization of stability. When the newly specialized sciences still adhered to Linnaeus's notion of "geographical niches" inhabited by species according to their God-given "place" or "station," when Thoreau's *Walden* emphasized the merits of steady lives in well-known places, and when John Muir would soon argue for preserving the ostensibly pristine California wilderness, such interlocking discourses revolved around the assumed value of stability in the nonhuman world and people's relationships to it.[11] George Perkins Marsh's *Man and Nature* (1864) illustrates how much these environmentalist arguments were tied to a denunciation of geographical movement:

Apart from the hostile influence of man, the organic and the inorganic
world are . . . bound together by such mutual relations and adaptations
as secure, if not the absolute permanence and equilibrium of both, a
long continuance of the established conditions of each at any given time
and place. . . . But man is everywhere a disturbing agent. Wherever he
plants his foot, the harmonies of nature are turned to discords. The
proportions and accommodations which insured the stability of existing
arrangements are overthrown. Indigenous vegetable and animal species
are extirpated, and supplanted by others of foreign origin, spontaneous
production is forbidden or restricted, and the face of the earth is either
laid bare or covered with a new and reluctant growth of vegetable forms,
and with alien tribes of animal life.[12]

Beyond its thinly veiled nativism that associates plants and animals with
people (paradoxically in an era when most environmentalists remained
unconcerned with the enforced displacement of Native Americans from
areas "protected" as wilderness), Marsh indicts human mobility as a threat
to "indigenous" species in "the stability" of their "arrangements."

On the other hand, the time's proto-ecological discourses were also inflected by a considerable commitment to mobility. After all, it was geologist
Charles Lyell's study of "the continual migrations of organisms over the
land and sea, . . . their shifting alignment in nature's economy," and his view
of subsequent geographical alterations as inherent to nature's dynamics,
that enabled Charles Darwin to interpret the conditions on the Galapagos
Islands as a "unique ecological system" created by "extraordinary migrations" and to develop a theory of adaptation critically based on changing
conditions and species mobility.[13] Moreover, several leading scientists made
their key observations en route, with publications such as Alexander von
Humboldt's *Personal Narrative of Travels to the Equinoctial Regions of the
New Continent* (1814–29) and Darwin's *Journal of Researches* (1839), better
known as *Voyage of the Beagle*, signaling their indebtedness to global mobility.[14] Numerous natural history essays, too, including Thoreau's "Walking"
(1862) and his more wide-ranging *A Week on the Concord and Merrimack
Rivers* (1849), *An Excursion to Canada* (1853), *The Maine Woods* (1864), and
Cape Cod (1865), embraced the genre of travel writing. Nineteenth-century

environmentalist discourses, then, were still characterized by a considerable plurality of perspectives regarding movement and mobility, while idealized notions of rootedness were already becoming more prominent, especially in popular discourses. An analysis of Dickinson's and Whitman's poetry in this nineteenth-century context reveals that both engaged with precisely the tension between mobility and rootedness at this watershed moment in the development of a modern ecological outlook and practice. While place played a central role in their writing about the nonhuman world, both embraced geographical mobility as an integral part of their environmental poetics.[15]

Dickinson and Whitman unsettle emerging notions of stable places as a litmus test for an environmentally attuned perspective in part by exploring geographies that are informed by such marked kinds of nonhuman movement that mobility becomes a quality of these places themselves. I'm not just referring here to the numerous poems in which Dickinson turns to "wide-wandering" insects and "returning" birds, or passages in which Whitman writes about a "migrating flock of wild geese alighting in autumn to refresh themselves" ("Our Old Feuillage," *WPP* 322) or a wild gander who "leads his flock through the cool night" ("Song of Myself," *WPP* 199). Apart from this shared interest in species that are obviously mobile or known to be migratory, they also talk about landscapes characterized by much more unexpected kinds of movement, so that fields, forests, and entire continents emerge as profoundly unsteady, indeed mobile sites of impermanent dwelling.

In the case of Dickinson, such constructions of places that are shaped by various kinds of "natural" mobilities in profound yet often unacknowledged ways have much to do with her interest in the movement of plants, a phenomenon that in itself emphatically unsettles popular notions of "natural" rootedness. The following poem is an excellent example:

> As if some little Arctic flower
> Opon the polar hem –
> Went wandering down the Latitudes
> Until it puzzled came
> To continents of summer –
> To firmaments of sun –

To strange, bright crowds of flowers –
And birds, of foreign tongue!
I say, As if this little flower
To Eden, wandered in –
What then? Why nothing,
Only, your *inference* therefrom!

(Fr 177)[16]

This 1860 poem has been read mainly allegorically, referring to issues of faith or the act of reading poetry, and historically, as commentary on the aurora borealis or Sir John Franklin's failed arctic exhibition.[17] Less often, critics have discussed its botanical resonance, pointing, for instance, to the "manmade movement of plants" caused by the import of species for gardening.[18] Yet the seemingly oxymoronic idea of a "wandering" flower can also be taken to refer to the botanical process of plant migration—the gradual change of habitat in floral species due to a shift in seed dispersal. Such floral movements were first discovered, also and especially with regard to the arctic, when the proto-Darwinian botanist Asa Gray suggested in 1859 that during the glacier epoch, "arctic climate" moved southward "nearly to the latitude of the Ohio," so gradually "that it did not destroy the temperate flora," bringing with it "a band of subarctic and arctic vegetation" some of which still survived "on the mountains of New York and New England."[19] One such plant is the saxifrage, a "little flower" common in New England, growing low to the ground with numerous small blossoms. My point here is not that Dickinson knew about Gray's discovery—although it was widely discussed at the time, and later also mentioned in Higginson's "The Procession of Flowers"—but that this context highlights how the poem's reference to floral movement, for all its prominent symbolism, creates an unsteady geography that is ecologically suggestive precisely because of such mobility.[20]

First of all, it is notable that Dickinson depicts a plant—commonly the symbol of a sedentary life—not as intricately related to its local surroundings as in many of her other poems, from "There is a flower that Bees prefer" (Fr 642) to "Pink, small, and punctual" (Fr 1357), but as autonomously moving across the continent. This alone invests all areas affected by this flower's migration with the quality of mobility, from the polar environment it has left, via the regions it has passed through, to its new habitat, be that New England or a place further south. From such a perspective, the "strangeness" and "foreignness" of the other flowers and birds that this "wandering" plant encounters in "Eden" may not only reflect the outlook of a newly arrived "Arctic" specimen unfamiliar with more temperate natural systems, but also suggest that these "foreign"-looking species may themselves not be indigenous to this place but have moved there at some point, further adding to the mobility of this poem's geography. Indeed, because in the logic of this poem plants are conceivable as mobile, underscored by several verbs of locomotion, any geographical area populated by plants is potentially invested with mobility. The poem here both responds to and radicalizes how her contemporaries talked about the new idea of plant migration. Higginson, in his 1862 reaction to Gray, would still insist on a principal floral rootedness, pondering "the sweet, blind instinct with which *flowers cling to old domains* until absolutely compelled to forsake them," and would remain more local than global in his view that the "humble movements of our *local* plants may be laying up results as important, and may hereafter supply evidence of earth's changes upon some *smaller scale.*"[21] Dickinson's vision of arctic, temperate, and tropic places as interconnected through potentially ubiquitous, even universal, floral movements shares Higginson's fascination with plant migration, yet is closer to young John Muir's more radical perception—expressed just a few years later during his 1867–68 walk across large parts of the United States—that certain mountains serve as "highways on which northern plants may extend their colonies south-ward," with great numbers of "enterprising" Northern and Southern plants gathering in "many minor places of meeting along the way."[22] Much like Muir's note, her poem pushes beyond the local, is devoid of nostalgia for lost rootedness, and imagines large-scale plant movements as integral to the world of botany.

Second, it is noteworthy that in spite of the poem's overlapping layers of mobility, physical places remain part of Dickinson's concern—indeed, the poem's ecological suggestiveness depends at least partially on this dimension. The speaker's references to the "Arctic," "polar," "Latitudes" and "continents" keep geography from dissolving into the realm of the purely symbolic, so that the novel idea of floral mobility can unsettle this poem's placeness without completely undoing it. This insistence on place includes the vision of "Eden," which resonates as a metaphor for a botanically diverse "Southern" naturescape as much as the other way around. At the time, such an Edenic view of this earth played a prominent role in Higginson's natural history prose, which tried to reconcile biblical dogma with new scientific paradigms by linking botanical phenomena to the trope of Heaven on Earth. It was also prominent, later, in John Muir's conservationist essays, which routinely referred to choice wilderness areas as a Garden of Eden. Dickinson's poem echoes and adapts such religiously infused but ultimately place-oriented gestures as she imagines a flower's mobility both as spiritual and as transcontinental journey.

Third, the poem's way of calling attention to the potentially radical implications of such a transcontinental plant migration, underscored by the opening "As if" and the speaker's refusal to formulate a conclusion, also challenges some of the broader eco-political inflections of considering mobility as a deviation from the norm. When Humboldt speculated about links between floral distribution and people's adaptations to climactic conditions around the turn of the nineteenth century, he still did so from an overall emancipatory perspective.[23] In the mid-nineteenth century, however, such transferrals became part of nationalistic debates and acquired xenophobic overtones: nativist arguments "naturalized" restrictive notions of people as being rooted in a specific territory, often by way of floral metaphors. If the poem's rhetoric of "strange" and "foreign" species resounds with notions of cultural otherness, its principal embrace of unexpected plant movements also undermines Western notions of sedentariness in ecological *and* cultural terms, inviting readers to consider migration as an equally "natural" process. Overall, this seemingly innocuous poem calls attention to dynamic landscapes whose various levels of movement—human and nonhuman, anthropogenic and not—constitute a formative part of their ecology. As such, it rethinks notions of rootedness at a cultural moment when such notions were becoming increasingly codified in environmental discourses and beyond.

This debate highlights how, in his poetry, Whitman also evokes places whose unexpected levels of mobility constitute a critical part of their ecological setup. A prominent case can be found in one of his signature poems, "Out of the Cradle Endlessly Rocking." So far, ecocritics have mainly stressed that the poem creates "a specific place" in which a "symbolic bird is endowed with a habitat, a history, a story of its own," that the boy is sensitive "to finer perceptions of the landscape's details," that Whitman links "quiet and careful observation of nature" to feelings of sympathy, and that the agency of shoreline and bird contribute to a "dynamic sense of place."[24] But if the poem's environmental overtones emerge from its attention to geography, it seems crucial that what defines this place, and provokes the speaker's attention, are this seashore's unusually mobile features. This has less to do with the dynamics of the ocean with its "white arms out in the breakers tirelessly tossing," or the play of shadows and weather upon the beach, than with the poem's core interest in two "guests from Alabama." Apart from their often-discussed political implications, the presence of Southern birds on Paumanok is also environmentally interesting, especially if one considers that the geographical distribution of mockingbirds was changing in the mid-nineteenth century. The northern mockingbird (*Mimus polyglottos*)—a Southern species now common in large parts of the United States—slowly extended its range northward for more than a century, but it was precisely during Whitman's time that this shift was increasingly noticed and discussed. The *Atlantic Monthly* alone carried dozens of essays on the bird, many of which debated its changing range, from Wilson Flagg's "Birds of the Night" (1859) to Olive Thorne Miller's "A Tricksy Spirit" (1885).[25] The mockingbird's possible or potential presence beyond the South was so contentious that the popular 1869 field guide *The Birds of New England* included an entry on the species, but stressed that it was "so exceedingly rare" in the north "that it [could] scarcely be regarded otherwise than an accidental visitor."[26] What is more, this northward shift was part of the time's growing environmental concern, since it occurred "naturally" and as a result of human action, including the massive northward shipment of mockingbirds as pets.[27] Many mockingbird sightings in the North were actually attributed to cage escapes, while the species became severely decimated in certain parts of the South.[28] Although Whitman's "Out of the Cradle" does not express direct environmental concern, its focus on a pair of "exceedingly" rare Southern "guests," from a species slowly pushed northward and threatened in its Southern habitat, turns mobility into a formative feature of Paumanok's ecology, and of the South as well. Already early in the poem, the birdsong's reference to *"Winds blow south, or winds blow north,"* and *"Home, or rivers and mountains from home"* (*WPP* 389) suggests that Long Island does not form these creatures' regular habitat, creating a sense of geographical instability that is redoubled when the remaining "he-bird" calls for the lost female:

> *Blow! blow! blow!*
> *Blow up sea-winds along Paumanok's shore;*
> *I wait and I wait till you blow my mate to me.*
> . . . . . .
> *Hither my love!*
> *Here I am! here!*
> . . . . . .
> *Do not be decoy'd elsewhere,*
>   (*WPP* 389, 391)

This shore does not come into view as a familiar landscape populated by common New England species, but as an unruly site where the only bird is now a "solitary guest" that appears to be profoundly out of place. As such, the emphasis on the unusual movement of mockingbirds reconceptualizes Long Island as a realm of geographical mobility. If the poem indirectly joins debates about the northern range of mockingbirds, it does so by taking sides, if you will, with naturalists who were beginning to see a sedentary species as more mobile than previously assumed—such as Wilson Flagg, who wrote in 1859 that the mockingbird "may be gradually making progress northwardly, so that fifty years hence both of these birds may be common in Massachusetts"—rather than with those who insisted on its rootedness in the South—including Maurice Thompson, who still wrote in 1884 that "the nature of the mocking-bird is that of a resident more than that of a migratory bird, and I am inclined to name its true habitat semi-tropical."[29] By doing so, the poem not only embraces mockingbirds as migratory, but also casts Long Island as a place shaped by new patterns of mobility.

"Out of the Cradle" thus rethinks the stability of local places in ways similar to Dickinson's "As if some little Arctic flower"; although there is clearly a more existential quality to Whitman's piece—where a species' transgressive movement turns the potential new habitat into a site of isolation and death rather than a diversely populated paradise—the struggle for survival (mockingbirds in the North) and successful adaptation (arctic flora in the South) are, in Darwinian terms, two sides of the same coin. Moreover, for all its instability, this Long Island shore itself remains present and matters in the world of this text as a specific physical realm. In other words, the poem unsettles popular notions of lasting platial stability without undoing the idea of place as such in ways that are further comparable to the geographical dimension of Dickinson's poem about plant migration.

Finally, Whitman's attention to the plight of two anthropomorphized birds who shift into an area where they are not considered to be native also has larger eco-political ramifications. Clearly, his bird elegy foregrounds individual experiences of love and loss, without even hinting at such political concepts as "foreignness" and "exoticism"—mentioned, no matter how playfully, by Dickinson. Linking the traveling mockingbirds' fate to nativism, or, for that matter, to cultural diversity, would be equally mistaken. And yet both poems do intersect on the level of rethinking the "(un)naturalness" of nonhuman as well as human mobility. At the very least, the intensity with which the boy-turned-poet "absorbs" and "translates" the "sorrowful" song of the surviving Southern bird and subsequently identifies himself as "outsetting bard" puts pressure on claims about Whitman as essentially "a loyal son of the New York islands,"[30] an ecopoet of local groundedness. It also suggests that politically, what is at stake here is not just the closeness of Whitman's rooted or not so rooted environmental perspectives to supposed "tribal" place attachments,[31] but the suggestiveness of his often unstable platial position in terms of more wide-ranging issues of human migration that were widely discussed at the time. Looking back from here to Dickinson's arctic poem invites fresh perspectives on her ecopoetics of place as well, since the symbolic link between the far-traveling flower and flippant speaker suggests that her often-quoted mode of seeing "New Englandly" might involve a more mobile stance than often presumed. Both his Long Island and her New England speaking positions are, for all their local orientation, also mobile insofar as both poets talk about and often identify with species whose regional ties are not as stable as commonly assumed, unsettling precisely the places through which they seem to ground their environmental imagination. Dickinson and Whitman, then, imagine mobility as a vital part of specific geographies that are dynamically linked to larger transregional, even transcontinental networks of movement and change, subtly pushing against a solidifying environmentalist rhetoric of "rootedness" in nonhuman and human realms and undoing the logic of stability that informs both.

A second, related manner in which Dickinson and Whitman unsettle popular equations between platial stability and ecological wholesomeness is by letting their speakers move across the land in ways that recast such mobility as a constitutive element of environmental perception. Here they assume almost opposite positions, considering that some of Dickinson's poetic walks revolve so closely around the home and garden that they seem to stay largely put, while Whitman's mode of imaginatively gliding or skipping from place to place, across vast distances, and even off into space has little in common with more mundane forms of travel or migration. And yet both of them construct what I would call a mobile sense of place, and formulate fine-tuned insights into the environmental possibilities and limitations of a mobile way of being in the world.[32]

With Dickinson, it is again a flower poem that provides one of the strongest examples:

It bloomed and dropt, a Single Noon –
The Flower – distinct and Red –
I, passing, thought another Noon
Another in it's stead

Will equal glow, and thought no more
But came another Day
To find the Species disappeared –
The Same Locality –

The Sun in place – no other fraud
On Nature's perfect Sum –
Had I but lingered Yesterday –
Was my retrieveless blame –

Much Flowers of this and further Zones
Have perished in my Hands
For seeking it's Resemblance –
But unapproached it stands –

The single Flower of the Earth
That I, in passing by
Unconscious was – Great Nature's Face
Passed infinite by Me –

(Fr 843)

Earlier readings have discussed this 1864 poem as revolving around "a red rose of love" or an unknown symbolic referent, assuming that the speaker's intense suffering cannot be explained by a lost flower.[33] Others have pointed out that the poem evokes daylilies, whose oversight signifies a missed transcendental revelation, and that apart from its language of botany and plant geography, the poem is informed by an environmental ethics of paying attention to the seemingly familiar, expressed through profound regret over its absence.[34] But the poem's core concern over the causes and consequences of having missed a flower also resonates with the time's proto-ecological discourses in ways that propel the question of human mobility into the foreground. Thoreau, for instance—whose extraordinary familiarity with the flora of his native Concord is often linked to his insistence on staying put—repeatedly reflected on the intense movement that botanizing required; as Ray Angelo has pointed out, in his 1856 *Journal* entry for December 4, he "described the great lengths he went to at times to ascertain the exact date a particular flower opened—'running to different sides of the town and into neighboring towns, often between twenty and thirty miles in a day.'"[35] Moreover, Thoreau "made possibly his most significant contribution to New England botany" not in Concord, but when "he ascended Mt. Washington, New Hampshire—the highest peak in New England—and prepared the most detailed list of plants by zones that had ever been made for this site."[36] And yet he seems to have ultimately favored an environmentalism of local situatedness: "Many a weed here stands for more of life to me than the big trees of California would if I should go there."[37] What I am interested in here is how the environmental import of Dickinson's flower poem, with its defining tension between place attentiveness and inattentiveness, similarly revolves around conflicting views of human mobility.

At first glance, the poem's overt moral message of not mindlessly "passing" by what lies close at hand seems to suggest that the speaker's very movement is at least partially responsible for the inattention she comes to regret so deeply. This negative connotation of mobility is redoubled when she declares that "Much Flowers of this and further Zones / Have perished in [her] Hands / For seeking it's Resemblance – ": accentuated by a lexicon that combines the sentimental language of flowers with the proto-ecological discourse of plant geography ("this and further Zones"), these lines imply that new walks in the neighborhood and beyond, or through gardens and greenhouses with local and exotic specimens—or the search for pressed specimens in letters from faraway places—not only failed to bring her close to such a flower again, but caused substantial destruction ("perished") and "blame." The speaker concludes that "lingering" would have been wiser in all these instances, once more repeating the critique of having moved. However, all of the environmentally sensitive insights this poem expresses also *depend* on physical movement. It is during a habitual walk that the speaker first notices, no matter how briefly, the presence of an extraordinary plant; it takes another visit to the same place to realize that this species blooms only very briefly; and the new kinds of movement inspired by her search for a similar plant generate a supreme level of attention concerning the links between "Species" and their "Locality," which in itself turns out to be not as stable as she expected, since the flower's "disappearance" resonates in temporal as well as spatial terms. Without movement, none of these insights are to be had, so that human movement leads to oversight and insight, damage and concern, with an emphasis on the latter.

Compared to Thoreau's reflections about occasional oversights, about the astonishing number and length of walks required to ascertain a plant's flower date, and about his occasional dependence on other people's geographical explorations,[38] Dickinson is both more uncompromising in sounding out the mobility-related failure to perceive a unique botanical phenomenon, and paradoxically also more affirmative of human movement. Where Thoreau's notes ultimately privilege expressions of local attachment, Dickinson's poem, while deeply invested in a flower's "stead," "locality," and "place," begins and ends with the passing of the speaker, mirrored in the passing of "Great Nature," and overall reimagines place and people's sense of place as deeply, perhaps inherently mobile in ways that challenge and contradict the sense of rootedness that it also yearns for. While "It bloomed and dropt, a Single Noon – " is clearly also about time, the poem intersects reflections about the passing of the seasons with fresh ideas about passing through a specific place, foregrounding how the speaker's—and the flower's—very mobility gives meaning to a landscape in ways that create a multilayered, and decidedly mobile sense of place.

Whitman similarly unsettles notions of people's local "rootedness" without relinquishing his environmentally resonant investment in place. Although he explores this kind of environmental instability in several poems, it is particularly striking in "O Magnet-South." This 1860 poem has been noted for its exuberant praise of southern landscapes, usually in terms of Whitman's prewar "rhetoric of conciliation"; from an ecocritical perspective, I have argued earlier that its nostalgia functions as a preservationist gesture, but at the price of far-ranging political myopia.[39] What has remained unexplored is the speaker's way of registering natural particulars from a perspective of passionate movement, up and against the poem's more sedentary longings. It is again instructive to think about this tension in conjunction with the time's environmental discourses, which included ecologically invested travel narratives. For instance, the conservationist philosophy of Thoreau's disciple John Muir was deeply informed by numerous excursions—in and around Yosemite Valley, through the American South, and to South America and Alaska—and many of his texts testify to a lifelong passion for extended journeys. In the posthumously published account of his 1867–68 *Thousand-Mile Walk* from Indianapolis to Florida he wrote that he "had long been looking from the wildwoods and gardens of the Northern States to those of the warm South," and found that he "could enjoy traveling . . . in the midst of such beauty all [his] life."[40] At the same time, however, the trained botanist always yearned to "linger" longer, and ultimately committed himself to conservation in California. This interplay between the urge to continue traveling and an intense interest in local detail enabled several of Muir's ecological insights, a context that makes Whitman's mobile poem of the South resonate in fresh ways.

In "O Magnet-South," human mobility again seems to be responsible for the all but cursory attention to the land's geographical particulars. Compared to Dickinson's "It bloomed and dropt," whose speaker explicitly links the oversight of a flower to her own physical movement, the negative inflection of mobility remains more subdued here—both the poem's original title "Longings for Home" and its culminating wish to "never wander more" imply an unspecified regret over ever having left; and when the speaker imagines to "cross the hummock-land or through pleasant openings or dense forests," to "coast off Georgia . . . coast up the Carolinas," and "pass rude sea-headlands and enter Pamlico sound through an inlet" (*WPP* 584–85), his very restlessness prevents a more in-depth engagement with the landscapes in question. At the same time, however, the speaker's movement is also the basis for the poem's multilayered environmental insights, in ways that are structurally similar to Dickinson's poem, despite the marked difference in voice and geographical range. This speaker's imaginative journey across various parts of the South enables something like a composite vision, which includes a broad range of species and geographical formations that together characterize the region in its diversity. Also, the trans-regional mode of reentering the South from the North makes the perspective inherently comparative, drawing attention to relevant markers of difference that distinguish the Southern landscapes from Northern ones; the assemblage of "parrots in the woods, . . . the papaw-tree and the blossoming titi," and of "live-oak . . . yellow-pine, the scented bay-tree, the lemon and orange, the cypress, the graceful palmetto" foregrounds details that are both stereotypical and suggest the mobile speaker's discriminating attention to regionally distinct flora and fauna. Finally, the erratic movements still allow for occasional pauses, and time to pay more detailed attention—be it to "A Kentucky corn-field" with "the tall, graceful, long-leav'd corn, slender, flapping, bright green, with tassels, with beautiful ears each well-sheath'd in its husk" (*WPP* 584–85), or to the intensely alive system of swamps that lies at the heart of the poem.

This mode of rushing through an entire region to absorb a number of its finer geographical features in passing is not unlike Muir's Southern travel narrative, as in this characteristic entry:

Discovered two ferns, *Dicksonia* and a small matted polypod on trees, common farther South. Also a species of magnolia with very large leaves and scarlet conical fruit. Near this stream I spent some joyous time in a grand rock-dwelling full of mosses, birds, and flowers. Most heavenly place I ever entered. The long narrow valleys of the mountainside, all well watered and nobly adorned with oaks, magnolias, laurels, azaleas, asters, ferns, Hypnum mosses, Madotheca . . . . Obtained fine glimpses from open places as I descended to the great valley between these mountains and the Unaka Mountains on the state line.[41]

The point here is not that Whitman's poem has merit as a descriptive nature essay, but that it amplifies a formative environmentalist tension between stationary and mobile views of the nonhuman world. "O Magnet-South" expresses a vision of regional reinhabitation, of a life in and with the natural environment based on rest, that is both created and undone by the very mobility of the speaker and his ever-changing relationship to the land. This constellation corresponds with the one in Dickinson's "It bloomed and dropt," whose speaker wishes she had "lingered" more, although movement is a defining part of her life in place. Dickinson and Whitman, then, both develop speaking positions and modes of perception that establish a sense of place in their very mobility. In conjoining visions of various places, and of specific places at different times, their poems accentuate the rhythms of particular landscapes and of people's environmental perception—based on human mobility.[42]

Attending to the role of mobility in Dickinson's and Whitman's environmental imagination opens fresh perspectives for reading their poetry and for reading them together. In particular, comparing their work within the larger framework of their time's proto-ecological discourses suggests that questions of mobility, rather than being marginal or antithetical to their ecopoetics, are in many ways central to the green resonances of their art. The mid-nineteenth century marked a moment when the new sciences, natural history essays, and preservationist arguments critically revolved around matters of place *and* mobility, before environmentalist discussions became largely dominated by the perspectives of equilibrium ecology and a popular green localism, both of which privileged notions of stability, if not stasis, in the nonhuman world and human-world relations and perceptions. Precisely at this transitional moment, Dickinson and Whitman developed intensely mobile views of plants, animals, places, and human-place relations that are both in conversation with these broader cultural negotiations and intersect with each other on a number of levels. Both of them test the possibilities and limitations of casting mobility as a formative characteristic of places on different scales and of an ecologically oriented subjectivity.

Whitman and Dickinson construct unexpected plant and animal migrations that evoke mobile places, and speaking positions that express a self-consciously mobile sense of place. Additionally, both address issues of mobility in ways that complicate the environmental resonance of their work. These include intersections between race and ethnicity and mobile perspectives of the larger-than-human world, and explorations of collective rather than individual movements, such as the westward expansion and colonial explorations. A discussion of these issues would further contribute to a more nuanced understanding of Dickinson's and Whitman's mobile ecopoetics, and serve as an additional reference point for an ecocriticism that is interested in transnational networks and global flows of people, objects, and ideas, without necessarily relinquishing its analytical investment in place. While Dickinson's and Whitman's visions certainly were informed by white middle-class perspectives, Western notions of science, and colonialism, both also addressed questions of migration, travel, and other kinds of human and nonhuman mobility in ways that productively challenge the environmental imaginary of their own time as much as of ours—as Dickinson once put it, "We must travel abreast with Nature, if we want to understand her, but where shall be obtained the Horse – ."[43]

Hyperbole and Humor in Whitman and Dickinson

ANDREW DORKIN AND CRISTANNE MILLER

THERE IS A LONG, IF SOMEWHAT SPORADIC, HISTORY OF SCHOLAR-
ship acknowledging both Whitman and Dickinson as humorists.[1] Still, these
poets' exaggerated or hyperbolic claims are often read seriously, making
Whitman seem egotistical and Dickinson depressed or without self-esteem.
In this essay, we argue that the figure of hyperbole is both intrinsically linked
with humor and a key element in what makes both poets' work at once col-
loquially familiar and radically disorienting. For Whitman and Dickinson
the use of hyperbole extends other features of their work that defamiliarize
and disorient readers' values, perceptions, and cognitive processes, while
simultaneously creating the effect of a privileged, sympathetic community.
Whitman famously writes, "I might not tell everybody but I will tell you,"
and in later editions of *Leaves of Grass*, he repeatedly addresses his reader
as "camerado" (*WPP* 1855, 45; 1891–92, 454).[2] Dickinson almost identically
addresses a general reader as though utterly singular—"Then there's a pair
of us! / Don't tell!"—in her much-quoted "I'm Nobody! Who are you?"
(*EDP* 128 [Fr 260]). This bond with the reader is crucial because their
hyperbole and humor can be difficult to apprehend and can have jarring
effects; rather than ridiculing others or satirizing nineteenth-century life,
Whitman and Dickinson use humor to encourage readers to think through
the challenges of their poetics and poems.

Though largely underappreciated either as a literary or philosophical
tool, hyperbole has enjoyed renewed theoretical attention recently. Christopher D. Johnson, for example, seeks to redeem hyperbole's potential

significance in the face of the banal or superficial exaggerations that pervade casual conversation, focusing on "exceptional" rather than colloquial usage.[3] Yet, as so often happens when scholars, in pursuit of the serious, brush aside the trivial, humor also gets swept away. Whitman and Dickinson provide ample evidence in their poetry that hyperbole may function as a serious fulcrum for thought and affect specifically through its humorous aspects—not in opposition to or as divorced from them. Even when Whitman's and Dickinson's hyperboles are not straightforwardly comical, the tension between serious themes or literal readings and the possibility of humor is fundamental to many of their effects. Both poets construct a broad range of types of hyperbole: from the obvious comedy of simple exaggeration to hyperbole dealing with topics so grave that the humor is largely submerged—or hyperbole so entwined in metaphor that it all but disappears in the metaphor's unexpected equivalences. Building on the work of recent hyperbole scholarship but refocusing on the humor of hyperbole, this essay focuses first on the poets' comic uses of hyperbole in relation to popular forms of mid-nineteenth-century humor, demonstrating that even such apparently simple use is complex in its implications. It then turns to the more subtle and intricate dynamics of hyperbole's heuristic leap and the humor that mediates it in the work of both poets.

Introducing "unserious" constructions of language, as William Solomon puts it, especially in poems with profound cultural, psychological, or epistemological implications, alters the cognitive work of a poem.[4] Hyperbole is a particularly effective tool for this kind of mental swerve or gymnastics because it disrupts normal scales or avenues of conception. It introduces the "Splinter" that Dickinson tells us can send a brain careening from its normal "Groove" into uncharted territories as unstoppably as a river overflowing its banks, "When Floods have slit the Hills – / And scooped a Turnpike for Themselves – " ("The Brain, within its Groove"; EDP 286 [Fr 563]). We propose that hyperbole warrants a place among the "radically redescriptive" experiments through which poetry, as Jed Deppman puts it, can make us "ready to rethink what we knew, either in the limited sense of reconsidering beliefs and trying on redescriptions or in the deeper one of rethinking how and why we rethink and redescribe at all."[5] Whitman writes, "What is known I strip away .... I launch all men and women forward with me into the unknown" (*WPP* 1855, 79). With more obvious humor, Dickinson defamiliarizes through equivalencies that level the great rather than elevating the common: "The Queen, discerns like me – / Provincially – " ("The Robin's my Criterion for Tune – "; *EDP* 126 [Fr 226]). Both gestures make the reader reassess what can be known and how to value it comparatively in the scale of worlds or nations.

Ronald Wallace is the only critic to write at length about humor in both Whitman and Dickinson. In *God Be with the Clown: Humor in American Poetry*, Wallace describes Whitman as *alazon* and Dickinson as *eiron*, Aristotelian terms for the characters of Greek Old Comedy. For Wallace, the *alazon* is a backwoodsman or Kentuckian figure of boastful foolishness and the *eiron* is distinctly Yankee in stereotype, Socratic, and often a "witty self-deprecator."[6] Focusing on persona, he describes each poet as a character in a comic plot, using hyperbole or understatement to criticize and celebrate themselves. "In much American comic poetry," Wallace writes, "the *alazon* is both fool and god-figure, requiring a careful balance of acceptance and rejection on the part of the reader"; two functions of the *alazon*, ridicule and celebration, merge in Whitman.[7] In contrast, according to Wallace, "Dickinson's characteristic mode of self-mockery is deflation, claiming to be less than she is. She knows she is not the simpleminded character she poses as, and we know that she knows it, but the pose of powerlessness gives her a power she couldn't claim somberly"—as feminist scholars have also claimed in relation to Dickinson's deployment of the feminine gender role.[8]

Whitman's language is easily compared to that of tall tales, such as Thomas Bangs Thorpe's 1841 "The Big Bear of Arkansas." In this story, the "Big Bear" describes Arkansas to some skeptical gentlemen on a steamboat as "the creation state, the finishing-up country—a state where the *sile* runs down to the centre of the 'arth, and government gives you a title to every inch of it? Then its airs—just breathe them, and they will make you snort like a horse. . . . Just stop with me, stranger, a month or two, or a year if you like" and then, he implies, you'll think like he does about Arkansas.[9] In 1855 Whitman writes, "Stop this day and night with me and you shall possess the origin of all poems" (*WPP* 1855, 28). When he further describes himself as "a kosmos" or asks "Who goes there! hankering, gross, mystical, nude?" or proclaims "I have pried through the strata and analyzed to a hair, / And counselled with doctors and calculated close and found no sweeter fat than sticks to my own bones," he echoes the tones of tall-tale humor (*WPP* 1855, 50, 45).[10] In such lines, Whitman uses humor to persuade readers that every aspect of humanness should be celebrated on microscopic and cosmic scales.

Dickinson also uses the language of comic hyperbole—and in several registers besides the self-deprecating. In "She sights a Bird – she chuckles – ," for example, Dickinson describes a bird-stalking cat as having "Hopes so juicy ripening – / You almost bathed your Tongue – ." The cat's anticipation is frustrated, however, when the bird flies away, in dramatic metaphorical and abstracted hyperbole: "Bliss disclosed a hundred Toes – / And fled with every one – " (*EDP* 185 [Fr 351]). In "I think I was enchanted," Dickinson describes the transformation of the world after reading Elizabeth Barrett Browning; everything becomes oversized: "The Bees – became as Butterflies / The Butterflies – as Swans – "; she experiences "Lunacy of Light" and nature's tunes sound like "Giants – practising / Titanic Opera – " (*EDP* 308 [Fr 627]). Just as Whitman's humor shares elements with Southwestern tall tales, what Wallace describes as Dickinson's Yankee humor has a popular counterpart in the anonymously authored poems written in comic Yankee dialect that were published in the newspaper she read daily, the *Springfield Republican*. "A Sunnit on the Big Ox" (April 19, 1856), for example, hails a "4 thousand pounds" "tremenjous boven nuggit" in mock-heroic bad spelling: "What a lot of mince pize yude maik," concluding with a chaotic confusion of hyperbolic categories by calling it a "prodigious reptile" and "great and glorious insect." Dickinson's Yankee tonality comes out in poems such as "I reckon – When I count at all – ," which concludes grandiosely that "Poets" so "Comprehend the Whole" that "Sun . . . Summer . . . [and] the Heaven of God . . . look a needless Show" in comparison (*EDP* 292 [Fr 533]).

Whitman's and Dickinson's use of hyperbole and humor departs from that of tall-tale tellers and comic dialect speakers in that hyperbole is for them not just a matter of authorial pose; it is integral to the structure and language of their poetry. Here we differ from Wallace, who presents humor and exaggeration in both poets as expressing a persona's, but in effect the poet's own, thoughts and feelings. Such characterization reflects a common, limited view of hyperbole that Audrey Wasser attributes to Aristotle: "In this view, hyperboles reveal less about the objects they refer to than about the character of the person who uses them."[11] Our focus instead is on hyperbole that has ontological and epistemological, not plot and character, implications. Hyperbole in Whitman and Dickinson takes on a heuristic function in the verse by transporting readers beyond standard conceptions or modes of understanding, while at the same time creating an empathy of understanding (or of frustration) that lies specifically in the figure's humor, distinguishing it from similarly disjunctive figures. Both poets use forms of exaggeration bordering on the comic to destabilize conceptions and assumptions and thereby potentially reorient their audiences.

Humor provides both writers with a tonal flexibility that helps disrupt assumed categories of understanding—opening the possibility for new thought—just as the author of the "Big Ox" sonnet, or "Sunnit," makes us think ironically and earnestly about economies of scale and consumerist values: something is "great" because we can make a lot of sausages, oxtail soup, and pies from it. In language that illuminates Whitman's play with tone and his characteristic challenge to assumed economies of value and scale, Johnson describes hyperbole as "waver[ing] between self-mockery and earnest epideixis. Its quantities strain to bridge the gap between microcosm and macrocosm and thereby leave the reader wavering indefinitely between laughter, admiration, and scorn."[12] Whitman writes, "My embryo has never been torpid"; "For it the nebula cohered to an orb . . . . the long slow strata piled to rest it on . . . . vast vegetables gave it sustenance, / Monstrous sauroids transported it in their mouths and deposited it with care" (*WPP* 1855, 80). Any visualization of this scene, involving an embryo ferried by "vast vegetables" and dinosaurs' mouths into the present, indeed strains to bridge various gaps in ways of thinking about identity or nationhood in time and space. For Whitman, size and quantity are markers of value, the mundane is also epic, and the boundary between the micro- and macro-cosmic is often humorously fluid.

Drawing on the work of other theorists such as Paul Ricoeur, Joshua R. Ritter describes the "metafunction" of hyperbole precisely in terms of such "reorientation out of disorientation."[13] Hyperboles may respond to an existing source of disorientation, such as the insufficiency of language or concepts to represent the world, or when "language or thought must transcend epistemological and ontological boundaries in order to describe the magnitude of an extraordinary perspective or situation."[14] A poet may also use hyperbole to cause disorientation where familiarity or complacency inhibits understanding and insight. When it effects a paradox, for example, hyperbole "stretches the imagination through its extravagance and in one's ambiguous apprehension of it, because it is only in the obscure space of 'para' that one is disoriented enough to surrender presuppositions about thought and reality, thereby preparing the way for a newly reimagined perspective."[15] The reader's "ambiguous apprehension" of hyperbole is thus crucial to its effect; etymologically an "overshooting" or "throwing beyond," hyperbole is constructed in terms of error.[16] On one front, hyperbole hazards being misperceived as literal or true, as a lie or as "bullshit."[17] At the same time, it may so profoundly succeed in disorienting that readers cannot reorient themselves: as a mode of radical figuration, hyperboles must strike a precarious balance if we are to "find them valuably post-intelligible rather than gratuitously pre- or unintelligible."[18]

According to Johnson, hyperbole "often precipitates a heuristic experience in which imaginative and cognitive limits are tested."[19] Ritter similarly describes the heuristic nature of hyperbole when he posits that "the enormity of a particular exigence may be such that one of the only tropes capable of communicating the incommunicable is the one that so adamantly risks miscommunication."[20] Most theories represent communication as attempting to build a bridge of meaning between the user and the receiver; hyperbole, as a form of humor, throws us at least momentarily off that bridge and into the river's cognitively chaotic ride.[21] As a kind of shortcut, practically sufficient but suboptimal and risky, hyperbole offers poet and reader a heuristic leap by which to mediate the gaps between thought, word, and world.

In their recent cognitive theory of humor, Matthew Hurley and his coauthors, Daniel Dennett and Reginald Adams, suggest that humor's function is primarily para-heuristic, responding to potential errors created by the automatic heuristics that permit us to filter sensory input, reason inductively, make assumptions, and generate expectations.[22] In their model, humor is the process or mechanism of reconciling mental spaces, not merely the mirth that results from discovering cognitive inconsistencies or errors. Gregg Camfield similarly theorizes humor as a "capacity," "state," or "mood" prior to its resolution:

Humor opens the mind to discordant mappings. It is, in essence, the capacity to hold in mind conflicting conceptions without choosing between them. . . . To recognize incongruity is to return categories to an equal footing and to allow a new grouping of their component categories to manage cognitive dissonance. Within the state of humor itself, that management is mainly tolerance, suspension of the need for resolution.[23]

Once the reconciliation of categories, hierarchies, or other mental spaces has occurred, Camfield posits, humor has passed; this is why a joke is often only funny the first time we hear it. Dickinson deploys hyperbole to describe this effect in "The Riddle that we guess" when she asserts, "Not anything is stale so long / As Yesterday's Surprise" (*EDP* 550 [Fr 1180]).

Because hyperbole is a risky heuristic leap and humor's function is to mitigate the risk of such leaps, the relation between hyperbole and humor is both intimate and fraught: hyperbole is vulnerable to humor, which mediates its passage from disorientation to reorientation, and to the possibility of laughter. In hyperbolizing, a speaker always risks being ridiculed. One might thus rebut Dickinson by asserting that, in fact, many things are staler than "Yesterday's Surprise," resolving the error of its representational shortcut by dismissing the hyperbole as absurd. To laugh in this situation is to laugh at the hyperbolist for such faulty thinking. However, a very different kind of humor response is possible if the reader sympathetically entertains the possibility that "Yesterday's Surprise" could be the stalest of phenomena; in attempting to reconcile such a claim into our own understanding of the world, or even to tolerate its surprising juxtapositions or errancy, we implicate ourselves in its hyperbole and its humor. If we genuinely "try to think with" a Dickinson or Whitman poem—"to explore the thinking of which the poetry is the necessary byproduct"—we humor the poem and laugh or smile empathically with it, which is to say, ultimately at our own thoughts.[24] Suzanne Juhasz, Cristanne Miller, and Martha Nell Smith similarly claim that the reader contributes to establishing the humor in a text: "To appreciate the full range of Dickinson's humor, one must be able to conceive of her as a sharp critic of her world."[25]

Both poets use hyperbole to juxtapose or collapse boundaries between the profound and mundane, spiritual and physical, genteel and grotesque;

the humor in these hyperbolic comparisons comes not from any depiction of flaws (to be ridiculed) but from the performance of flawed categorizations and binaries (to be reconceived). In some respects, the two poets have distinct patterns of hyperbolizing—for example, Dickinson tends to complicate hyperbole with metaphor, while in early poems Whitman deploys a steady stream of hyperbolic equivalences. But while Whitman's hyperbole often seems to serve a larger persuasive or rhetorical project, both poets use the figure to produce a diversity of effects, reminding us, as Johnson does, that "hyperbole does not always aim to persuade. Sometimes it would astonish or create other emotional or cognitive effects. Sometimes the hyperbolist cultivates lasting ambiguity."[26] In the hands of these poets, hyperbole and humor spur the reader to think openly, critically, and with empathy about the politics, ironies, and paradoxes of physical being and human, spiritual consciousness in the mid-nineteenth century.

Hearing the humor in Whitman's hyperbole helps us to realize the disorienting edge of his radical claims. Rather than saying that the body is superior to religion, he claims, "The scent of these arm-pits is aroma finer than prayer" (WPP 1855, 51). He says not that preachers are ineffective but that "a mouse is miracle enough to stagger sextillions of infidels"—that is, a creature typically feared or despised is so marvelous in its construction that it could convert more people than inhabit the globe (WPP 1855, 57). This leaves open what it means to be an "infidel" or what happens when infidels are "stagger[ed]," but the hyperbole deliciously elevates the mouse (perhaps punning on "church mouse") above even the greatest preacher or priest of any religion, none of whom could convert or "stagger . . . infidels" through the mere fact of being alive—or at least no more than the least rodent might. In section 6 of "Crossing Brooklyn Ferry," Whitman claims that "I too knitted the old knot of contrariety, / Blabb'd, blush'd, resented, lied, stole, grudg'd, / Had guile, anger, lust, hot wishes I dared not speak"— using forceful verbs and nouns. Then he continues, "The wolf, the snake, the hog, not wanting in me." The efficiency of this cognitive disorientation is remarkable: for example, the "hog" signals greed; by claiming hog-ness (that is, the extreme of greed and a purely animal, therefore rationally uncontrolled, behavior), Whitman identifies these "hates" and "Refusals" as simultaneously comic, nightmarish, and utterly natural (WPP 1891–92, 311).

Larger-than-life descriptions or portraits—Whitman's "friendly and flowing savage," his "barbaric yawp"—powerfully redefine our conception of the possibilities for perceiving and being in the world, if we allow ourselves to think about how they are both outrageous and true (*WPP* 1855, 71, 87).

Richard Chase asserts that "Song of Myself" is a "comic drama of the self," "on the whole comic in tone"; Wallace finds the poem to be structured as comedy.[27] We would add that its structure is also based in hyperbole. Hyperbole offers itself as a link between Whitman's more-than-rhetorical gestures and his not-quite metaphorical or ironic voice.[28] As Whitman states in his preface, he sets out to prove that "the United States themselves are essentially the greatest poem," in part by constructing a flexible speaking "I" that represents an individual, the collectivity of individuals, and the concept of the nation—that is, any and therefore all manifestations of Americanness (*WPP* 1855, 5).[29] The project attempts to unify the United States by constructing a representative but shape-shifting speaker who repeatedly embodies and performs the principles that are fundamental to democracy, as Whitman understood it: equality, personal and political liberty, and the possibility of "commensurate" representation—such that a poet, and perhaps a political body, might be "commensurate with a people" (*WPP* 1855, 7).[30]

The hyperbolic humor of this project is, however, explicitly distinct from ridicule. In his preface to the first edition of *Leaves of Grass*, Whitman rejects ridicule and exaggeration: "Of the human form especially it is so great it must never be made ridiculous"; "Exaggerations will be revenged in human physiology" (*WPP* 1855, 19). This distaste for the sharp wit epitomized in ridicule was common in Whitman's time; as Camfield asserts, "Virtually every moral philosopher or every popularization of moral philosophy published in America in the nineteenth century embraced 'humor' as it attacked 'satire' and 'wit.'"[31] In *The Senses of Humor*, Daniel Wickberg navigates the nineteenth century's fluid terminologies of humor, especially its identification of wit with exaggeration but humor with the representation of truth; "popular consciousness associated humor with reality, understood in concrete and empirical terms, and associated wit with unreality, understood as abstraction and idea-based."[32] Thus Whitman's defense of the body against caricature and ridicule does not contradict his repeated hyperboles of grandeur and greatness due to the latter's deep investment in the accumulated details of truth and reality.

Whitman's firm belief in the possibility of representation to change a national culture extends to language generally, in ways that profoundly shape his hyperbolizing. Although many hyperboles stem from a perceived insufficiency of language, in his 1855 *Leaves of Grass* Whitman appears to have complete confidence in his language's—and his own—ability to express the greatness of America, which he catalogs and epitomizes. "The English language befriends the grand American expression. . . . it is brawny enough and limber and full enough," he assures his reader; "It is the medium that shall well nigh express the inexpressible" (*WPP* 1855, 25). This faith in language extends to hyperbole as a structure that does not merely exaggerate—that is, misrepresent or disfigure—reality or possibility, but renders commensurate life and death, the cosmos and the leaf of grass, and all things that appear disparate or paradoxical.

Whitman's grand experiment in extended hyperbole in the poem eventually titled "Song of Myself" disorients his readers so radically that even when reoriented they find it difficult to judge the exaggeration on which his hyperbole depends. If exaggeration is defined as an inexact relation to (subjective) truth, and hyperbole is a heuristic figure that deploys a disorienting exaggeration in order to reorient, identifying a hyperbole as such requires a stable ground against which to assess a claim's truth and intent: one must first determine whether it exaggerates. Out of context, the phrase "considering a curl of smoke or a hair on the back of my hand as curious as any revelation" seems exaggerated and humorous in its absurdity (*WPP* 1855, 74). However, in the world of *Leaves of Grass*, in which we find repeated declarations of universal commensurability, the ground against which we might evaluate this statement's degree of exaggeration falls away. What would normally look like exaggeration or paradox begins to resemble a tautology. Our sense of the line's humor remains, but it is transfigured from skeptical amusement at the line's absurdity into empathic appreciation of the curiosity it depicts—or into a tensely pleasurable seesawing between the two: "the reader wavering indefinitely" between smiling adoption of the poet's perspective on the greatness of all living things and the hilarity such a statement about a hairy hand as revelatory of divinity would provoke in other contexts.[33]

This basic structural grandness underlies the self-conscious hyperbolic humor that occurs throughout this poem. For example, Whitman writes:

A tenor large and fresh as the creation fills me,
The orbic flex of his mouth is pouring and filling me full.

I hear the trained soprano . . . . she convulses me like the climax of
    my love-grip;
The orchestra whirls me wider than Uranus flies,
It wrenches unnamable ardors from my breast,
It throbs me to gulps of the farthest down horror,
It sails me . . . . I dab with bare feet . . . . they are licked by the
    indolent waves,
I am exposed . . . . cut by bitter and poisoned hail,
Steeped amid honeyed morphine . . . . my windpipe squeezed in the
    fakes of death,
Let up again to feel the puzzle of puzzles,
And that we call Being.

                                      (*WPP* 1855, 54–55)

Here the hyperbolic similes "large and fresh as the creation" and "like the climax of my love-grip" ease the reader into the fully metaphorical hyperbole of the following lines: the "orchestra whirls me wider than Uranus flies," "throbs me to gulps of the farthest down horror," and so on. This mix of celestial, orgasmic, seafaring, and painful metaphors—in which the speaker (and by extension the reader) becomes the object of the actions the orchestra performs, have a surreal quality that is humorous if one attempts to visualize this hallucinating, ecstatic, terrifying succession of feelings or experiences: the orchestra "whirls . . . wrenches . . . throbs. . . sails . . . expose[s] . . . cut[s] . . . squeeze[s]" its listener. If we read skeptically, we laugh at such nonsense. If we read sympathetically, we may smile at the fact that this far into his poem of hyperbolic iterations Whitman can still astonish us with his figures, but we are too caught up for any element of ridicule. With his speaker, we have been wittily and disorientingly again cajoled into feeling the sublime "puzzle of puzzles / And that we call Being."

Whitman's later poems use far less hyperbole, or the hyperbole lacks a comic edge, because the poet engages projects that make both this trope and humor less appropriate. This is not to say there is no humor in the later poems. "After All, Not to Create Only" (1871) exemplifies a late use of humor. Here, Whitman summons a "Muse" to "migrate from Greece and Ionia" to the "New World" so that he may introduce her, "the illustrious Emigré," to "Columbia"; though her path is strewn with confusing, foreign sights and sounds, she ably makes her way—"By thud of machinery and shrill steam-whistle undismay'd, / Bluff'd not a bit by drain-pipe, gasometers, artificial fertilizers"—so that he can see her "here, install'd amid the kitchen ware!" at the National Industrial Exhibition of the American Institute, for which he wrote and at which he read the poem.[34] Here Whitman deploys many of his favorite humorous techniques at once: a boastful hero undaunted by any challenge, whose description seems to have one foot in the *Iliad* and the other in "The Big Bear of Arkansas"; what Wallace calls out-of-place or "clown" words from traditionally nonpoetic discourses ("gasometers"); and surprising juxtapositions of categories, domains, values, and scales—as in the image of the ancient, mythical goddess dropped into the realm of kitchen pots.[35] We laugh with the muse at her disorientation because we can empathize with it—who hasn't felt ill at ease with domestic technologies at some point?—and because she heroically overcomes it.

When Whitman revised the poem as "Song of the Exposition" for the 1881 *Leaves of Grass*, he curiously removed nineteen satirical lines, including a passage directly preceding his description of the migrating, kitchen-bound muse, in which he describes contemporary poetry as "a terrible aesthetical commotion":[36]

With howling desperate gulp of "flower" and "bower,"
With "Sonnet to Matilda's Eyebrow" quite, quite frantic;
With gushing, sentimental reading circles turn'd to ice or stone;
With many a squeak, (in metre choice) from Boston, New York,
    Philadelphia, London;

In purging the 1881 "Song of the Exposition" of nineteen lines, including this hyperbolic parody of contemporary poetry as containing bad rhymes

and meter and trivial or sentimental conceits, Whitman eliminates much
of the poem's satirical edge, a revision consistent with his general shift away
from the humor and hyperbole of his earlier projects.

Juhasz, Miller, and Smith analyze Dickinson's wit, teasing, cartooning,
and use of camp grotesqueries across a broad range of her poems and letters
as aspects of her "comic power" but give no attention to the poet's use of
hyperbole (which also extends across the decades of her writing), perhaps
because Dickinson's hyperbole is often of *not* having or of smallness. In a
poem copied in late 1862, she writes, "It would have starved a Gnat – / To
live so small as I –" (*EDP* 223 [Fr 444]). Another poem mocks the heroic
martyrdom celebrated in much Civil War writing and debunks the glory
of human dying by comparing it to that of toads and gnats. The first stanza
reads:

> A Toad, can die of Light –
> Death is the Common Right   [The] mutual – · equal –
> Of Toads and Men –
> Of Earl and Midge
> The privilege –
> Why swagger, then?
> The Gnat's supremacy is large as Thine –
>   (*EDP* 166 [Fr 419])

In other poems, she writes (not always with humor), "I was the slightest in
the House" (*EDP* 236 [Fr 473]) or "I was a Phebe – nothing more – . . . I
dwelt too low that any seek" (*EDP* 460 [Fr 1009]). A late poem comically
describes a single "Bird" as carelessly producing a "Note" so powerful that
it shocked the entire universe. After crossing "a thousand Trees" to find
the one that suited "His Fantasy," this bird "squandered such a Note / A
Universe that overheard / Is stricken by it yet – "—or, as Dickinson wrote
in alternative final lines, "A Universe's utter Art / Could not it imitate – "
("Upon his Saddle sprung a Bird"; *EDP* 653 [Fr 1663]).

Often Dickinson asserts such singular smallness to reverse obvious categories of worth. One small bird carelessly produces music or "Art" beyond
anything else the universe can muster—or, as she writes in another poem,

"One note from One Bird / Is better than a Million Word – " (*EDP* 615 [Fr 1478]).[37] In "A solemn thing – it was – I said – ," what the speaker calls "the size of this 'small' life – / The Sages – call it small – " suddenly "Swelled – like Horizons" in the speaker's "breast." The poem concludes by pointedly undercutting the wisdom of sages: "And I sneered – softly – 'small'!" (*EDP* 161 [Fr 307]). The hyperbolic swelling of pride reverses expected categories of worth for this female speaker invisible to the world's authorities. Similarly, in a late poem sent to two friends, "They might not need me, yet they might – ," the quatrain concludes: "A smile so small as mine might be / Precisely their necessity – " (*EDP* 717 [Fr 1425]). In the previously mentioned "I reckon – When I count at all – ," the opening disclaimer of attention to comparative worth, spoken in the idiom of inelegant Yankee shrewdness, provides the foundation against which the poet's later claim of "Poets – All – " becomes humorous (*EDP* 292 [Fr 533]). The poet says, as it were, in my characteristic diffidence I rarely think of the great values of being, but when I do I place myself (or "Poets") at the top of the list.

As some of these examples indicate, Dickinson often uses hyperbole, with its humorous edge, to imagine states as serious as pain and death. "It would have starved a Gnat – " probes the inexpressibility of hunger—physical and metaphysical—through exaggerated smallness. Hyperbole about hunger is ubiquitous in colloquial speech ("I'm starving," "I could eat a horse"), but unlike the everyday hyperbolist, Dickinson juxtaposes micro and macro scales, expressing the enormity of her speaker's hunger through the miniscule figure of a gnat—much as she implicitly celebrates the importance of life by reminding the reader (in "A Toad, can die of Light – ") that the "Gnat's supremacy" in death "is large as Thine – ."[38] As Shira Wolosky observes, "often in Dickinson, terms of measure—lesser and greater—are difficult to gauge."[39] Dickinson's shifting scales disorient by exceeding the reader's conception of normal degrees or parameters of hunger; this is an effect that commonplace hunger hyperboles lose in becoming idiomatic. If "It would have starved a Gnat – " is only vaguely humorous, it is not for lack of freshness or surprise; this absurd comparison to a tiny insect with a funny name would perhaps be laughable were it not dampened by starvation and suicide:

It would have starved a Gnat –
To live so small as I –   [To] dine
And yet, I was a living child –
With Food's nescessity

Upon me – like a Claw –
I could no more remove
Than could coax a Leech away –   [could] modify [a Leech]
Or make a Dragon – move –

Nor like the Gnat – had I –
The privilege to fly
And seek a Dinner for myself –   [And] gain
How mightier He – than I!

Nor like Himself – the Art
Upon the Window Pane
To gad my little Being out –
And not begin – again –

Though her life and portion are "small," the speaker does not claim to be smaller than a gnat; in fact, the force of the hyperbole depends on our recognition that "a living child," though smaller than a "Dragon," is vastly larger than a gnat, which should be able to "live" and "dine" on a proportionately small—indeed, a microscopic—diet. The poverty and insufficiency she feels is therefore absolute, not merely relative to her size.

Yet its relative nourishment is only the beginning of what makes the gnat "mightier" than she, for the tiny gnat has two means to escape its hunger: "to fly / And seek a Dinner" elsewhere or to commit suicide "Upon the Window Pane." Each of these options draws attention to the fact that this hyperbole, like so many of Dickinson's, is entangled in metaphor: it is not only that the speaker's portion would not literally have starved a gnat, but that the hunger depicted is not literally for "Food" or "Dinner." In the first case, while the child certainly cannot fly, it is not clear what restricts her from seeking nourishment elsewhere: what is this horizon, and what binds her within it? Her characterization of the gnat's second escape route, to die "and not begin – again – ," points to immortality as a key distinction between humans and gnats: like the gnat, the speaker could kill herself, but unlike the gnat, her being—and, apparently, her hunger—would not cease. A hunger that follows you into the afterlife is no physical hunger, then, but something spiritual or intellectual. The poem's evocations of limited perception (in the figure of the gnat, which is just barely—and only fleetingly—visible to the human eye), limited perspective (in the "Window Pane," which is not deadly to the human, but does mediate her view of the outside world), and limited access (in the speaker's inability to seek food elsewhere) together suggest that the hunger depicted is for consumption of what lies beyond those limits. Situated by the poem's past tense construction and its references to being a child, the reader, having leaped with the hyperbolist into disorienting scales and realms of gnats and dragons, emerges in a very familiar space—childhood—radically reoriented. Here the edge of humor is slight and bleak but, as in Whitman's passages where hyperbole thrusts the reader into extremes of feeling, the disorienting tension between sympathetic identification with the speaker and skeptical or commonsense distancing from the absurdity of the comparison aligns the poem's figure with some of the functions of humor.

In a more obviously comic poem, "If you were coming in the Fall," Dickinson describes how she'd handle being deprived of her beloved for a period from months, seasons, years, or centuries to apocalyptic periods—in itself a hyperbolic and comic structure to portray longing since, until the last stanza, the length of time separating them is reified as something trivial that might be easily laid aside or discarded. In stanza four, for example, she writes:

> If certain, when this life was out –
> That yours and mine, should be –
> I'd toss it yonder, like a Rind,
> And take Eternity –   [And] taste
>   (*EDP* 188 [Fr 356])

At the poem's conclusion, however, uncertainty about how long the lovers must be apart "goads" the speaker like a "Goblin Bee," a figure that retreats from comic to nightmarish exaggeration: this bee that has not yet stung is not just irritating like the one that buzzes around us on a summer day but tormenting like a creature of dark legends. The "Goblin Bee" shifts the poem's focus from love to cognition: we can manage suspense or grief only when we can anticipate it will have an end rather than threatening some worse "sting" to come.

Exaggeration is often a part of Dickinson's portraits of macabre humor. She imagines "A still – Volcano life – " that erupts like a siren's "Coral" smile, "And Cities – ooze away – " (*EDP* 253 [Fr 517]); confusion resembles a moment of uncontrolled space travel: a speaker heads out "upon Circumference – / Beyond the Dip of Bell – " ("I saw no Way – The Heavens were stitched"; *EDP* 320 [Fr 633]); the distance between lovers is as flimsy as a "filament" or "Vail" but with "every Mesh – a Citadel – / And Dragons – in the Crease – " ("I had not minded – Walls – "; *EDP* 283 [Fr 554]). On the more obviously comic side, and to return to the "bee," the suggestively ministerial "Buccaneers of Buzz" subsisting on "Fuzz ordained – not Fuzz contingent – " are hilarious because of the way the combination of hyperbolic personification, alliteration, and rhyme busts open theological questions about whether Jesus's death was divinely ordained: perhaps in the grand cycles of life such things matter no more than "Buzz . . . . Fuzz . . . Fuzz" ("Bees are Black, with Gilt Surcingles – "; *EDP* 600 [Fr 1426]).

People who knew Dickinson during her lifetime describe her as a humorist: on March 23, 1891, Susan Dickinson comments that the poems published to date have left out "her witty humorous side." In his 1891 *Atlantic Monthly* essay on her letters, Thomas Wentworth Higginson comments that his epistolary relationship with the poet during her lifetime "gave [him] no opportunity to see that human and humorous side of her which is strongly emphasized by her nearer friends." And her childhood friend Emily Fowler Ford repeatedly writes of Dickinson's comic side, her "glinting playfulness": "she certainly began as a humorist."[40] In 1889 Whitman said to friends in Camden, "I pride myself on being a real humorist underneath everything else"; similarly, Whitman edited the following warning into Richard Maurice Bucke's biography of him: "I believe that it has been assumed by the critics that he [Whitman] has no humor. There could not be a greater mistake."[41] The hyperbole and humor we have described helps put such claims into context: given how complex the affective purpose of each poet's hyperboles can be, readers might easily miss their humor "underneath everything else"; at the same time, by recognizing their artful hyperbole, we can better see the "humorist" in each poet. For although their writing remains distinct from the more obvious comedy of their (and our) peers, Whitman and Dickinson deploy hyperbole to participate, on their own terms, in some of the same riddles and paradoxes of human nature, thought, and communication that preoccupied the popular humor writers of their day.

In 1855—the same year in which Whitman boasted like a tall-tale protagonist about the English language's ability to meet any task—the California humorist John Phoenix published "A New System of English Grammar," a story premised on the narrator's conviction that "the adjectives of the English language [are] not sufficiently definite for the purposes of description" (187).[42] In his quest for a better alternative, the narrator becomes "acquainted with every ancient and modern language" but to no avail, until he finds himself in the office of a phrenologist, who examines his head and evaluates his qualities on a scale of 1 to 12: "Size of Head 11 . . . Self-Esteem ½ . . . . Mirth 1" (188, 190). This gives the narrator his eureka-moment, and he quickly enumerates a "great system" by which to improve our adjectives:

In the first place, "*figures won't lie.*" Let us then represent by the number 100, the maximum, the *ne plus ultra* of every human quality—grace, beauty, courage, strength, wisdom, learning—everything. Let *perfection*, I say, be represented by 100, and an absolute minimum of all qualities by the number 1. Then, by applying the numbers between, to the adjectives used in conversation, we shall be able to arrive at a very close approximation to the idea we wish to convey; in other words, we shall be enabled to speak the truth. (190)

By replacing figures that "*lie*" with the kind of figure that "*won't,*" the narrator's system seems to make exaggeration impossible. And yet, in the story he includes as a demonstration of his system, hyperbole and humor reemerge quickly:

As a 19 young and 76 beautiful lady was 52 gaily tripping down the sidewalk of our 84 frequented street, she accidentally came in contact—100 (this shows that she came in close contact) with a 73 fat, but 87 good-humored-looking gentleman . . . Gracefully 56 extracting herself, she received the excuses of the 96 embarrassed Falstaff with a 68 bland smile, and continued on her way. But hardly—7—had she reached the corner of the block, ere she was overtaken by a 24 young man, 32 poorly dressed, but of an 85 expression of countenance . . . "Madam, at the window of the toy-shop yonder, you dropped this bracelet, which I had the 71 good fortune to observe, and now have the 94 happiness to hand to you." (Of course the expression "94 happiness" is merely the young man's polite hyperbole.) (191)

As the narrator acknowledges, the society that uses his exacting system immediately develops hyperbolic idioms and expressions; his model passage ends with "their happiness, of course, being represented by 100" (191). But his story is hyperbolic long before "94 happiness"; his entire system exaggerates the extent to which human qualities—abstract or concrete— can be quantified: the reader who tries to calculate a "68 bland smile" or a man "32 poorly dressed" finds hilarity on the path from disorientation to reorientation.

The hyperboles in Whitman and Dickinson seldom yield such full laughter, in part because their experiments do not reorganize language or understanding into simple systems of quantity or value. In each case, their hyperbole must be understood in relation to the assertions, metaphors, or narratives that contextualize it and to the larger directions of the poet's thought. Whitman's faith in language may lead him to enact disorientation more than respond to it, but his hyperboles are constructed from details of the physical and social worlds of his time that point us directly back to new orientations—of gender, races, politics, the value of labor, and the value of physical, sexual being in the world. Dickinson's hyperboles seem more localized than programmatic and are often blended with, or complicated by, metaphor, so that they respond to disorientation in one respect and enact it in another, simultaneously, often dizzyingly. Consequently, we do not always immediately recognize the extent to which hyperbole (and humor) play a role in her deft philosophical and psychological dissection or analysis of consciousness, human behavior, and issues of ideology, belief, desire, and suffering. As with Whitman, her disorientations always provide at least the possibility of reorientation, although not always on sure ground.

In a late essay, Whitman praises "the wit—the rich flashes of humor and genius and poetry—darting often from a gang of laborers, railroad-men, miners, drivers, or boatmen! . . . You get more real fun from half an hour with them than from the books of all 'the American humorists.'"[43] For both poets, humor was not a genre or style of writing but an integral part of thought and experience, of the life of language, and of the world; as both poets remind us through their repeated invocations of audience, humor is, after all, something we bring to the text as well as something the text offers us—a disorienting thought.

Radical Imaginaries
Crossing Over with Whitman and Dickinson
BETSY ERKKILA

One's-Self I sing, a simple, separate person,
Yet utter the word Democratic, the word En-Masse.
—Walt Whitman, *Leaves of Grass* (1867)

The Soul selects her own Society –
Then – shuts the Door –
To her divine Majority –
Present no more –
—Emily Dickinson, Fr 409 (1862)

A DECADE AGO, AMONG AMERICAN SCHOLARS, THOSE WHO WORKED
on Walt Whitman and those who worked on Emily Dickinson tended to
divide into two distinct groups. Those who worked on Whitman, almost
exclusively men, rarely ventured into Dickinson studies, which was dominated mostly by women, and those who worked on Dickinson had little to
say about Whitman, except to negate his spread-eagle poetics and politics
in comparison with the serious experimental art of Emily Dickinson. In
recent years, as this collection and the historic conference it embodies make
clear, this appears to have changed. But as someone who began my career
by crossing over, focusing in my classes and scholarship on both Whitman
and Dickinson, I would like to begin by imagining what a social and poetic
encounter between the bard of Manhattan and the belle of Amherst might
have looked like.[1]

Whitman might solicit intercourse with Dickinson as a woman waiting
to breed a hardy race of poets and democratic children as he does in "A
Woman Waits for Me":

A woman waits for me, she contains all, nothing is lacking,
Yet all were lacking if sex were lacking, or the moisture of the right
man were lacking.
. . . .
Without shame the man I like knows and avows the deliciousness of
his sex,
Without shame the woman I know I like knows and avows hers.

(*WPP* 258–59)

Dickinson would likely flee, as she does the "Silver Heel" of the erotically overbearing "Sea" "Man" she encounters in "I started Early – Took my Dog – " (Fr 656). But Whitman would persist:

It is I, you women, I make my way,
I am stern, acrid, large, undissuadable, but I love you,
I do not hurt you any more than is necessary for you,
I pour the stuff to start sons and daughters fit for these States, I press
with slow rude muscle,
I brace myself effectually, I listen to no entreaties,
I dare not withdraw till I deposit what has so long accumulated
within me. (*WPP* 259)

Dickinson would be put off by the collectivity and impersonality of Whitman's love call. Driven by a "suppressed and ungratified desire for distinction," according to her childhood friend Emily Fowler Ford, Dickinson would find Whitman vulgar "like a Frog," low class, and more interested in sex and breeding than "women," love, or her in particular (Fr 260).[2] She had nothing against sex; she too dreamt of "Wild nights – Wild nights!" but it was more dreamy, romantic, and personal. She liked the tease and the foreplay, especially with her sister-in-law Sue, who inspired many of her poems. "Wild nights – Wild nights! / Were I with thee," Dickinson writes:

Rowing in Eden –
Ah – the Sea!
Might I but moor – tonight –
In thee!

(Fr 269)

Unlike the sexually and rhetorically prone woman, or women, of Whitman's "A Woman Waits for Me," Dickinson's woman lover is active, athletic even, as she joyously rows in a "Sea" of orgasmic feeling and fantasizes entering and mooring herself within—rather than being penetrated by—her lover. Dickinson was more likely a top than a bottom, and in her poems she occasionally speaks as a man rather than a woman. Although Whitman's "A Woman Waits for Me" celebrates a healthy, athletic, and sexually charged female being who had been unnamed by his culture, the speaker of his poem is insistently, and even embarrassingly, phallic and nationalistic. In other poems, such as "Song of Myself," "The Sleepers," and especially the "Calamus" poems, Whitman fluidly assumes both male and female roles, often revealing his preference—contra Dickinson—as bottom rather than top.

What I want to suggest by this opening sexual and poetic encounter between Whitman and Dickinson is that while they have been treated as diametrical opposites of each other by literary critics, she an essentially private poet raised in a genteel upper-class household in rural Massachusetts, and he an essentially public political poet raised in a working-class household in Brooklyn and the bustling city of New York, both were not only sex radicals but radical imaginaries in the nineteenth-century United States. As different as they may seem, their lives and works and the various "myths" and critical contests that have attended their reception are often surprisingly parallel, in conversation with each other, and mutually illuminating in relation to the major political, social, sexual, racial, and cultural struggles that marked their time and ours. In this essay, I want to sketch out several instances of personal and poetic intercourse between Whitman and Dickinson as a provocation to our conversations about the many crossings between them.

Politics

While it is certainly true to say that Dickinson was not an overtly political poet in the same sense that Whitman was, it is simply not true to say that she had no politics and no ideological investment in a particular order of power. Dickinson was, in fact, born into a more publicly active and politically engaged family than Whitman. Whereas Whitman's father was a house builder, a party Democrat, and a Thomas Paine radical, Dickinson's father,

Edward Dickinson, was a conservative Whig who served as a state representative, senator, and a member of the Massachusetts Governor's Council in
the 1840s. Between 1853 and 1855, at a time of intensified struggle over the
issue of slavery, he served as a representative to Congress from the Tenth
District of Massachusetts. Edward Dickinson was a possible candidate for
governor of Massachusetts in 1859 and a nominee for lieutenant governor
in 1860 and 1861. Later, in 1873, only a year before his death, he was elected
again to serve in the Massachusetts General Court.[3]

Like Whitman, who was raised among brothers named George Washington, Thomas Jefferson, and Andrew Jackson Whitman, Dickinson lived
in a political house. Although she did not share her father's public political
commitment, as I have argued in "Emily Dickinson and Class," she shared
many of his class values and social fears in response to Jacksonian democracy, the masses, foreigners, the Irish, Negroes, labor, reform, and westward
expansion at a time when the aristocratic class-based values of the past were
being eroded under the pressure of an increasingly democratic and industrial
capitalist society of new money and new men.[4]

Dickinson's political values and fears are evident in a letter she wrote to
her brother Austin from Mt. Holyoke College in 1847, in which she mocks
the state of political non-knowledge and removal in which girl students are
kept as she queries Austin for information about the political happenings
of the time:

> Wont you please tell me when you answer my letter who the candidate
> for President is? I have been trying to find out ever since I came here &
> have not yet succeeded. I don't know anything more about affairs in the
> world, than if I was in a trance. . . . Has the Mexican war terminated
> yet & how? Are we beat? Do you know of any nation about to besiege
> South Hadley? (*L* 16)

Dickinson's intense engagement with "affairs in the world," especially the
Mexican War (1846–48), which many New Englanders saw as an imperialist land grab aimed at extending slavery and the "Slave Power," and the
presidential campaign, which would result in the election of Zachary Taylor
and a major Whig victory in 1848, suggests that one of the reasons she left
Mt. Holyoke after only one year is that she felt isolated and removed from

a whole world of political "affairs" and dialogue to which she had grown accustomed in the Dickinson house. Written at a time when the Massachusetts legislature had resolved that the Mexican War was "unconstitutionally commenced by order of the President,"[5] Dickinson's letter mocks the politics of manifest destiny and President Polk's expansionist ambition to annex Mexico; it also registers a more local Whig fear that New England was itself under siege, not by the republic of Mexico, but by the nationalist, imperialist, and proslavery forces of Polk and the Democrats.

Whereas Dickinson was a student at Mt. Holyoke College, one of the first colleges for women in the United States, Whitman was schooled as a printer's apprentice, journalist, and later editor of the Brooklyn *Daily Eagle* (1846–48), where he wrote articles in support of the laboring masses, social reform, and the expansionist policies of President Polk, including the Mexican War. In 1848, however, Whitman was fired by the *Eagle* owner when he "split off with the radicals" in opposing the expansion of slavery into the western territories. At about the same time, Dickinson "split" with the religious establishment at Mt. Holyoke Female Seminary, where she was found "without hope" of religious salvation.[6] She returned home in 1848, after only one year.

The American 1848

The Compromise of 1850, which extended slavery into the territories and strengthened the Fugitive Slave Law by requiring that fugitive slaves be returned to their Southern masters, sent Whitman literally raging into verse. Under the pressure of political events, his savage attack on congressmen who supported slavery rather than freedom and his celebration of the Revolutions of 1848 in four poems published in 1850 broke the pentameter and began to move toward the free verse line of *Leaves of Grass*. "God, 'twas delicious! / That brief, tight, glorious grip / Upon the throats of kings," Whitman declared in "Resurgemus," the earliest of his poems to be included in the 1855 *Leaves of Grass* (*WWA*).[7]

At the same time that Whitman was celebrating the revolutionary struggle for liberty as part of the natural law of the universe, Dickinson inaugurated her own revolution against the orthodox sexual ideologies of her time. She resisted marriage, rebelled against domestic ideology, and saw housework as a plebeian interference with her writing. Mocking the politics of housework—"mind the house – and the food – *sweep* if the spirits were low"—and the true womanly ideals of "meekness – and patience – and submission," Dickinson issued her own revolutionary manifesto in a letter to her friend Jane Humphrey written in January 1850:

> Somehow or other I incline to other things – and Satan covers them up with flowers, and I reach out to pick them. The path of duty looks very ugly indeed – and the place where *I* want to go more amiable – a great deal – it is so much easier to do wrong than right – so much pleasanter to be evil than good, I don't wonder that good angels weep – and bad ones sing songs. (*L* 30)

As Dickinson's identification of her desire to write with Satan suggests, at a time when the Calvinist orthodoxy of the fathers was breaking down, she retained the language, imagery, and conscience of New England Puritanism without the faith. "Christ is calling everyone here," she wrote to Humphrey again in 1850, "and I am standing alone in rebellion" (*L* 35). While her friends and family converted to the Congregational religion during the many revivals that passed through Amherst and the surrounding community in the 1840s and 1850s, Dickinson refused to give herself up and become a Christian.

Living in a time of major political, social, religious, and epistemological breakdown perhaps best signified by the political collapse, blood violence, and ongoing social questions raised by the Civil War, Dickinson, who was eleven years younger than Whitman, dedicated herself to writing at about the same time that Whitman did, not as a retreat into privacy but as a radical act of the imagination, a higher order of culture, and a powerful means of talking back to, with, and against her democratic age.

Radical Imaginaries

On or about July 4, 1855, Whitman published the first edition of *Leaves of Grass*. Designed by Whitman and printed at his own expense, everything about the book was revolutionary: the volume was oversized with clusters of leaves embossed on its dark green cover; its title, which was printed in gold, sprouted lush sperm-shaped roots and leaves, suggesting the motifs of the body, sex, fertility, and regeneration that figure throughout the poems. The title page bears no author's name, only an engraved frontispiece of himself as a day laborer, a common man who speaks as and for rather than apart from the people. "The attitude of great poets is to cheer up slaves and horrify despots," Whitman announced in a twelve-page preface that sounds the cry of revolt implicit in the design of the 1855 *Leaves (WPP* 17).

The twelve poems that follow the preface make good Whitman's declaration of literary independence. Defying the rules of rhyme, meter, and stanza division and breaking down the distinction between poetry and prose, Whitman's verse rolls freely and rhythmically across the page. The long opening poem, later "Song of Myself," and the five poems that follow are all entitled "Leaves of Grass," while the last four poems, separated only by two horizontal bars, are untitled. All of the poems appear to flow together as part of a single florid growth entitled *Leaves of Grass.* The poet's epic subject is not Virgil's arms and the man, but the self that is at the center of the American myth of origins. "I celebrate myself," Whitman begins:

> And what I assume you shall assume,
> For every atom belonging to me as good belongs to you.
> *(WPP* 1855, 27)

The opening *I* and the closing *you* are the bounds of an agonistic arena in which the poet commands, questions, challenges, wrestles, fondles, and makes love to the reader, finally sending him or her into the world bearing the seeds of democratic creation.

Whitman had inky fingers: he presided over every aspect of the material and poetic production of the 1855 *Leaves of Grass,* including the reviews, three of which he wrote himself. "An American bard at last!" he exuded in the *United States and Democratic Review:* "One of the roughs, large, proud, affectionate, eating, drinking and breeding, his costume manly and free."[8]

Whitman played the market and failed to gain an audience for his radical poems. Dickinson refused to go to market. "Publication – is the Auction / Of the Mind of Man – " she wrote in a poem that associates print publication with blackness, wage slavery, and the degradations of both the slave auction and the capitalist marketplace:

> Poverty – be justifying
> For so foul a thing
>
> Possibly – but We – would rather
> From Our Garret go
> White – unto the White Creator –
> Than invest – Our Snow –
>
> (Fr 788)

Making use of the language of both antislavery and artisan republican protest against wage labor as a new form of slavery to constitute herself and her writing as part of an elect community of whiteness, Dickinson resists the "foul" values of the commercial marketplace: "reduce no Human Spirit / To Disgrace of Price – " (Fr 788). Her refusal to publish was not so much a private act as it was an act of social and class resistance to the commercial, democratic, and increasingly amalgamated and mass values of the national marketplace.

If Whitman looked upon his poems as material seeds of present and future artistic and democratic creation, Dickinson described her poetry as another form of letter writing and "News" addressed to her "countrymen":

> This is my letter to the World
> That never wrote to Me –
> The simple News that Nature told –
> With tender Majesty
>
> Her Message is committed
> To Hands I cannot see –
> For love of Her – Sweet – countrymen –
> Judge tenderly – of Me
>
> (Fr 519)

Here as elsewhere in her writing, Dickinson presents her poetry not as a "private" production but as a form of "public" address—a "letter to the World"—whether imaginary or real. Like Whitman, Dickinson was also engaged in her own form of material production and "publication." Between 1858 and 1864 she copied over 800 of her poems onto folded sheets of stationery, which she then bound into 40 hand-sewn booklets. Binding 4 to 5 folded sheets of paper together in groupings of 18 to 20 poems, Dickinson, in effect, converted traditional female thread and needle work into a different kind of housework and her own form of productive industry. She appears to have been engaged in a kind of home or cottage industry, a precapitalist mode of manuscript production and circulation that avoided the commodity and use values of the commercial marketplace.[9]

Along with the manuscripts that she produced and bound with string and thread herself, Dickinson also engaged in a more aristocratic form of "publication" by circulating her poems in letters to her friends. While only eleven of her poems were "printed" during her lifetime, including seven in the *Springfield Republican*, beginning in the early 1850s Dickinson, like Whitman, broke down the distinction between poetry and prose by circulating hundreds of her poems in letters to a select republic of "countrymen" that engaged her in dialogue with some of the most powerful cultural and social figures of her time.[10] Her network of known correspondents included Samuel Bowles, the editor of the *Springfield Republican,* one of the most influential newspapers in the country, and an outspoken supporter of antislavery, women's suffrage, the Republican Party, and Abraham Lincoln; Josiah Gilbert Holland, the literary editor of the *Springfield Republican,* a founding editor of *Scribner's Monthly* in 1870, and popular author of numerous novels and books, including a *Life of Abraham Lincoln* (1865); Thomas Wentworth Higginson, a well-known writer, Unitarian minister, liberal Republican advocate of abolition and women's rights, and a colonel who led one of the first regiments of black troops during the Civil War; Thomas Niles, the editor of Roberts Brothers, a major publishing house in Boston; Judge Otis P. Lord, a leading figure in Massachusetts politics and law; and Helen Hunt Jackson, one of the most highly acclaimed women writers of her time.

Homoerotic Poetics

The heteronormatizing mythologies that have attended the critical reception and criticism of Whitman and Dickinson have obscured the extent
to which homoerotic love was at the very origins of their poetic voice and
vision. Whitman supposedly fell in love with an octoroon on his trip to
New Orleans in 1848, and as suggested in his poem "Once I Passed through
a Populous City," this New Orleans romance inspired his poems. Dickinson supposedly fell in love with a married minister, Charles Wadsworth,
on a visit to Philadelphia in 1855, and it was her lifelong love of him that
inspired her to withdraw from society, wear white, and devote herself to
poetry. Both of these "myths" fly in the face of the reality of same-sex love
in their lives, letters, and poems. Whitman's "Once I Passed through a
Populous City" was originally addressed to a man rather than a woman, so
romances with other women have been proposed; and there is no evidence
that Dickinson even met, let alone fell in love with Wadsworth in 1855, so
other men have been proposed.

And yet, as early as his temperance novel *Franklin Evans: or, The Inebriate*
(1842), Whitman evoked the urban subculture of sexual cruising and man
love to which he would seek to give voice in *Leaves of Grass*: "Through me
forbidden voices, / Voices of sexes and lusts . . . . voices veiled, and I remove
the veil" (*WPP* 1855, 50). At the outset of his long opening poem, later "Song
of Myself," Whitman insists on the body, sexuality, and love between men
as the site of ecstasy, vision, and poetic utterance:

I mind how we lay in June, such a transparent summer morning;
You settled your head athwart my hips and gently turned over
    upon me,
And parted the shirt from my bosom-bone, and plunged your tongue
    to my barestript heart,
And reached till you felt my beard, and reached till you held my feet.
                                                            (*WPP* 1855, 28–29)

Rather than posing cocksucking and mysticism as antithetical readings, as
past critics have done, I want to suggest that this passage is representative

of the ways the languages of sexuality and spirituality, same-sex love and love between men and women, private and public, intermix and flow into each other in Whitman's work.[11] It is unclear finally whether Whitman is describing sexuality in the language of spiritual ecstasy or a mystical experience in the language of sexual ecstasy, for he seems to be doing both at once. What is clear is that the democratic knowledge the poet receives of an entire universe bathed in an erotic force that links men, women, God, and the natural world in a vision of mystic unity is associated with sexual and bodily ecstasy, an ecstasy that includes but is not limited to the pleasures of cocksucking among men. Giving tongue is associated at once with sexuality, including sexuality between men, democracy, spiritual vision, and poetic utterance.

In the early 1850s Dickinson and her friend and later sister-in-law, Susan Gilbert, began writing poems together. Despite the later efforts of Dickinson's brother Austin literally to cut out and mutilate the traces of his sister's lifelong love relationship with Sue, it is clear from Dickinson's extant letters and poems that it was Dickinson's explosive and transgressive love for Sue that called forth and validated the volcanic persona who would emerge in her poems as "Loaded Gun" and "Vesuvius at Home."[12] In her multiple incarnations as "absent lover" and a "real beautiful hero," "Imagination" and an "Avalanche of Sun," an "Emblem of Heaven" and the "garden *unseen*," Gilbert served finally as a bewitching muse-like presence who poeticized Dickinson's world and inspired her own art of song. "You sketch my pictures for me," Dickinson wrote Sue in 1853, "and 'tis at their sweet colorings, rather than this dim real, that I am used, so you see when you go away, the world looks staringly, and I find I need more vail – " (*L* 107).

In "One Sister have I in the house – ," one of Dickinson's earliest extant poems, she represents Sue as a bird whose "different" tune becomes a source of sustenance in the journey from adolescence to adulthood. In stanzas 3 and 4, she wrote:

> She did not sing as we did –
> It was a different tune –
> Herself to her a music
> As Bumble bee in June.

Today is far from childhood,
But up and down the hills,
I held her hand the tighter –
Which shortened all the miles –

Even in this sisterly song of praise, however, there are ambiguous references to a "hum" that "Deceives" and eyes that "lie," references that suggest that Sue's "different tune" was also a source of tension and struggle between them (Fr 5).[13]

Love Crisis

Sometime around 1858 both Whitman and Dickinson appear to have suffered a personal love crisis during the very years when the political union was moving inexorably toward the fracture and bloody carnage of civil war. The primary evidence for Whitman's crisis is a small sheaf of twelve poems of male intimacy and love that he copied into a notebook in spring 1859. First published by Fredson Bowers in 1953, and hailed as a "gay manifesto" by Herschel Parker and others over the past few decades, the exact nature of this love affair remains a mystery. Whitman may be alluding to a break with Fred Vaughan, who lived with or near him at the time they were written, or possibly with another man, or even several men over a span of time.[14] What is clear is that these poems represent a revolutionary break with the past and a radical new departure in literary, sexual, and social history in their moving evocation and affirmation of the hitherto unnamed and unnamable bonds of erotic passion, love, and affection among and between men. The poems also record a crisis of poetic vocation in "Live Oak" V, in which the poet renounces his earlier desire "to strike up the songs of the New World" in order to pursue his relationship with his lover. "I can be your singer of songs no longer—," the poet writes: "I have found him who loves me, as I him, in perfect love, / With the rest I dispense—" ("Live Oak, with Moss").

The primary evidence for Dickinson's love crisis is a sequence of three "Master" letters, written between 1858 and 1861 with no evidence they were ever posted, in which she presents herself in the figure of "Daisy," a "Bird" hit by a "bullet," and someone with "a Tomahawk in my side," to a mysterious unknown "Master." Although much critical ink has been spent seeking to identify which man broke Dickinson's heart, these letters read more like a metaphysical complaint against the nature of things, perhaps addressed to God or some other patriarchal Master of the universe. The real source of Dickinson's wound may be her loss of Sue to religion, marriage, and family, a story she movingly retells in "Ourselves were wed one summer – dear":

> Ourselves were wed one summer – dear –
> Your Vision – Was in June –
> And when Your little Lifetime failed,
> I wearied – too – of mine –
>
> (Fr 596)

Although Dickinson used the term in other poems of the time, the syntactical oddness of "Ourselves" in this wedding poem to another woman suggests the "difference" of their female marriage—the autoerotic awakening to an enriched consciousness of self that a woman may feel in loving someone who is like rather than different from herself. Dickinson's poetic construction might be paraphrased to read: we married ourselves when we married each other, a phrasing that recalls the auto- or homoerotic mirroring of self that Whitman evokes in the opening poem of the 1855 *Leaves of Grass* when he asks: "Is this then a touch? . . . . quivering me to a new identity, ... My flesh and blood playing out lightning, to strike what is hardly different from myself" (*WPP* 55). While Whitman's free verse line is very different from Dickinson's, the ellipses that he used in the 1855 *Leaves of Grass* are similar to Dickinson's dashes in rhythmically marking—and expressing—pause, break, and sometimes fracture.

Sue's vision in "June" appears to telescope two events: her profession of faith in August 1850 and her marriage to Dickinson's brother, Austin, in July 1856. Associating their relationship with the creative bloom of summer, Dickinson experiences her loss of Sue to religion and marriage as a kind of social death in which Sue is "yielded up" to the masculine and heteronormative orders of husband and God (*L* 93). The speaker overcomes her own experience of death and waste by yielding "her" self—not to man or God—but to the "light" and call of her poetic muse:

And overtaken in the Dark –
Where You had put me down –
By Some one carrying a Light –
I – too – received the Sign –

Having received the "Sign" of her poetic vocation as another kind of religious and marital vow, Dickinson describes the difference of her own
election in lines that suggest the heroism of her rededication and the anguish of her loss:

'Tis true – Our Futures different lay –
Your Cottage – faced the sun –
While Oceans – and the North must be –
On every side of mine

'Tis true, Your Garden led the Bloom,
For mine – in Frosts – was sown –
And yet, one Summer, we were Queens –
But You – were crowned in June –
(Fr 596)

Whereas Sue's life is contained within the daily round of cottage and sun,
Dickinson lives sterile and witchlike, on the margins, facing the open spaces
of "Oceans" and "the North."

Once again Sue is associated with the creativity and bloom of a garden,
but it is a garden circumscribed by the round of the male order signified by
sun/son. The reference to Sue's "Bloom" may refer to the birth of her son,
Edward, on June 19, 1861. Like Whitman sowing the seeds of his poems,
Dickinson sows her own garden—her poems—in "Frosts" that suggest the
cold and desolation of her separation from Sue, her existence on the margins
of the social order, and a barrenness that gives birth to poems rather than
children. In their separation, Dickinson suggests that both have lost some of
the potency of their primal bond together when they were "Queens" under
another law. And thus, the "crown" of power Sue receives as the Bride of
Christ and man is also a crown of limits, suffering, and thorns.

The story is not unlike the story Whitman tells in his 1859 elegy "A

Word Out of the Sea" (later "Out of the Cradle, Endlessly Rocking"), with its dark undertone of the "fierce old mother" the sea whispering "Death, Death, Death, Death, Death" in response to the former joy of the he-bird and the she-bird nesting their "four light-green eggs." Identifying with the he-bird's loss of his mate, Whitman bids farewell to male/female love, marriage, and family, and rededicates himself to his poems as the expression of unsatisfied love:

> O you singer, solitary, singing by yourself—projecting me,
> O solitary me listening—never more shall I cease imitating,
>   perpetuating you,
> . . . .
> Never more the cries of unsatisfied love be absent from me,[15]

On the eve of the Civil War, both Whitman and Dickinson appear to intersect in practicing a compensatory poetics in response to the "real reality" of human loss, misery, and "Death" ("Calamus" 2, *LG* 1860, 344).

Representing herself as the "Empress of Calvary," in an 1861 poem Dickinson evokes her dedication to her art as an alternative form of marriage and religion:

> Title divine, is mine.
> The Wife without the Sign –
> Acute Degree conferred on me –
> Empress of Calvary –
> Betrothed, without the Swoon
> God gives us Women –
>   (Fr 194)

Whereas for Whitman in the 1860 *Leaves of Grass*, Death is "strong and delicious," associated with the "angry moans" of "the fierce old mother" the sea as the generative source of a " thousand response songs" and "My own songs, awaked from that hour" (*LG* 1860, 275, 277), for Dickinson, Death is an exigent male figure, a signifier of the all-powerful "He," the "Blond Assassin" and sadistic bringer of loss, pain, change, and the finality of Death as Death against whom and in competition with whom she writes her poems.

"I had a terror – since September – I could tell to none – ," Dickinson wrote in April 1862, "and so I sing as the Boy does by the Burying Ground – because I am afraid – " (*L* 261). Whatever the sources of Dickinson's "terror"—a personal love crisis, a failure of religious belief, the advent of the Civil War, the collapse of an older New England social order, the horrifying prospect of everlasting "Death," metaphysical angst, or all these together—her poems powerfully register the disintegrative emotional and psychic effects of social transformation and political crisis that marked Dickinson's years of greatest productivity during and after the Civil War. In the 1860 *Leaves of Grass*, Whitman registered a similar terror of America as graveyard rather than garden. "O give me some clue!" he asked "the savage old mother," the sea, in "A Word Out of the Sea":

O a word! O what is my destination?
O I fear it is henceforth chaos!
O how joys, dreads, convolutions, human shapes, and all shapes,
    spring as from graves around me!
O phantoms! you cover all the land, and all the sea!

O I cannot see in the dimness whether you smile or frown upon me.
                              ("A Word Out of the Sea," *LG* 1860, 276)

Although Whitman would later delete this passage from "Out of the Cradle Endlessly Rocking" on the occasion of the American centennial in 1876, on the eve of the Civil War, Whitman's prospect and the "terror" of annihilation that gives rise to song were much closer to Emily Dickinson.[16]

The Civil War

The massive bloodshed, carnage, and horrific loss of human life during the Civil War tested Whitman's democratic faith and deepened Dickinson's searing critique of American providential history. Whitman visited the sick and dying soldiers in Washington hospitals, suffered the amputation and violence of the war physically and psychically, and wrote poetry.

Although critics have traditionally emphasized Dickinson's isolation from the war and history and the merely personal sources of the crisis she suffered in the years immediately preceding and following the start of the war, as scholars such as Shira Wolosky and others have powerfully argued, in poems such as "'Tis so appalling – it exhilarates –" and "Revolution is the Pod," the war crisis appears to have set "Fright at Liberty," inspiring Dickinson to a "Bloom" of creative power in the very midst of the "over Horror," "rattle" of "Systems," and "Death" signified by the Civil War (Fr 337, Fr 1044).[17] Of the 1,789 poems in Franklin's variorum edition of *The Poems of Emily Dickinson,* over half were written during the years of the Civil War between 1861 and 1865; and of these, almost 300 were written in 1863, a year of crisis and turning point in the war, when even Union victories such as Gettysburg had become scenes of horrific bloodletting and mass death on both sides.

"I, myself, in my smaller way, sang off charnel steps," Dickinson wrote during the war (*L* 298). For Dickinson, the Civil War became the larger historic ground against and through which she enacted her own "charge within the bosom" against "The Cavalry of Wo – " ("To fight aloud, is very brave –," Fr 138). The massive carnage, suffering, and death of the Civil War propelled Dickinson into further doubts about republican destiny, divine providence, and the nature of things, a fuller withdrawal from society, and a renewed dedication to art as a higher order of culture. Against the self-sacrificial patriotism of local "soldier-hearts" like Frazar Stearns, an Amherst boy who died in the war—"His big heart shot away by a 'minie ball'" (*L* 255)—and against Lincoln's public rhetoric of blood sacrifice for the cause of Union or the sin of slavery, several of the poems Dickinson wrote during and after the war express doubt about the larger meaning and value of war, suffering, and sacrificial death.

In "It feels a shame to be Alive – / When Men so brave – are dead –," the speaker wonders if the sacrifice of human lives "In Pawn for Liberty –," or for the United States ("for Us"), is worth the price:

The price is great –Sublimely paid –
Do we deserve – a Thing –
That lives – like Dollars – must be piled
Before we may obtain?

Are we that wait – sufficient worth –
That such Enormous Pearl
As life – dissolved be – for Us –
In Battle's – horrid Bowl?

(Fr 524)

Similarly in "My Portion is Defeat – today –," Dickinson presents a starkly realistic evocation of the "Bone and stain" of the battlefield—of "Moan" and "Prayer" and "Chips of Blank – in Boyish Eyes"—but the scene has no meaning beyond "Death's surprise, / Stamped visible – in stone –" (Fr 704). Dickinson resists Lincoln's redemptive reading of the Civil War in the Gettysburg Address (1863) and the Second Inaugural Address (1865) as a blood sacrifice for "a new birth of freedom" or a "mighty scourge" sent by a "true and just God" to rid the nation of "American Slavery."[18]

When Whitman returned to poetry with the publication of *Drum-Taps and Sequel to Drum-Taps* in 1865, he sought, like Lincoln, to locate the butchery and unreason of the Civil War within a redemptive narrative of democratic sacrifice and rebirth. But in poems such as "A March in the Ranks Hard-Prest, and the Road Unknown," his dark and unmeaning prospect is closer to Dickinson's. The army of soldiers marching in darkness along an unknown road come upon a "large old church" made into "an impromptu hospital," where pews become beds for soldiers, the gleams of light amid "shadows of deepest, deepest black," and the hellish cast of flame and smoke all reflect an ambivalent response to the war as a site of redemption and a descent into hell. The soldier stops momentarily to minister to the wounds of a fellow soldier:

At my feet more distinctly, a soldier, a mere lad, in danger of bleeding
   to death (he is shot in the abdomen,)
I stanch the blood temporarily (the youngster's face is white as a lily,)

(*WPP* 440)

Unrelieved by any larger teleology that would give meaning and significance to the "bloody forms" of war, the soldier is swept back into the ranks marching in darkness along an unknown road:

But first I bend to the dying lad, his eyes open, a half-smile gives he me,
Then the eyes close, calmly close, and I speed forth to the darkness.

(*WPP* 440)

The half-smile of the dying lad represents a sustaining gesture of comradeship, love, and human affirmation—possibly redemptive—shooting its light into the surrounding darkness as the soldier falls back into line and speeds onward into the night.

Here, as in his elegy for the death of President Lincoln, Whitman resists any larger religious vision; he insists on a fully secular account of the war in which the passions of manly love and comradeship and the everyday heroism of ordinary men and boys—the common and unknown soldiers who fought the war, North and South—become the only hope for the future of democracy in America.

Immortality

For both Dickinson and Whitman, the Civil War represented a trial, a crucible, a darkness from which neither fully returned in the post–Civil War period. If "Boston had solved the universe," as Adams wrote in *The Education of Henry Adams*, Emily Dickinson had not.[19] In a poem written toward the close of her life, she expresses the pain of living in an era of unbelief using the same figure of amputation that Whitman had used to evoke both the war's carnage and the dismembered Union:

Those – dying then,
Knew where they went –
They went to God's Right Hand –
That Hand is amputated now
And God cannot be found –

The abdication of Belief
Makes the Behavior small –
Better an ignis fatuus
Than no illume at all –

(Fr 1581)

167

Unlike Dickinson, Whitman did not mourn the death of God, but he did lament the apparent loss of faith in Democracy amid the aggressive selfism, greed, and economic and political scandal of the Gilded Age and beyond.

Both poets became critics of a decline, a loss, in post–Civil War America, she from a conservative country point of view, he from the point of view of ordinary laborers and the democratic radicalism of his antebellum years. Although Dickinson sees "New Englandly" and Whitman sees from the point of view of the increasingly disenfranchised urban workers, both make use of similar figures—artisans, laborers, craftsmen, art—to emblematize a set of individual and communal values that have been lost. At a time when the local Amherst economy was being pressed into the production of cash crops for the national market, Dickinson's "The Products of my Farm are these" links poetic creation—"With Us, 'tis Harvest all the Year"—with the self-sufficiency and barter of an older agricultural economy (Fr 1036). In "Sparkles from the Wheel," Whitman identifies with the "works" and "copious golden jets" unleashed by "a knife-grinder" at "his wheel," displaying a craftsmanship rapidly being replaced by wage labor and the assembly line values of speed, profit, and efficiency (WPP 514).

In the post–Civil War years, Whitman and Dickinson may have had much more to say to each other. And it wouldn't have been about sex. After his paralytic stroke in 1872, Whitman moved to Camden, New Jersey, where he still had his "boys" and his art; and Dickinson withdrew into the Dickinson Homestead, but she still had her art and her community of friends. "Some – Work for Immortality – / The Chiefer part, for Time – ," Dickinson wrote in 1863, setting the new commercial economy of money, exchange, and free-flowing cash—"The Bullion of Today"—against the "Slow Gold," "the Currency / Of Immortality – " she associates with the transcendent work of art. "One's – Money – One's – the Mine – ," she writes, invoking contemporary political debates about the gold standard as opposed to the free circulation of greenback notes (Fr 536). While Dickinson's "Work for Immortality" and the forms in which she circulated it look backward toward a set of Federalist and country values embodied in the figure of George Washington, her work also looks forward to the increasing valorization of art as an aesthetic object separate from the messiness of politics and history that came to be the dominant mythos of literary modernism and that still shapes the ways Dickinson's work is interpreted today.[20]

Whitman worked for "Immortality" too, but the immortality he sought was not aesthetic or transcendent. As he suggests in "Poets to Come" (1867), the immortality he sought would be achieved somewhere down the road, in poets and readers who would carry on the work of democratic creation: "I myself but write one or two indicative words for the future, / I but advance a moment only to wheel and hurry back in the darkness" (*WPP* 175). But even here, in this seemingly public poem, Whitman evokes a persona, a poet, who is as coy, dark, and enigmatic as Dickinson.

By reading Whitman and Dickinson in private and public, as poets whose unsettled and unsettling *interiors* existed *inside* rather than *outside* the political and social struggles of their times, I have tried to move beyond the "public" and "private" frames that have too often structured past approaches to their work. I have tried to suggest some of the new social and aesthetic perspectives that might be opened by reading—or more properly rereading—the relation between Whitman and Dickinson *within* the social and political histories that they lived, suffered, wrote about, and resisted.

Queer Contingencies of Canonicity
Dickinson, Whitman, Jewett, Matthiessen

JAY GROSSMAN

1

FOR MANY READERS SINCE ITS PUBLICATION IN 1941, THE OMISSION of Emily Dickinson from F. O. Matthiessen's landmark *American Renaissance: Art and Expression in the Age of Emerson and Whitman* is among its most egregious and often-noted shortcomings.[1] So imagine my surprise to have found a letter from 1931 in which Matthiessen insists upon Dickinson's necessary place in the following year's survey of American literature for Harvard undergraduates. Matthiessen writes to his partner, Russell Cheney, about a meeting with his Harvard colleague Kenneth Murdock regarding the syllabus for their co-taught American literature course:

> The actual scheme of the course, between you and me, struck me as very conventional. Far too much attention to the early part. As much time given to Irving as to Thoreau! No lecture on Henry Adams, none specifically on Sarah Jewett or Emily Dickinson until I asked for them.[2]

A decade before *American Renaissance*, Matthiessen expresses dismay at Dickinson's exclusion from a conventional undergraduate canon, although from our perspective his linkage of Dickinson to, or as an alternative for, Sarah Orne Jewett may be what is most in need of explanation, because these two writers now occupy such distinct canonical registers. Their juxtaposition is, among other things, an emblem of just how thoroughly American literary canonicity is under construction in the first few decades of the twentieth century, and gives us a sense as well of the indefinite literary-historical space into which *American Renaissance* will so powerfully insert itself a decade later. In what follows I take this letter as a point of departure for rethinking Dickinson's exclusion by demonstrating that her poetry exists in a far more complex relation to Matthiessen's Emerson and Whitman than her exclusion from *American Renaissance* might suggest. This is an essay, then, about the contingent relations and analogies that underwrite the canon of nineteenth-century American literature as it is constructed in the twentieth century. It is also an essay that, in the end, looks for alternate terms of canonization for Emily Dickinson in what has come to seem an unlikely place: the canon-making work of F. O. Matthiessen, where she mostly does not appear, and where the figure of the canonical American poet is usually Whitman (or, as will become clear, Whitman-as-Emerson).[3]

But first a few more words about Matthiessen's curious pairing of Dickinson and Jewett, whose canonical fortunes, even at the time of Matthiessen's letter to Cheney, and certainly from the perspective of almost a hundred years later, are clearly moving in opposite directions. Indeed, the canonical discrepancy between the poet and the novelist will become, by the time of *American Renaissance* in 1941, so divergent that Matthiessen himself will call Jewett a "minor talent"[4] just twelve years after he had himself published a whole monograph on her. In that 1929 book's penultimate paragraph, he once again links Jewett's canonical significance to Emily Dickinson. All of which serves as an important reminder that Dickinson's canonical standing is also in flux during this period, as Anna Mary Wells's 1929 survey, "Early Criticism of Emily Dickinson," makes apparent: Dickinson is, Wells concludes, "one of the most interesting of our minor poets."[5]

The Jewett book's lengthy penultimate paragraph is Matthiessen's strongest statement of the Jewett/Dickinson pairing:

The distinction and refinement of Sarah Jewett's prose came out of an America which, with its [Boss] Tweed rings and grabbing Trusts, its blatantly moneyed New York and squalid frontier towns, seemed most lacking in just these qualities. They are essentially a feminine contribution, and the fact that they now appear more valuable than anything the men of her generation could produce is a symptom of what had happened to New England since the Civil War. The vigorous genius of the earlier golden day had left no sons.[6]

Matthiessen's gender and class assumptions, as well as his politics, are patently on display here. As a budding socialist Matthiessen laments the "Tweed rings and grabbing Trusts" that are undoing the possibilities of more equitable, if possibly fanciful, economic relations. He recognizes a feminine, New England "distinction and refinement" that gestures toward Ann Douglass's feminization thesis of 1977 and that also offers a gendered solution, in the Jane Tompkins mode, to the corruption and predations of the American moneyed class.[7] Finally, the passage seems also to be taking heed of the carnage of the Civil War; it's not only that women like Jewett are now out-writing the generation of New England men following the war, but also that there are fewer men left alive to be writing in the first place.

Matthiessen's analysis turns more overtly literary in the rest of the paragraph.

Emily Dickinson is the heir of Emerson's spirit, and Sarah Jewett the daughter of Hawthorne's style. In the whole group of proud Brahmins whom Miss Jewett knew, and revered as far wiser and stronger than herself, there is not one with her severity of form and subtle elimination. Their words are heavy and diffuse, lacking balance, lacking concentration. And so they are sinking slowly, while hers go lightly forward, and she takes her place next Emily Dickinson—the two principal women writers America has had. (*SOJ* 151–52)

In Matthiessen's account Jewett and Dickinson obliterate a panoply of American Victorian writing men, some of whom—including William Dean Howells, John Greenleaf Whittier, Richard Henry Dana, Jr., and James Russell Lowell—nevertheless play prominent roles in the biographical story Matthiessen tells in *Sarah Orne Jewett*. At the same time, as if preparing the way for *American Renaissance*, the governing categories for defining excellence and achievement remain indicatively, starkly male: Emerson and Hawthorne wholly underwrite the terms of Matthiessen's appraisal. And yet Dickinson and Jewett persist—if (only) as "women writers"—at

173

paragraph's, and book's, end. To speculate on how this unlikely pairing came to be is the task of this essay's ending. Before turning to that issue, however, I first take a closer look at Matthiessen's interest in Dickinson, as well as the terms within which his understanding of her writing sharpens our understanding of his reading of Emerson's and Whitman's poetry.

2

It turns out that Matthiessen's enthusiasm for Dickinson goes back even further than the 1931 letter to Cheney. In a letter written in 1924, just after the two men met, Matthiessen glosses for his painter partner what he has been reading en route to their planned rendezvous in Italy:

> All the way up in the train this evening between snatches of Emily Dickinson (do you know her? a really significant American poet of the late nineteenth century. A great depth and freedom of spirit that is just being recognized) I kept saying to myself: the next train you get onto, you will be headed for Rat.[8]

("Rat" is Matthiessen's nickname for Cheney.) The year 1924 is thus when Matthiessen is not only making Dickinson's literary acquaintance, but also when he and Cheney meet aboard the ocean liner *Paris* and begin their relationship. His characterization of Dickinson's "great depth and freedom of spirit" provides the first instance of the affirming terms that recur in a number of Matthiessen's encounters with her work across his scholarly writing.

In 1950, for example, a decade on the other side of *American Renaissance*, in his editor's introduction to *The Oxford Book of American Verse*, Matthiessen once again offers support for the necessity of Dickinson's inclusion, once again in relation to Emerson:

> Emerson's fertility is further attested by the fact that his pure eloquence enkindled Emily Dickinson. "The little tippler leaning against the sun" drew one source of her inspiration directly from his symbolical [poem] "Bacchus." She, incidentally, can be represented by the greatest number

of poems because these scarcely take up a quarter of the pages required for an adequate suggestion of Whitman. Since her books were all published after her death, and her editors have allowed into print all the casual fragments she jotted on the backs of envelopes, it has seemed important to winnow out here only her most finished pieces. We may thus perceive her art at its best.[9]

Presciently, if a bit skeptically, Matthiessen seems here to foresee manuscript collections like *Radical Scatters* and *Gorgeous Nothings*, and maybe even the *Dickinson Electronic Archives*. He shows us how Emerson figures for Dickinson, too, as "the cow from which the rest drew their milk," the memorable phrase about Goethe that Matthiessen repurposed in *American Renaissance* to characterize Emerson's centrality to his Big Five (Emerson, Thoreau, Hawthorne, Melville, Whitman). Emerson persists for Matthiessen in providing the governing analytical terms even for those authors like Dickinson who stand at the margins of his Renaissance.

As is well known, Whitman is for Matthiessen the paradigmatic instance of Emersonian discipleship: he is the figure, as Matthiessen puts it, "who set out more deliberately than any of his contemporaries to create the kind of hero whom Emerson had foreshadowed in his varying guises of the Scholar and the Poet" (*AR* 650). Imitation is the governing trope for Matthiessen's understanding of Whitman's encounter with Emerson, as when he finds Whitman ventriloquizing Emerson's famous opening formulations about language from *Nature:*

When [Whitman] tried to make his meaning plainer by giving examples of how many "of the oldest and solidest words we use, were originally generated from the daring and license of slang," he showed that what he was really thinking of was something very like Emerson's first proposition about language—that words are signs of natural facts. (*AR* 520)

These, then, are the keynotes to Matthiessen's approach: "It is not hard to find, for what they are worth, passages in Whitman running parallel to most of Emerson's major convictions about the nature of art"; "the main contours of Emerson's doctrine of expression . . . are unmistakable, and unmistakably Whitman's as well" (*AR* 523).

But that curious phrase, "for what they are worth," may be worth paus-
ing over, because it marks Matthiessen's suggestion that, when it comes to
the poetry itself—the field in which genuine critical evaluation means the
most for Matthiessen—both Dickinson and Whitman may have Emerson
beat. In the contrast between, on one hand, Emerson's poetry, and, on the
other, Whitman's and Dickinson's, important differences cannot be denied:

> Thus Whitman seems to show the very dichotomy between the ma-
> terial and the ideal, the concrete and the abstract that we observed in
> Emerson's remarks on language. Nevertheless, when we look at their
> poems, it is obvious that Whitman often bridged the gap in a way that
> Emerson could not. The whole question of the relation of Whitman's
> theory and practice of art to Emerson's is fascinating, since, starting
> so often from similar if not identical positions, they end up with very
> different results. (AR 522)

One of these central differences emerges around the depiction of the body
and of sex more generally:

> Whitman's language is more earthy because he was aware, in a way that
> distinguished him not merely from Emerson but from every other writer
> of the day, of the power of sex. In affirming natural passion to be "the
> enclosing basis of everything," he spoke of its sanity, of the sacredness of
> the human body, using specifically religious terms. . . . No matter how
> happily inconsistent Emerson might be on other matters, [the] basic po-
> sition of the idealist was one from which he never departed. (AR 523–24)

So the template here becomes clear in Matthiessen's treatment of both
Whitman, and, as we shall see, Dickinson. Matthiessen emphasizes what
might be called underlying philosophical or theoretical similarities that
hearken back to Emerson, but a chasm with Emerson opens up once actual
poetry enters the equation.

Matthiessen extends his analysis of Dickinson's poetic distinction from
Emerson in a 1945 *Kenyon Review* essay, "The Problem of the Private Poet,"
by taking Dickinson's "I'd rather recollect a Setting / Than own a rising Sun"
(Fr 1366) as a point of departure:

Whether or not she was consciously balancing her ablative case against Emerson's emphasis upon "the optative mood," the difference between wishing for a more radiant future and accepting the finality of removal is the difference between these two poets, marking the distance traversed between the beginning and the end of the New England renaissance. It marks also why Miss Dickinson possessed the dramatic, indeed, the tragic sense so lacking from Emerson's radiant eloquence.[10]

In 1945 Emerson remains at, or as, every seeming origin of consequence: in this formulation Dickinson takes part in a lowercase "r" renaissance—one still tied to Emerson's "optative mood," which is the phrase that names the opening section on Emerson in *American Renaissance*, if also one that is named for a more delimited geographical space. She now marks the end of a renaissance she had been excluded from only four years earlier.

Across *American Renaissance* Matthiessen discusses Dickinson only three times—fewer times than Goethe, Whittier, or even Samuel Johnson—but on these occasions he compares her poetry favorably to Emerson's, as I have already begun to suggest. One important instance occurs in a long discussion of the relation of the metaphysical poets to Emerson. This is in fact how we know it is the 1930s, when Matthiessen is writing *American Renaissance*, because T. S. Eliot's reorienting essay on the metaphysical poets from 1921 is still reverberating:[11]

By contrast [to the metaphysicals], Emerson's poems can hardly be said to have any structure at all. He could capture the surprise of a moment, but he could hardly hold onto it long enough to suggest its density. . . . [He] could pick up some of the stones that these earlier poets used, and handle a few of their tools, but he could not build in their style. . . . Moreover, the tensions of their religious belief, their struggles between doubt and acceptance, made their utterance dramatic where his was simply ejaculatory. Emily Dickinson's poems, because they have such tension, are much more authentically in the metaphysical tradition than Emerson's are. (*AR* 115)

Matthiessen goes on to identify what it is Dickinson does well, as well as the poetic traits she shares with Emerson as forebear:

Many of [Emerson's] values were . . . hers also—especially where they concerned the integrity of the mind and the sufficiency of inner re-sources. . . . [Dickinson's] best poems display an excruciated awareness of the matching of good against evil, which was foreign to Emerson's temperament . . . and her conceits, unlike many of his, do not dissipate in every direction, since they are subordinated to a central issue. (*AR* 115)

Matthiessen engages Dickinson in fairly extensive detail in book 1 of *American Renaissance,* then, and seems invested in differentiating her practice, and, tellingly—though she is Emerson's "heir"—her *success,* from Emerson's, much in the same way he describes a Whitman who "bridged the gap" in ways Emerson never could.

All of which is to say that Matthiessen is a careful and considered reader of Dickinson's poetry, perhaps more so than we have been led to expect. In the *Kenyon Review,* he extends his discussion of Emerson's poetic practice to Dickinson by employing the famous keyword from Emerson's 1855 letter to Whitman:

Yet whatever Emily Dickinson's debts to the 17th Century, it should never be forgotten that Emerson was the great figure in her *foreground,* and that her conception of poetic language, of how "the word becomes one with the thing" in the moment of inspired vision, was basically his. (Matthiessen, "PP" 593–94, my emphasis)

Within the schemes of poetic lineage presumed across these extracts, Dickinson starts to emerge as Emerson's closest disciple. Indeed, it is an under-recognized aspect of *American Renaissance* that—notwithstanding how rarely she is mentioned—Dickinson, and not Whitman, sometimes comes to the fore when Matthiessen goes looking for a better, more nu-anced fulfillment of Emersonian poetics. Matthiessen can find his version of Emersonian poetic excellence when he reads Dickinson, something that he rarely finds in Emerson's own poems, and only intermittently sees in Whitman's.

Which is not by any means to say that Dickinson displaces Whitman. Whitman occupies a place of tremendous importance within the schema of *American Renaissance*; he is, of course, the sole subject of the concluding book 4, and, as I have argued elsewhere, his writings play a crucial, even determinative intertextual role for Matthiessen and Cheney as they forge a relationship in the culturally uncharted waters of male-male affection. Whitman's "Calamus" poems in particular occupy a position very near the substantive emotional center of the Matthiessen/Cheney relationship, especially in the early years. Whitman's words, the example of his life lived in the company of men, his conception of comradeship, and his erotically charged and affectionate depictions of male bodies, all function importantly as the two men jointly devise their own version of male-male physical and emotional intimacy.[12]

It is nevertheless instructive to note the instances in which Matthiessen invokes Whitman, as if by rote, and even on occasions when it seems that Dickinson would provide better evidence, or would seem to be a better choice, for the plausibility of his arguments tying Emerson and Whitman together. Against, for example, what he calls "Emerson's instinctive shying away to country solitude," Matthiessen at one point juxtaposes "Whitman's eager abandonment to sprawling New York in its iron age" (*AR* 543), which has the effect of redoubling the distinctions between Emerson's Concord and Whitman's Mannahatta, even within the scope of the larger argument that usually tries to rein in Whitman's excesses or differences in the service of Emersonian discipleship. Another way of saying this would be to note that a description of Emerson's "instinctive shying away"—not, it must be said, the first phrase that comes to mind when describing Whitman in virtually any context—would seem naturally to call to mind Dickinson's life lived apart in Amherst, on Main Street, often at home, though Matthiessen once more reaches to the example of Whitman. Or again: Whitman, Matthiessen writes, had gone even further than Emerson "in throwing overboard church and dogma" (*AR* 544), though we might point to an otherworldly, buzzing fly, or the alternative trinity of "the Bee – / . . . the Butterfly – / And . . . the Breeze – " (Fr 23), to signify Dickinson's own no-less-powerful theological insurrections. So there is a way in which Matthiessen's attention to—and, as I have argued about his personal life, his reliance upon—Whitman sometimes obscures his view of Dickinson, even as he seems to favor, in the aggregate, her poetry over his.

The question of religious faith and dogma initiates a notorious passage in *American Renaissance* that begins with a comparison of Emerson and Whitman's distinct versions of "religious assurance"; Emerson's, Matthiessen writes, is "mildly innocent," though it is also "unleashed from all control in dogma or creed." This somewhat oxymoronic "unleashed" "innocence" contrasts unfavorably with Whitman's "confused and bombastic" tendency to proclaim "the individual as his own Messiah," a claim that launches the rest of an impassioned paragraph that traverses through Nietzsche and Dostoevsky until it lands on Hitler: "When the doctrine of the Superman was again transformed, or rather, brutally distorted, the voice of Hitler's megalomania was to be heard sounding through it" (*AR* 546). Against this escalation, though, and in a kind of rhetorical recovery from it, Matthiessen's appreciation of Dickinson once again lurks in his depiction of Whitman at his best "not when he was being sweeping, but when contemplating with delicacy and tenderness some object near at hand" (*AR* 547). I say "lurks" because this appreciation of Whitman covertly resembles what Matthiessen admires about Dickinson in the *Kenyon Review*: "her expectant intimacy with nature" ("PP" 589), and what he calls Dickinson's "way of writing [that] continued to illustrate [Emerson's] conception of the Poet. That she believed no less than he that poetry could be written only in all-sufficient moments of inspiration . . ." ("PP" 591–92). So here is a Dickinson in tacit competition with Whitman, or at least those parts of Whitman that Matthiessen wishes, in some contexts, that the New York poet had more successfully "leashed."

This Whitman/Dickinson rivalry raises the stakes for thinking about the contingencies of canonization, and leaves us with a resonant question: what if Dickinson had been treated more fully by Matthiessen in *American Renaissance* and in keeping with the way that she emerges approvingly in this 1945 essay, as the more Emersonian Whitman he sometimes sought? What would the story of American literature that we have inherited look like if these threads in Matthiessen's later writings had come together earlier, or been brought to fruition in a later work? How might our Dickinson—not to say our Emerson or Whitman—look different if Matthiessen had found a way to include her in his 1941 canon-building tome, especially in light of how seriously he takes her work as a poet, and how invested he seems to be in establishing the nature of her poetic achievement?

Indeed, the privacy he is talking about in "The Problem of the Private Poet" is, at least explicitly, an almost entirely bibliographical and textual one. Writing about the publication of Mabel Loomis Todd and Millicent Todd Bingham's *Bolts of Melody* in 1945, Matthiessen has no patience for the biographical speculations and family gossip that pepper the introduction, though he is pleased that "Mrs. Bingham no longer engages in that favorite guessing-game of the twenties, 'Who was Emily Dickinson's lover?'" ("PP" 584). Here is the way Matthiessen's 1945 essay begins:

> According to the advance agents, a historic event occurred this spring in the annals of American literature, and we are the richer by over six hundred more poems by "Emily." Nearly everyone who writes about her plunges at once to cozy first-name calling with this poet who did not enjoy such liberties when she was alive and could prevent them. ("PP" 584)

From the outset Matthiessen is interested in displacing a patronizing familiarity. He is instead centrally focused on the editorial issues involved in securing the proper poetic text, not in biographical-psychological speculation: "The only portions [of Bingham's account] indispensable to our knowledge of the poet," Matthiessen declares, "are those chapters which extend the already grim picture of the state of the printed text of her poems" ("PP" 586).

For Matthiessen the problem of the private poet has to do primarily with the editorial questions that arise because of the unprinted, unregularized, and uncertain provenance of the poems that have been published as Dickinson's through an often vexed and sometimes compromised editorial lineage. His term "private" refers not to the secret backstory of Dickinson's sexual or psychological predilections; it is instead a figure for the editorial inconsistencies that the texts have suffered at the hands of a range of variously intentioned editors and intermediaries:

> Hitherto it has been generally assumed that the Higginson-Todd editions gave their poems as Emily Dickinson wrote them, but it now appears that the case was more complicated. In her chapter called "Creative

Editing," Mrs. Bingham recounts the dilemma with which the original editors felt themselves confronted. They wanted to present their poet to the world, but they did not want the world of the nineties to find her too queer, and there was the problem of her eccentric syntax and grammar, to say nothing of her rhymes. ("PP" 587)

Thus is the question of Dickinson's private "queerness" contained by thinking through the extreme contingencies of the Dickinson text, whether fair copy or foul.

And yet: I think some of what is happening in Matthiessen's curiously insistent pairing of Jewett with Dickinson is his awareness that these two women's shared, non-normative, never-married life stories are themselves aligned, even as they are allied with his own. Writing in the 1940s, of course, Matthiessen did not have the editorial tools we today take for granted— neither the compilation of Dickinson's intimate, and intimately editorial, correspondence with her sister-in-law Sue in *Open Me Carefully*, nor Sewall's extremely cautious broaching of the question of homosexuality in his 1974 compendious biography, nor even the relative luxury of Johnson's *Complete Poems* which, for all its problems, did not appear until 1955.[13] So he lacked many of the resources we rely upon for fleshing out a "queer" reading of Dickinson, whether at the level of the life or the line. But what Matthiessen did have, as I have begun to suggest, was the analogue of his distant cousin Sarah Orne Jewett's life lived apart from the strictures of heteronormativity,[14] as well as the example of his own life, which took both Whitman's writings and Jewett's long-term relationship with Annie Fields as its model. By insistently pairing Dickinson's work to Jewett's, whose own queer life he knew and had written about in detail—that is, when he was not himself simply living another version of it with Russell Cheney—Matthiessen signaled the possibilities of Dickinson's alternative, quasi-queer canonization, even in the very gesture of insisting that the question of privacy was first and foremost always only an issue with regard to the establishment of legitimately authoritative texts. Because, after all, and as he had written passionately to Cheney, how could what's private legitimately have anything to do with anything else?

Marriage! What a strange word to be applied to two men! Can't you hear the hell-hounds of society baying full pursuit behind us? But that's just the point. We are beyond society. We've said thank you very much, and stepped outside and closed the door. (Matthiessen to Cheney, September 23, 1924, Matthiessen and Cheney, *R&D* 29)

It was left to one of Matthiessen's most astute queer students, the poet Adrienne Rich, to fulfill the implicit promise of these complex scholarly traces and these closed doors by definitively identifying the consequences of queer Dickinson's life, even as her teacher Matthiessen had worked in the 1920s to construct and reconstruct Jewett's, and, not incidentally, his own.[15]

3

Adrienne Rich commended in print on more than one occasion Matthiessen's importance in teaching her how to read poetry and to conceptualize its place in the world. She also acknowledged Matthiessen's political beliefs as well as his status as a gay man.

> Francis Otto Matthiessen, a socialist and a homosexual, was teaching literature at Harvard when I came there. One semester he lectured on five poets: Blake, Keats, Byron, Yeats, and Stevens. That class perhaps affected my life as a poet more than anything else that happened to me in college. Matthiessen had a passion for language, and he read aloud, made us memorize poems and recite them to him as part of the course. He also actually alluded to events in the outside world, the hope that eastern Europe could survive as an independent socialist force between the United States and the Soviet Union; he spoke of the current European youth movements as if they should matter to us. Poetry, in his classroom, never remained within the realm of pure textual criticism.[16]

Neither Dickinson nor any woman poet appears in the syllabus Rich describes, though the course must have been taught a number of years after Matthiessen's conversation with Murdock about the undergraduate lectures. Perhaps because of his own status as a sex/gender outsider, it must have been difficult for Matthiessen as early as 1931 to have insisted to his colleague about the importance of teaching women writers like Dickinson and Jewett—sex/gender outsiders in their own right—by an all-male faculty to an all-male student body. (It gets only more complicated when we recall that Kenneth Murdock played a prominent role in the so-called Harvard Secret Court that expelled some gay students in a scandal from 1920, though this occurred before Matthiessen arrived in Cambridge, and I'm not certain he ever knew about Murdock's role.)[17]

Likewise Matthiessen's convictions a decade later, in the 1930s when he is writing *American Renaissance*, seem not to be strong enough to bring women fully into the public text of his canon-forming book, despite the sex/gender issues sometimes foregrounded in his analyses of a Melville, a Whitman, even a Thoreau. And yet, to hear Rich tell it, Matthiessen prepared a way forward. "I was exceptionally well grounded in formal technique, and I loved the craft," she writes in another essay in which she names Matthiessen as one of her teachers of Eliot, whose poetry nevertheless leaves her cold.[18]

When Matthiessen writes about Dickinson, he keeps his focus wholeheartedly absorbed in the value and the achievements of the poetry itself. Only perhaps in the curious alignment of Dickinson with Jewett do we find traces where Matthiessen's interest resides elsewhere, in a tacit acknowledgment that Jewett and Dickinson might have shared more than their on-again/off-again roles as "the two principal women writers America has had" (*SOJ* 152). In two places in her groundbreaking 1975 essay "Vesuvius at Home," however, Rich tacitly brings into view the complex processes Matthiessen put in motion. In the first of these instances, the larger context sets the scene: "[Dickinson's] niece Martha told of visiting her in her corner bedroom on the second floor at 280 Main Street, Amherst, and of how Emily Dickinson made as if to lock the door with an imaginary key, turned, and said: 'Matty: here's freedom.'"[19] The immediate context for the quotation is that "Matty" (or "Mattie," as it was usually spelled) is the nickname of Dickinson's beloved Susan's daughter, Martha. Not least of the resonances in the anecdote is the sense it conveys that, writing in the 1970s, Rich imagines for Dickinson an artistic and psychic freedom in the same enclosed space that generations of other, often male critics, though not Matthiessen, had demonized, rendered pathological, or understood to be only privative.

"Matty" was also F. O. Matthiessen's nickname, as Rich knew.[20] Twice in the essay that as much as any other in the second half of the twentieth century cleared a new space for Dickinson—as "a figure of powerful will, not at all frail or breathless" ("Vesuvius," 160), "the importance, and validity, of [whose] attachments to women may now, at last, be seen in full" (162),[21] "one of the two mid-nineteenth-century American geniuses, and a woman, living in Amherst, Massachusetts" (159)—twice in this essay the name of Rich's admired Harvard teacher arises. And in so doing, she imagines creating a new world for her mentor Matthiessen as well.

On its second repetition, the invocation of the nickname gains added resonance:

"Matty: here's freedom," I hear her saying as I speed back to Boston along the turnpike, as I slip the turnpike ticket into the toll-collector's hand. I am thinking of a confined space in which the genius of the nineteenth-century female mind in America moved, inventing a language more varied, more compressed, more dense with implications, more complex of syntax, than any American poetic language to date; in the trail of that genius my mind has been moving, and with its language and images my mind still has to reckon, as the mind of a woman poet in America today. ("Vesuvius," 163)

These lines from an essay that helped to recalibrate Dickinson's place in the literary canon—like her mentor had done thirty years earlier—also channel a poet's voice speaking to a long-lost teacher. "Matty" is given a restored place in an essay that frees Dickinson, once and for all, from a heteronormative patriarchal literary heritage, but it is not by any means only Dickinson's, or only her own, liberation with which Rich is concerned. Rather, this is a freedom for a life lived beyond the protocols of the normative by Matthiessen himself. This is the student teaching her teacher, much as the beloved Whitman had always insisted, and which is a renaissance of a wholly different kind.

Whitman, Dickinson, and Their Legacy of Lists and "It"s

VINCENT DUSSOL

But could It teach it?[1]

is there any gender
"accouche! accouchez! out with it!
is there any gender
(finish)
acheve! achevez! out with it!"[2]

INDIRECTION—DICKINSON'S "ANGLED ROAD" (Fr 899)—SOMETIMES
works best: a fragment in French author Georges Perros's *Papiers collés II*
suggests the special relationship that seems to link lists to indefinites in
Walt Whitman's and Emily Dickinson's poetry:

> There is something that the language we use . . . is very far from ap-
> proaching, be it at the acme of communication, something which does
> not belong to us but concerns us, something like the Christians' god,
> and Christ's "Do not touch me."
>
> There is something which resists such communication, which will
> not hear of *it* but which keeps worrying us day and night . . . something
> insatiable, something immeasurable, always ahead always behind and
> never standing at attention in the present . . . .
>
> There is something that demands that mankind say it, the human
> being precisely, because it is a cripple by birth and its being chosen for a
> victim shows discernment in the chooser that gave it something to speak
> about without giving it the means to do so . . . .
>
> There is something gnawing at mankind, which enables it to die
> before its death and live after its life; which enables it to be—if only but
> a little—there.

187

The sea the sky trees birds, as well as nothing natural, what do we know about it, nothing will ever console me for this absence, the diffuse absence of this in everyone's speech, in any speech, no, nothing that beats to the other rhythm and for the love of which I would die, nothing will console me for all this which has never, which will never tell me anything, I am waiting for this something which will make me live for the love of it, and if I die badly, as a stupefied drunkard would, what will be to blame if not that ever unutterable something which only mankind can say to mankind, beyond all horizons.[3]

Perros's fragment makes clear the way a list based on the reiteration of indefinites can stand halfway between the urge to express what is most elusive about the human being and the consciousness that it is bound to remain an impossible, frustrating, but exhilarating attempt. Indefinites—here "something" and the single highlighted "it"—are traces of the forced compromise struck by the human speaker on the brink of the ineffable. Walt Whitman and Emily Dickinson translated the experience of that confrontation in ways that differ but share common features, most notably the combination of lists and indefinites ("it" in particular) to give body to the idea that we mean more than we can say.

Instances of the dialectics of the detailed epic list and the vague "it" can be observed in twentieth-century American poetry, suggesting that this thread in the fabric of Whitman's and Dickinson's work was consciously picked up. Specific reasons for doing so seem related to the nature of the poems in which the configuration is found: if only through their ambition, their scale, and their authors' wish to "make it cohere" even loosely, in suite-like fashion, those poems point toward the epic.

The epic is inseparable from a totalizing gesture. While the epic features of Whitman's nation-defining, all-embracing *Leaves of Grass* have been widely acknowledged, such is not the case with Emily Dickinson's poems, the obvious reason being their brevity. Yet I believe that a case can be made for an unmistakable epic thread in her poetry.[4] Her 1,789 poems in the Franklin edition can be viewed as so many tesserae coming together as the portrait of a heroic woman who, despite repeated descents into a private hell, always returned, never giving up. Like most epic figures, she is representative of a people: the often silenced nineteenth-century woman, absent from public space. Her poems, which show her maintaining a watch on her times, crystallize and magnify that figure's frustration but also document a thousand facets of a single woman's private space, a space in which Dickinson would *not* let herself be confined. More literary reasons for exploring Dickinson's epic leanings include her frequent reference to Revelation, the Bible's most epic book, in which the hero who ensures victory "is called The Word of God" and the power of words is figuratively represented by "a sharp two-edged sword" coming out of a mouth, a phrase echoed in Dickinson's "There is a word / Which bears a sword" (Fr 42).[5] Similarly, Elizabeth Barrett-Browning's *Aurora Leigh*, a long verse-novel with a poet-heroine praising the epic, is known to have held lasting appeal for her.[6] Dickinson's resistance to the publishing world may have been partly fueled by these heroic literary models. Many war-related images in her poetry give evidence of her pugnacity, ironic or otherwise, as in "To fight aloud, is very brave – / But *gallanter*, I know / Who charge within the bosom / The Cavalry of Wo – " (Fr 138).

Catalogs, that is to say lists with a poetic intent, are also an essential feature of epics, and Dickinson's poems frequently include lists, if only short ones. But I will show that she also gives clues as to the reasons for the limited length of her lists. I believe it can be argued that her often prominent use of the indefinite "it" is probably both a conscious and an ironic substitute for other possible translations of the ineffable, longer lists among them. On the other hand, Whitman's use of the indefinite "it" testifies to an unslaked and fully embraced thirst for exhaustiveness. Between these two manners of showing awareness of language's impossible completion, later poets traced their own ways. Understanding the two sources of this "tradition" provides useful evidence of the complementarity of the poetic list and the indefinite "it," or what I call the list/it pair.

Dickinson's Thing about "It"

The first track on the CD of one of France's currently most popular bands, Christine and the Queens, is a song entitled "iT," written in English: surprisingly (it's just a song) but fittingly, given its title, it refers to Emily

Dickinson.[7] It is tempting to think that Dickinson had a thing about "it"; lines five to eight of "Beauty – be not caused – It is – " (Fr 654) go:

> Overtake the Creases
>
> In the Meadow – when the Wind
> Runs his fingers thro' it –
> Deity will see to it
> That You never do it –

In this poem about the elusive character of Beauty, the indefiniteness of "it" effectively conveys that elusiveness. Additionally, the epiphora of "it" evokes a barrier materializing the impossibility for anyone to trespass certain limits in the chase for beauty: all forcible efforts are bound to crash against a wall. What most interests me here is the sheer repetition of "it." The threefold end-of-line (rhyming) return of this vaguest of function words is unusual enough that we must assume it was meant to call attention to itself. The three rhyming pronouns carry different antecedents: while the first one clearly refers to "the Meadow," the second one is non-referential and part of a phrase, what linguists call a dummy object; the third may equally refer to the overtaking of the creases in the meadow as an instance of unachievable attempt or be the dummy object in the phrase "do it," that is, to succeed. This first example makes "it" appear to be a skeleton substitute, as one would talk of a skeleton key. It can replace any word, and so refer to anything or everything, as well as stand for what has no meaning (a dummy object). As such, it is economical in the extreme and makes lists superfluous. In fact, it could almost be said to constitute a list all by itself.

In *A Poet's Grammar*, Cristanne Miller has shown how Dickinson's use of the two-letter "it" runs the whole gamut of its possible functions and opens onto a wide range of meanings.[8] Writing about "We dream – it is good we are dreaming – / It would hurt us – were we awake – / But since it is playing – kill us" (Fr 584), Miller first describes "It" as a "ubiquitous, unplaceable, and contentless subject," then goes on to suggest that in the second line, the "grammatical subject eerily becomes akin to something like God"; Miller adds: "'It' often acquires extraordinary significance in

Dickinson's poems because it remains absolutely mysterious and absolutely feared and desired."⁹ Miller's analytical inventory leads one to the conclusion that for all its diminutive and unprepossessing aspect, "it" is used by Dickinson most visibly to point to essentials of the human experience, condition, and thinking. This may be linked with what is perhaps the most immediate reason for the second-to-none foregrounding of function words in Dickinson's poetry pointed out by Miller: an occasional skeptic's and an instinctive contrarian's playful reversal at the Bible's expense.

Numerous words are italicized in the edition of the King James Version of the Bible Dickinson owned, now made available online by Harvard University.¹⁰ The italics indicate those words that were added by the translators to help the reader make sense of the text.¹¹ Most of the words in italics are function words, but italicizing makes them stick out. Though by no means the most frequently italicized, "it" is among them. Is it a stretch of the imagination to think that the large number of function words given extraordinary prominence in Dickinson's poetry may partly be traceable to their heavy italicizing in the King James Version of the Bible, which Dickinson seems to have read more than any other book? As Jack Capps reports, "biblical quotations in her letters and poems far exceed references to any other source or author."¹² To give but one example, she would have read and known of this passage in Ecclesiastes in which "it" is italicized four times: "Then I beheld all the work of God, that a man cannot find out the work that is done under the sun: because though a man labour to seek *it* out, yet he shall not find *it;* yea farther; though a wise *man* think to know *it*, yet he shall not be able to find *it*."¹³ This biblical example incidentally confirms the idea that Dickinson's use of "it" stands for a constant human concern: what lies beyond mankind's understanding.

It is very likely that Dickinson would have known about the reason for italicizing words in the King James Bible. And it involved a paradox: the italics did not bring a word's high importance to the reader's special attention but rather its lower status, as an import into the original text for readability's sake. This reversal might well have appealed to one who was to write "The Bible is an antique Volume – / Written by faded Men" (Fr 1577), and it may have contributed to Dickinson's striking use of function words in her verse. Function words are often central to her poetry, making "it" the perfect touchstone; this grammarian's dummy-word is turned into the ultimate placeholder, the final signifier or supreme fiction, at the outer limit of the expressible.[14] Having "it" refer in turn to God *and* death is also clearly a way to pay God back in his own coin, as the phrase would have it.[15]

Always keeping things fluid, Dickinson placed her ironical transfigurations of "it" side by side with instances where "it" merely serves as the anaphoric list-like marker used in posing a riddle as in "It's like the Light –" (Fr 302) or "It sifts from Leaden Sieves –" (Fr 291). These Dickinson poems are often grouped under the label "definition poems." But in that "it" is typically the opening word in this category of poems, the enigma rather than the clarification is highlighted: even when the solution of the riddle is finally given, these short implied lists carry irony, since they point to the original absence of a center.

Dickinson's 1850 Valentine poem, the first and longest poem of hers we know, is rich in lists. Its speaker draws on the list-like form of Genesis to make her point about the intended pairing of all beings and things in creation. At this very early stage of Dickinson's writing, the list is positively associated with God, despite its darker aspects: "The *worm* doth woo the *mortal*, death claims a living bride" (Fr 1): Dickinson plays at listing all of God's creations, in making her point that everything has a mate except the "you" she addresses. The possibility of such a "reading of the roll" is not questioned in this poem where she assumes complete order in the universe. Such is not the case in the rest of Dickinson's poetic oeuvre: later, she relies on lists or list-effects, but the general brevity of her poems runs counter to the totalizing intent that is a prime function of a literary list. In "I reckon – When I count at all – " (Fr 533), she calls attention to the fact that she is making a list but only the better to show her (speaker's) impatience with it: after "the List is done –", *she* is quickly done with it, showing how it boils down to one essential: poetry. What follows the conclusion to the first part of the poem ("So I write – Poets – All – ") is a point-by-point reexamination and undoing of the original list, the extension and hierarchy of which no longer matter; poetry-governed comprehension of its items is now the priority, and the loosening of the vertical organization enables those items to combine in a richer, more narrativized way.

The "more-is-less" message, suggesting that "totalness" does not depend on size (extension) but on intensity ("Utmost"), is also found in the tightly packed form, so unlike a list, of

> All I may, if small,
> Do it not display
> Larger for the Totalness –
> 'Tis Economy
>
> To bestow a World
> And withhold a Star –
> Utmost, is Munificence –
> Less, tho' larger, poor –
> (Fr 799)

"Small" can hold "all," just like the short function words ubiquitous in Dickinson's poetry outdo the infinity of lists.

To reformulate, it could be argued that Dickinson's favoring of "it" or equivalent indefinite placeholders was for her an economical way of ensuring terseness. "It" would be one of the ways to "reduc[e] the ratio of what is stated to what is implied" and *not* give in to the facility of the apparent largesse of lists.[16] This usage is the mark of her ironic consciousness of the impossible rounding of circumference, including that supposedly offered by scripture: there's no reaching "Further than Riddle ride," so it's best to content oneself with the implicit fullness of "it" (Fr 1068).[17]

Whitman: The Poet of Lists

In contrast to Dickinson, Whitman is a list poet. A mere glance through Emerson's programmatic essay "The Poet" verifies what different scholars have noted about the prominence of lists in Transcendentalist writing: "The habit of conveying ideas by means of a barrage of linked analogies is distinctively transcendental," Buell writes.[18] If only for that reason, it is no wonder that Emerson should have hailed Whitman's 1855 *Leaves of Grass* as a work meeting his agenda and expectations. His never once using the words "poet" or "poetry" in his letter to Whitman is proof enough of the acknowledgment of the absolute novelty of the poetry: "I find incomparable things said incomparably well, as they must be."[19] "Song of Myself" uses long lists for poetic effect. Over the successive editions of his book, Whitman kept reorganizing his work toward increasing cogency, turning it more and more into the catalog of a life. No less significantly than Dickinson, however, Whitman also uses "it" and other indefinite placeholders as complements to his lists.

Drawing from the novelist Georges Perec's research, the Montaigne scholar Bernard Sève notes a paradox about lists: while they are aimed at taking a full inventory, that goal is never reached, much to the relief of those drawing the lists.[20] That the whole world could be confined in one list would indeed be terrifying. Complete(d) lists suggest death, as Dickinson implies in "They Dropped like Flakes – ," where God's "Repealless – List" (Fr 545) refers to the death toll of a Civil War battle. The realization that most lists cannot be complete, that something eludes the listing, is welcome: this may be why a lyrical anaphora using "it" surfaces in the antepenultimate section of "Song of Myself": "it is Happiness." Nearing the end of the poem, the poetic persona acknowledges the fact that, despite the trappings of completion (the 52 sections, as marked in the 1867 edition), his account of himself is bound to remain incomplete. Yet the tone of the passage is anything but resigned or weary. Listing approaches to or hints of the item he claims to have "missed" sounds elevating: "I do not know it . . . . it is without name . . . . it is a word unsaid, / It is not in any dictionary, utterance, symbol"; "Something it swings on more than the earth I swing on" (WPP 1855, 86).[21] The thrill of incompletion continues to the end despite the apparently conclusive final line of the section as it offers not one but five different ways of identifying the "it." The very diverse identifications provided leave the mystery intact and are as many invitations to go on grappling with it.

The unnamable elicits similar fervor in a more elaborate treatment of how to approach what cannot be known or said in two passages of "A Song for Occupations": I "offer the value itself," the speaker states before launching into the anaphoric paean:

There is **something** that comes to one now and perpetually,
It is not what is printed, preach'd, discussed . . . . it eludes discussion
  and print,
It is not to be put in a book . . . . it is not in this book,
It is for you whoever you are . . . . it is no farther from you than your
  hearing and sight are from you,
It is hinted by nearest and commonest and readiest . . . . it is not them,
  though it is endlessly provoked by them . . . . What is there ready
  and near you now?
You may read in many languages and read nothing about it;
You may read the President's message and read nothing about it there,
. . . .

I do not know what it is except that it is grand, and that it is
  happiness,
And that the enclosing purport of us here is not a speculation, or
  bon-mot or reconnoissance,
And that it is not something which by luck may turn out well for us,
  and without luck must be a failure for us,
And not something which may yet be retracted in a certain
  contingency.
                              (*WPP* 1855, 90–91, emphasis mine)

The sense of incompleteness itself is seen here to generate a passionate list. Similarly, in Dickinson's "Before I got my eye put out – " (Fr 336), the speaker's mention of "finite eyes" creates a positive tension by limiting the potentially infinite catalog: "the Sky . . . The Meadows . . . The Mountains . . . All Forests – Stintless Stars – / As much of noon, as I could take – / Between my finite eyes – // The Motions of the Dipping Birds – / The Morning's Amber Road – ."

For both writers, incompleteness leaves room for meaning to wander. Whitman's "it"s celebrate that open road of a semantic space or horizon. Unsurprisingly, "democracy" makes one of the best matches for the elusive "subject" of "A Song for Occupations": it is within everybody's reach, does not rely on special knowledge, is owned by no one, but the "nearest, commonest, readiest" constantly revitalize it (*WPP* 357); and, like American democracy, in Whitman's 1855 hopeful view, it is there to stay forever and is independent of contingencies. It would explain why the rhetoric of apophatic theology (describing something by negation) is recycled, given the sacred character of the reference.[22] Dickinson's "it"s are more often about helplessly tackling ultimate meanings through duplicating the world's enigma, out-Godding God (and scripture) at their little guessing-games, with death (Dickinson calls it "Murder by degrees" in "The Whole of it came not at once – ," Fr 485) as the price players must pay for definite answers: "I shall know why – when Time is over – / And I have ceased to wonder why – " (Fr 215) tells this story in a tone that sounds deceptively light at first, only to end on a more painful note "that scalds [her] now!" Whitman's resort to "it" in "Song of Myself" and "A Song for Occupations" is paralleled in the final editions of *Leaves* by what Whitman calls a "poemet"—entitled "The Unexpressed," the first line of which goes: "How dare one say it?" "It" here is no longer multi-referential as it was in "Song of Myself," since it meekly carries the poem's title as its antecedent (*WPP* 638, 653). But the epiphora of "lacking," also the poem's final word, brings the point home: casting doubt on the all-encompassing power of epics, the whole poem is like a belated version of the youthful "it"s of the 1855 book: a key part of the "cluster" that is to conclude all previous ones (*WPP* 637), it signals the end of the listing. But this ultimate capstone creates once again the reassuring and necessary hole in the whole that makes Whitman's lists always open, never static: a feeling heightened by the constant impression with Whitman's poetry of being spoken to an addressee.

In *Trying to Think with Emily Dickinson*, Jed Deppman notes an important difference between Dickinson and Whitman with regard to what he calls "the Webster-Worcester lexicographical furor [in nineteenth-century America]. Unlike Walt Whitman . . . who enjoyed reading different editions of dictionaries, considered writing one himself . . . looked for his own coinages in new editions and drew up long lists of words, Dickinson, despite close family ties to the Webster family, did not get swept up in the politics of lexicography."[23] Allowing for this difference enriches the perspective on the relation of lists to the "it" and to the question of the inexpressible in the two poets.

Whitman was generally comfortable with what remained unsaid for, put briefly, quasi-political reasons linked with his democratic ideals. As he writes in *The Primer of Words*: "For in manners, poems, orations, music, friendship, authorship, what is not said is just as important as what is said, and ~~gives as out~~ holds just as much meaning" (*Daybooks,* 746). Thrilled as he was at the "subtle something there is in the right name—an undemonstrable nourishment" (*Daybooks,* 756), he could rest contented with what cannot be verbalized or transmitted. That there exist inexpressible things is all for the better. Whitman's "it"s are a linguistic horizon. But his view of the English language as essentially dynamic must also have determined this easy acceptance of the limitations of expression as he viewed them as a historical and therefore moving frontier: "As for me, I feel ~~many~~ a hundred realities, ~~perfectly well~~ clearly determined in me, that words are not yet formed to represent." "Of ~~all~~ words wanted, the matter is summed up in this; When the time comes for them to represent any thing or any state of things, the words will surely follow" (*Daybooks,* 746, 745). One thing is sure: Whitman's lexicographer's work was on a par with his epic ambitions. A list in a notebook starts: "Dictionary/ Democracy/ America" (*Daybooks,* 811).

Unlike Whitman with his lists of words in the daybooks or *Specimen Days* (*WPP* 791), Dickinson never did a regular lexicographer's groundwork. Yet Jed Deppman calls her "Amherst's Other Lexicographer" because her some 250 "definition poems" make up "a lexicon of her own" and these often ironic, lyric definitions challenge the view of language as "semantically stable, referential [and] sanctioned by God" then held by professional lexicographers like Noah Webster.[24] From that angle too, granted that a defining characteristic of epics has been their "accompanying role in support of a community's evolvement of a new structure or of a new becoming," it would make sense to speak of a long-range epic impact of Dickinson's oeuvre in the reshaping of sensitivities.[25] But, if I may be permitted an oxymoron, the epic, political impact of her heroic resistance took place through the lyric; her "epic" is comprised of all the minute lyric challenges she meets from her private space, enlarging the English language by carving into it to the limit while Whitman carpentered roomy new extensions for it.

The Legacy: Variations on "It" and the List

The topic of this study largely comes under what Umberto Eco, in *The Infinity of Lists*, names "the 'topos of ineffability.'"[26] "Faced with something that is immensely large, or unknown, of which we still do not know enough or of which we shall never know, the author tells us he is unable to say, and so proposes a list very often as a specimen, example, or indication, leaving the reader to imagine the rest."[27] Such is indeed the case in Dickinson's list-like "An altered look about the hills – " (Fr 90), which ends: "All this and more I cannot tell – / A furtive look you know as well – / And Nicodemus' Mystery / Receives it's annual reply!"

Numerous critics have written about Whitman's attempts at getting "beyond the limits of language altogether," his renewed attempts at expressing "that curious, lurking something."[28] In *Specimen Days*, Whitman wrote that he wanted "to justify the soul's frequent joy in what cannot be defined to the intellectual part, the calculation," which prompts Matthiessen to say: "Something like this feeling was the usual result of the transcendental conception that the idea is always greater than any expression of it" (*WPP* 947).[29] So there is nothing new under the sun, but that is precisely the point: "There is something that comes home to one now and perpetually," Whitman writes in the passage from "A Song for Occupations" quoted above. The old topic of the ineffable can be tweaked toward plotting a continuity of the complementarity of the list and the "it" in American poetry.

Were someone to attempt to plot a short history of what might be called the "Transcendental-it" / "Transcendental-list" couple in American literature, Wallace Stevens's "Notes Towards a Supreme Fiction" would appear as a necessary inclusion: short of ways to name that fiction, Stevens chose to use the vaguest of all pronouns to refer to it, breathing fresh life into the indefin-"it" while the poem's thirty sections can be regarded as a list-like attempt at giving substance and exhausting the idea of an ultimate signi-fied.[30] Like Dickinson's "it" pregnant with meaning, Stevens's "It" "Must Be Abstract," "Must Change," and "Must Give Pleasure."[31] Somewhat later, H. D. (Hilda Doolittle) provides the next example, an all-the-more telling one, as in *Trilogy*, she seems to stand equidistant from Whitman and Dickinson.[32] Pressed by her patron and guide in alchemical matters to name "'the jewel colour,'" the speaker first confesses to her inability to do so:

> a vibration that we can not name
>
> for there is no name for it;
> my patron said, "name it";
>
> I said, I can not name it,
> there is no name;
>
> he said,
> "invent it."
>
> > (*Trilogy*, 76)

She goes on to state her unwillingness to comply:

> . . . I do not want
>
> to talk about it,
> I want to minimize thought,
>
> concentrate on it
> till I shrink,
>
> dematerialize
> and am drawn into it.
>
> > (*Trilogy*, 77)

On one hand, these passages strikingly resemble Dickinson's "Beauty – be not caused – It Is – " (Fr 654): while there is less play on the flexibility of "it" in H. D.'s than in Dickinson's poem, a kind of helpless fascination with "it" may account for the speaker's threatening engulfment.[33] As in Dickinson's poem, the repeated "it" at the line break suggests an insurmountable barrier. On the other hand, this confrontation with "it" takes place in the context of a long poem, "Tribute to the Angels," which is the richest in series and lists of the three poems composing *Trilogy*, H. D.'s epic of war and peace. The speaker's unwillingness to describe the opalescent jewel as accurately as she can, repeats itself later on in the poem following her vision in a dream of "the Lady," a female savior whom she strives to release (as Susan Stanford Friedman puts it) "from traditional imagery as the Virgin Mother of God."[34] She does so through "a catalog of images she can recall," none of which can wholly capture the Goddess's novelty.[35]

In her article on "Mystical Experience in H. D. and Walt Whitman," J. W. Walkington convincingly demonstrates that Whitman's "Song of Myself" was a likely influence on H. D. as she wrote "Tribute to the Angels."[36] And indeed, the article ends on a climactic comparison of Whitman's resort to "it" in section 50 of "Song of Myself" with H. D.'s conspicuous use of "it" to end nine lines in the fragments of "Tribute to the Angels" quoted above. "The Whitman text furnishes us with a new way to read the undefined 'it,'" Walkington writes, which could stand for "the essence of the mystical experience."[37] Thus, triangulating H. D. with Whitman and Dickinson adds substance to the thesis that these two pillars of American poetry may have inspired dialectics of the "it" and the list. The pole of the list attached the list/"it" pair to the epic or long poem tradition.[38]

Like H. D.'s palimpsestic *Trilogy*, Rachel Blau DuPlessis's *Drafts*, now numbering over a hundred pieces, also belongs in the tradition of the American long poem. An H. D. scholar herself, and an early rediscoverer of H. D.'s work in the 1970s, she chose to entitle "Draft 1" "It."[39] In a study included in *Brouillons*, the volume of French translations of selected "Drafts" that he published recently, the French poet, translator, and critic Jean-Paul Auxeméry rightly relates this choice to the Poundian modernist "it."[40] But it is also likely to be a way for DuPlessis to go one step further than Whitman, Dickinson, and H. D. In placing the "It" piece at the threshold of *Drafts 1–38*, she acknowledges from the outset that she is aware of their poetic legacy on this point, that no matter how many drafts are drafted, there is to be no completion, no perfect expression and that "it" is the aptest signifier of this forever unsuccessful effort.

Four pages into the poem, the reader comes across Virgilian remains:

"CANO, can o, yes   no / conno- / tations of impurities fill the fold."[41]
The deconstruction of the epic notwithstanding, the link between the "it"
and the long poem is thereby hinted at and renewed.[42] And DuPlessis goes
at "it" from widely different angles, creating a list of sorts, extracted here
from the draft-like text:

> I
> is it (4)
>
> putt (pitting) the tiny word
> litt
> it . . . .
> spot a lite on
> it something
> alight with wings (5)
>
> It is the
> "it" characteristic of everything   Yes, read it! (8)
>
> . . . I
> want to be *in* it, but it is not for
> in it it
>
> *is* it. . . .
>
> it is sacred what you can do with it (8–9)
>
> it   is the definition of speaking
>
> gladness too is it, its weeping.
>
> Silence is not the only subversion; it is.
> (Drafts 1–38, 10)

"It" is all there, is it not? The frustration at the impossible definition that
leads one to yield to the temptation of tautology—"it // *is* it."; the belief

that "it" can capture the whole of human experience both intensively and extensively—"the / 'it' characteristic of everything"; the passionate wish to get at some ultimate essence—"pitting" and "putt[ing]" the "it" as though the tiny word could still be reduced to a more unbreakable kernel or gist (by ridding it of its "litt[er]") or, golf ball-like, was bound to lead to the hole at the center; the mystical and lyrical quest for light "it" may represent, as in "spot a lite on / it something / alight with wings" or "it is sacred what you can do with it"; the equating of "it" with language—"it is the definition of speaking."[43] To finish with DuPlessis's various ways of looking at "it," this temptation, already found in H. D.'s "Tribute to the Angels," to let subject and object melt into one: "I / want to be *in* it / . . . in it it" so that "I / is it." And "it" must give pleasure: "gladness too is it."[44]

Marina Camboni has pointed out that this mapping of the "it"/list(s) couple in American literature would be incomplete if it did not acknowledge Gertrude Stein, about whom the Beat poet Lew Welch wrote that "she was one of the few artists, perhaps the only artist, that put *it* all down."[45] Obviously she did not, but her writing does show a wish to exhaust the options offered by the generative power of language, giving one the impression that she is going over them all as you would with a list. And that involved an exploration of the power of function words in the making of meaning. *How to Write*, written between 1926 and 1929, is quite typical in these respects: many of its pages are literally dotted or pitted with "it"s. Can "it" summarize the story of mankind? "What is it. It is this. Once upon a time there was evolution. He made it. He made it he heard it he had it he and he meant it he meant it he is what they mean when they say it."[46] Gertrude Stein's writing was critical in paving the way for works such as DuPlessis's *Drafts*.

I want to conclude with the contemporary poet Ann Lauterbach, whose writing is deeply informed by Transcendentalism: a section of her essay "The Night Sky" quotes Beckett's *The Unnamable* in an epigraph: "It, say it, not knowing what. Perhaps I simply assented at last to an old thing."[47] What follows this, brings to brighter light the significance of the pronoun:

For me, the "it" is the fragment of reality out of which we each make our poems.
I have a phrase which I use often to express my sense of a work that has

exposed the
vitality at the core of making: *the it of it.* I think this is not
an entity, not a thing, but a force
around which everything else swirls; without *the it of it*
everything that swirls would be only an inchoate, inarticulate miasma.

We want to believe that language, as a vehicle of inclusion and closure,
can somehow contain/reflect all of the it, which of course is not
 possible.
Or rather,
language can and does contain all of it; one might say that what
 we know
and perhaps what we
believe is only
because of the bearing of
language, but we have learned that for every instance of this
 knowledge
(of it)
there is another, with another
portion of
it about to be.[48]

Quite as interestingly, Lauterbach writes in another section of her essay: "What is the 'it'? . . . It could be a list, turn the whole thing into a list, *this this this*, designate the place where desire harbors its value, its cost . . . only to conclude: 'It is not a list. The actual cannot settle into either a list or a sequence.'"[49]

Like H. D. and DuPlessis before her, Lauterbach responds to Whitman's and Dickinson's treatment of the "it"; her perception of the subject is even clearer than her predecessors' because she is the only one to formulate the connection between "it" and lists. In her view, the "it" transcends the list. Her "it of it" might seem to go even further toward an essentializing of "it." However, her identification of the "it of it" as a force added to her admission that the "it" keeps shifting its ground so that there is always a part of "it" that changes and eludes the boundaries of language, rightly keeps the

representation of these very abstract matters on this side of fluidity. Bill
Berkson makes the same point in passing in a poem he gave Éric Athenot
and Olivier Brossard for an anthology they gathered for the 150th anniversary of the first *Leaves of Grass*, when he has the speaker say, addressing
Whitman: "Surreptitious self is it. / We don't want 'It.'"[50] In refusing the
capitalized "It," Berkson reinjects elusiveness into what might be captured
and stunted. "It" shouldn't be essentialized. "It" must change. "It" reflects
Whitman's "problem and indirection" (*WPP* 399); it is a way to skirt Dickinson's "Acres of Perhaps" and, alongside the list, this indefinite pronoun
is the most laconic proof that "it" "is [indeed] the Ultimate of Talk / The
Impotence to Tell."[51]

In her book on Walt Whitman and Emily Dickinson, Agnieszka Salska
devotes a few pages to Dickinson's use of "it," which she presents as one of
the ways that this pronoun, like Dickinson's poems themselves, "serve[s] to
map the road by which the mind travels to meet the unknown [and] show
how consciousness impinges on the mystery's territory."[52] Shortly before the
end of the same chapter, she refers to "'Tis little I – could care for Pearls – "
(Fr 597) and "A House upon the Hight – " (Fr 555) as instances of poems
ending where they start and therefore suffering "from a lack of dynamism";
the author's final diagnosis is that "they resemble Whitman's catalogs without Whitman's sense of progression."[53] Lists and the "it" definitely seem to
invite joint examination.

To linguists, logicians, or philosophers, the relation between lists and the
"it" would boil down to the question of how to represent totality, how *omnis*
is different from *totus* or *quisque* or how intensive and extensive magnitudes
relate to each other. Dickinson and Whitman were writing in a century that
saw the flourishing of dialectics. Consequently, it would not be absurd to
look at the "it"/list pair from that point of view, as providing more evidence
of the percolation of German philosophy into nineteenth-century America.

What I set out to do in this essay was different. Georges Perros's fragment
helped me detect a possible affinity between lists and indefinite pronouns in
American poetry. I found the first and more obvious evidence in Whitman,
the "epic poet." The visible overlap with Dickinson's poetry comes in her
unique highlighting of function words: "it" in particular. This led me to
assume that lists might also occupy a special place in her poetry, a guess that

textual evidence confirmed and that led me to reconsider the description of Dickinson as an exclusively lyric poet. Éric Athenot addressed a similar question about Whitman, pointing out that the author of *Leaves of Grass* might variously be regarded as epic or lyric and that, in the final analysis, labeling him was of no special import.[54] In contrast, with Dickinson, it does make a difference to suggest that she might also be an epicist, because of the gendered connotations of epic. Going by what we know, Dickinson never read *Leaves of Grass*, but she read Barrett Browning's long poem *Aurora Leigh,* and her poems show traces of the epic genre and spirit. Moreover, the scale of Dickinson's oeuvre and the comprehensiveness in her coverage of life add to the impression that more than one person speaks. So why not think of her as an epic lyricist whose modest-looking "it"s often say it all?

Sections of H. D.'s *Trilogy* convinced me that here was a poet who had spotted (probably in Whitman) the importance of leaving room for the indefinite in an epic-like poem but, in Dickinsonian fashion, used "it" for enhancing the enigmas of life. American poets are fond of such conversations. These dialectics of the total and the minimal (but universal) placeholder, "it," have spawned a legacy among writers of long poems. Rachel Blau DuPlessis and Anne Lauterbach confirmed the validity of my hypothesis of a direct influence. There is no exhausting the meaning of the "it"/list pair within American poetry. Center and circumference? Checks and balances? Macrocosm and microcosm?

Two short extracts from very recent poems may serve as proof of American poets' continuing interest in the list and the "it." First, Trace Peterson writes: "To list is to enfold a new norm—that's what the outlaw spawns."[55] Sam Truitt writes:

> just the terror
>
> Of looking out
> At it
>
> Of it
> The unknown[56]

"Beginners"
Rereading Whitman and Dickinson through Rich's Lens

MARINA CAMBONI

Poetry was always for me a kind of probe into the unspeakable
because it was a way of speaking indirectly about things I could not
speak directly about.—Adrienne Rich

A poet is somebody free. A poet is someone at home. How should
there be Black poets in America? —June Jordan[1]

"BEGINNERS" IS THE THEORETICAL LOCATION IN ADRIENNE RICH'S
critical work where, taking as her starting point the eponymous poem
Walt Whitman first published in the 1860–61 edition of *Leaves of Grass*,
she develops a complex vision of American poetry while also building the
genealogical line that would ultimately include her own work.[2] That location maps the plural logic of the poet who is not only committed to the
truth of a "language intensified, intensifying our sense of possible reality,"
but whose "poetic imagination" is "radical, meaning root-tangled in the
grit of human arrangements and relationships: *how we are with each other.*"[3]
Her own poetry provides a concrete, complex, dialogic map of this location, and an instance of what Martha Nussbaum calls "poetic justice."[4] By
fostering "critical resilience" (Rich, *HE* 2) and inviting readers to question
given truths and to imagine the possible; by refusing to make her poetry
a social commodity, her criticism, like her poetry, is political, in the sense
Hannah Arendt gives to the word *politics*. Indeed, Adrienne Rich's poetics
is a politics of the dialogue that necessarily connects the plurality of subjects
who inhabit a common world. For her, as for Arendt, "not Man but men
inhabit this planet. Plurality is the law of the earth."[5] In this dialogic location

Dickinson and Whitman act as equally committed individuals who search for personal growth and collective change in the geographies of the land and of the mind, all the while exploring the contradictory historical and transhistorical worlds of possibility. For Rich, this space-time of possibility is the space of the world, and not only inherently American but inherently life-saving, political, and hence human.

As the twentieth-century heir of "this strange, uncoupled couple" (Rich, *WFT* 90), Rich did not simply respond to the "leaves" or "letters" they sent but, reinterpreting them, translated their poetry into her own and her own times'—our times'— moods and needs. In the eighteen years intervening between her very influential, first critical essay on Dickinson, "Vesuvius at Home: The Power of Emily Dickinson" (1975), and "Beginners," Rich not only left behind her essentialist and oppositional stances but slowly developed a mature definition of the politically committed poet. While she considered both Dickinson and Whitman geniuses, during the years of her pioneering feminist battles Rich favored Dickinson's metaphoric poetry, seeing in it both a proto-feminist gender rage and a powerful will that manifested as a Jungian masculine animus. Later, however, when shaping her own role of poet speaking to the larger community, Rich turned to Whitman's democratic vision and distanced herself from Dickinson, admitting that her "shattered language" represented a "partial vision," and her legacy was not "enough."[6] A third phase began for Rich when, having already earned power and authority as a poet, she built her own narrative line of American poetry, favoring antagonistic and visionary poets.

What follows is a discursive procedure that, while foregrounding three different phases in Adrienne Rich's interpretive process of Emily Dickinson's and Walt Whitman's work, also develops a personal interpretation of the relationship linking the three poets together. Building on the work of a number of Dickinson and Whitman critics, and on a long tradition of feminist criticism, and relying as well on the heuristic tools offered by Pierre Bourdieu's sociology, Yuri Lotman's semiotics of culture, and Alain Badiou's philosophy, my narrative follows the thread weaving Rich's search for truth into and out of Dickinson's and Whitman's texts.[7] My argument is that when Rich ceased to consider Dickinson and Whitman as opposites negating one another and envisioned them instead as relational complementaries she became a "beginner" herself, the poet capable of leaving behind the legacy both of nineteenth-century patriarchal sex-gender isolating antagonisms and of the separatist and oppositional logic of twentieth-century feminisms and ethnic and racial essentialisms.[8] Building her own poetics on the political and symbolic scaffold of the "two" and its potential for engendering the multiple, she could make space for the multiple poetries as well as the varied truths that interact, and conflict, in the United States and in our complex world.

While Rich's "Beginners" offers a response to Whitman's poem, as well as interpreting it as a paradigmatic text of dissident poetry, Whitman's "Beginners" provides a historical frame for an interpretation of Rich's poetics and her vision of poetry "as a resource to express and interpret contemporary experience and imagine a different future" (*HE* 36).

Truth

In one of her last and most Whitmanian essays, "Poetry and the Forgotten Future" (2006), Rich stated that "there is no universal Poetry . . . only poetries and poetics, and the streaming, intertwining histories to which they belong." In the following paragraph, she manifestly connects her pluralist conception of "poetries" both to Whitman's work and to political and cultural democracy (*HE* 134–35).

Whitman had repeatedly stated, since his 1855 *Leaves of Grass*, that "the truth in man is no dictum. . . . it is vital as eyesight" (*WPP* 1855, 143), also pointing out the inherent impossibility for an American poet to be content with, and accept past, Europe-based, truths. Finding well-established dictionary meanings and authoritative poetic practices inadequate vehicles for his American poetry, he set himself the task of shaping a language and a text made vital, that is, alive, not only through the eye but through all the senses a living being is provided with. Like Whitman, Dickinson appears to have valued life and the body over abstract truths. Writing to her Norcross cousins, she once stated that "each of us gives or takes Heaven in corporeal person, for each of us has the skill of life" (*L* 388), and she anxiously asked the critic Thomas W. Higginson to tell her whether her "Verse" was "alive" (*L* 260).

It is as a searcher for lived truth—as the title of her first collection of essays, *On Lies, Secrets, and Silence* (1979) makes clear—that, in the 1970s, Rich first revolted against the English language literary tradition handed down to her as she did also against patriarchal gender discrimination and the male modernist credo in poetry. As in the lines she quotes from Audre Lorde, she believed that it is the poet's commitment to truth that makes the "difference between poetry and rhetoric."[9] The persona speaking in "Double Monologue," a poem included in the collection *Snapshots of a Daughter-in-Law* (1963), can "no longer think / 'truth'" as "the most beautiful of words," even though she still acknowledges that "Sometimes, unwittingly even, / we have been truthful. // In a random universe, what more / exact and starry consolation?"[10]

A symptom, a chance event that, appearing like a star in a night sky, has the variety and impermanence of human experience, truth is, for Rich, something that can be only momentarily accessed. In this, she seems to join in the twentieth-century critique of the classical conception of truth as universal and existing ahistorically. As Jean-Claude Milner synthesizes it, in our time "truth not only proceeds from inexactitude but inexactitude is itself the form truth has acquired."[11] From an analogous stance, in the 1960s and 1970s Rich started to question the truth-value of language, reason, and universal poetry, and to scrutinize them from the point of view of a woman's experience, pointing out that "there is no 'the truth,' 'a truth'—truth is not one thing, or even a system. It is an increasing complexity" (*LSS* 187).

In search of personal and poetic guidance, Rich turned to Dickinson and explored "her complex sense of Truth" (*LSS* 183). Quoting Dickinson's famous line "Tell all the truth—but tell it Slant—," she observed that "it is always what is under pressure in us, especially under pressure of concealment—that explodes in poetry" (*LSS* 162).[12] Internal pressure was for her both the key into Dickinson's "dialect called metaphor" and the outcome of her "unorthodox, subversive . . . propensities" (*LSS* 161). Dickinson's metaphors taught Rich a lesson, which is not so much how to use a duplicitous language, but how to get to one's own mental and psychological power to *comprehend* the human, historically embodied self and question the sense of life and death.[13]

And, indeed, believing that "the unknown is the largest need of the intellect" (*L* 471), Dickinson had built metaphorical bridges, joining the known and the unknown, the finite and the infinite, language and silence, possibly to *comprehend* in her lines both the "'volatile' truth" and the hidden dimensions of human life.[14] In her own search for truth, however, Dickinson never forgot that not everybody would be able to face the crude truth that life was all that could be shared of eternity, that it was all that humanity could rely on to form an idea of immortality. "The Truth – is stirless – " (Fr 882), Dickinson writes in one poem, and in another, "Truth – is as old as God – " and "will endure as long as He." Contrary to religious beliefs and metaphysical conventions, however, her truth or God, "Himself is borne away / From Mansion of the Universe / A lifeless Deity" (Fr 795).

Dickinson's image of a lifeless deity evokes that of the lifeless god/ ancestor/father figure in the first paragraph of Whitman's 1855 "Preface," where "the corpse [is] slowly borne from the eating and sleeping rooms of the house" (*WPP* 1855, 5). And yet, Dickinson's image conveys an inherently different message from Whitman's. Closer in this to Friedrich Nietzsche's anti-metaphysical stance, Dickinson depicts a God apparently destined to disappear from the world altogether, emptying it of its eternal, universal truth. And if, in Whitman's allegory of a corpse taken out of the house to make space for an heir, he represents historical and geographical transformation within a fundamentally stable social and symbolic order, Dickinson shows little faith in that order, as Paul Crumbley points out.[15] Rather, she unmasks both the historical and metaphysical constructions of that truth, even though she manifestly also holds to them for ballast. For it is not only that, as Crumbley puts it, Dickinson "repeatedly advises readers . . . that truth illuminates the deceptions perpetuated by history," but, as Shira Wolosky articulately demonstrates, for Dickinson, as for Nietzsche, life is inherently in flux and unstable and we live in a world of becoming.[16]

Whether because she was disenchanted with the "prevailing wisdom of the era," as Roger Lundin argues, or because Dickinson valued individual life and the world ("To be alive – is Power – " [Fr 876]) more than established religion and the afterlife of resurrection, she could also, like Nietzsche, flaunt the "antichrist" persona in the face of religious piety and metaphysical values and beliefs (*L* 389).[17]

Geniuses

Though she had read and quoted from Dickinson's poetry, and even used Dickinson as a spokesperson in "I am in Danger, Sir," a poem of 1964, Rich had not engaged herself critically with her body of work until the 1970s. With "Vesuvius at Home," however, published in 1975 eleven years after the poem, she decided to set herself against contemporary scholarship and demolish popularized versions of Dickinson, like "The Belle of Amherst" (*LSS* 157).[18] Her essay, she wrote, would offer "a lesbian-feminist reading of her poetry and her life as the most accurate way to handle that otherwise confusing constellation of myth and fact surrounding her" (*LSS* 157).[19] An exploration of Dickinson's poetry in the light of her life meant for Rich a more faithful understanding of a woman's artistic achievement.

Together with "When We Dead Awaken: Writing as Re-Vision," "Vesuvius at Home" marked a turning point in both Rich's poetic work and her critical thinking, and broke new ground by initiating a woman-identified critical discourse that provided a non-edulcorate and non-formalist response to Emily Dickinson's poems. By claiming that feminist discourse should "illuminate the work of *any* woman artist" (*LSS* 158), Rich dismissed with a single word the patronizing logic that sets apart the "token" from all other women and brought about a forceful opening and democratization of the male-dominated "field of art."[20] Depicted as a woman with a wild imagination and a "powerful will" in "Vesuvius at Home" (*LSS* 160), Dickinson is also made to voice a repressed anger at the limitations women, and especially a woman with a bright mind, had to suffer in a patriarchal society.[21] Rich, who was at the time giving poetic and political vent to her own anger, read in Dickinson's poems an analogous emotion, also deeply rooted in her embodied experience as a woman. Anger, for Rich, was feeding Dickinson's revolt against the shared *doxa*, and making her "the breaker of rules the one / who is neither a man nor a woman."[22] This nineteenth-century poet, Rich argues, was capable of translating "her own unorthodox, subversive, sometimes volcanic propensities into a dialect called metaphor" (*LSS* 161).

Though opening the field of art to all women, however, Rich was not endorsing feminine women or nineteenth-century women's poetry in general. Rather, she was making a distinction between historical women and the intellectual and even philosophical woman artist, meta-historical and archtypically masculine in her search for truth. Coherently, she stressed Dickinson's poetry as belonging to "a class by itself" (*LSS* 17), the exceptionality of "a mind engaged in a lifetime's musing . . . a mind capable of describing psychological states more accurately than any poet except Shakespeare" (*LSS* 167), and the uniqueness of a poetry possessed by "the daemon" (*LSS* 173).

To build the image of a powerful Emily Dickinson, Rich resorted in her essay to the romantic conception of the poet as the "genius" who "knows itself" (*LSS* 160) and to Jungian psychology, representing her as a woman possessed by a masculine demon or lover (animus), an incarnation of "what Keats called 'The Genius of Poetry'" (*LSS* 174).[23] And it is in her portrait of Dickinson and Whitman as the "two mid-nineteenth-century American geniuses" (*LSS* 159) that Rich first associates the two poets in "Vesuvius at Home," considering them tutelary, demonic spirits, endowed with an original and originary generative, psychically androgynous power, which she could absorb through their poems. Hence, to them she turned as to American stars influencing her adventure as a poet, just like the persona in her poem "Orion," who addresses the hunter constellation as her "genius" (*Poems*, 95).

House and Home

Numerous poems in Adrienne Rich's collections owe their inspiration and images to Dickinson's poetry, but it is to the symbolism of *home* and *house*, and to her poem "From an Old House in America," that we must turn to find the location in her poetry where Dickinson and Whitman first meet. Rich wrote the poem in 1974, when she was working on "Vesuvius at Home" and on the poems she would include in her trailblazing collection, *The Dream of a Common Language,* published in 1978.

While in the first paragraph of "Vesuvius at Home" Rich introduces herself as an insect hovering "against the screens of an existence which inhabited Amherst" (*LSS* 158), as if Dickinson herself were a home, in the second paragraph, she quotes the famous statement Dickinson made in her 1856 letter to Elizabeth Holland, where she gives a partly ironic and partly concerned dramatization of her own and her family's move to the Dickinsons' Homestead on Main Street: "They say that 'home is where the heart is,' I think it is where the *house* is, and the adjacent buildings" (*L* 182).

Dickinson had placed home in her father's house. To explore Dickinson as *home* meant for Rich both to turn to Dickinson as the necessary American home for a female poet and to confront, and interpret, the material and symbolic building in which she had spent her life. For the Homestead ostensibly stood for Dickinson's father, Amherst, Massachusetts, and the American Anglo-Puritan historical context and culture.[24]

In "From an Old House in America," Rich herself comes to terms with the patriarchal "house" that symbolizes the United States. In it "Deliberately, long ago / the carcasses // of old bugs crumbled / into the rut of the window // and we started sleeping here" (*Poems*, 235). The first lines of the poem echo the sense of death and decay Dickinson conveyed, in another letter, through the images of "*wings* half gone to dust . . . an empty house . . . *last year's flies*" (*L* 184).[25] The old house Rich represents is silent and empty, like Dickinson's, yet marked with the telltale signs of the former presence of women and children. To that empty American house, the poetic persona returns "to comprehend a miracle beyond // raising the dead: the undead to watch / back on the road of birth" (*Poems*, 238). Intertextually connecting Rich and Whitman, the "miracle beyond raising the dead . . . the undead to watch" associates these lines with Whitman's image of the American poet, who "drags the dead out of their coffins" and "places himself where the future becomes present," in his 1855 "Preface" (*WPP* 1855, 13).

After Whitman chose to make Walt, the protagonist of his *Leaves*, the spokesperson for the men and women of his country, he also started to work on a poetic language molded out of the words of the American *vulgari eloquentia*, a literary vernacular that would be as different from "cultivated" British English as Dante's acclaimed vernacular Italian was from Latin.[26] It is when he first let magmatic sounds erupt, or "belch," out of Walt's volcanic body and made him "yawp" undistinguishable words from the top of the hill that was America, that the adventure of his idealized self began, and with it, the adventure of literature in the American grain.[27] By trying to build an American cultural self, however, he also opened a new path for world poetry.

In an analogous way, Adrienne Rich made her alter-ego poet both the speaker of shared truths and the contributor of women's words and life experiences to the English language. When in her lines we read of the poet's "drive / to connect. The dream of a common language," we hear in the background Whitman's self-empowering celebration in the first line of "Song of Myself." Her poems become the speech act of the poet empowering herself, and her readers, by claiming that the words of truth in her poetry are the location where the woman-poet and all women both meet and mirror one another. Like Whitman's Walt, the woman in her poems is the potential agent of the future, for women "stream / into the unfinished the unbegun / the possible."[28]

Yet, it is when Rich moves away from her white-woman, essentialist stance, and starts to identify with marginalized and oppressed minorities, that she rereads both Dickinson's and Whitman's work through such engaged poets of the left as Muriel Rukeyser, gay and black visionaries and radicals like Robert Duncan and James Baldwin, political thinkers like Antonio Gramsci, and dissident poets, women and men, from all the world.[29]

I & We

On her way to a more radical, leftist, perspective, Rich abandons what Susan Howe calls Dickinson's "Sovereign" I but which could be better represented as the Nietzschean "wild" self of the genius-artist outlined in "Vesuvius at Home."[30] She starts, then, to build the dialectical space where the exclusive and rebellious, self-affirming and masculine "I" coexists with the Whitmanian plural subjectivity, embodied in the "others" whose spokesperson he claims to be, or in the collective "you" to whom his songs are addressed. In "Notes toward a Politics of Location" (1984), Rich writes:

> *You cannot speak for me. I cannot speak for us.* Two thoughts: there is no liberation that only knows how to say "I"; there is no collective movement that speaks for us all the way through.[31]

Only two years separate the essay from the talk Adrienne Rich gave at the 1986 Emily Dickinson Centennial Conference in New Jersey, now available in the *Dickinson Electronic Archives*, where she read "The Spirit

of Place," a poem in which she manifestly takes her leave not so much of
Emily Dickinson as of that part of Dickinson's work she had needed to
write her woman-identified poetry. And yet, a long quotation from one
of Dickinson's letters reveals the new role Rich will call her to play in the
future. "*All we are strangers . . . And Pilgrims! . . . We are hungry, and thirsty,
sometimes — We are barefoot — and cold—*" Dickinson writes, and her words
offer Rich what Martha Nell Smith calls "irreverent . . . opportunities."[32]

Rewriting and re-contextualizing Dickinson's words in "In the Wake of
Home," Rich transforms the nineteenth-century religious abstractions of
Dickinson's metaphors into today's embodied immigrants, homeless, Afri-
can Americans, opening the metaphorical space to include their languages
and dialects, yet again imaginatively expanding the field of poetry: "What if
I told you your home / is this continent of the homeless / . . . / of languages
tabooed / diasporas unrecorded / . . . / What if I tell you your home / Is this
planet of warworn children."[33]

It is in this context of social awareness, political engagement, and human
commitment as a poet that Rich turns to Whitman, the cosmopolitan New
Yorker, who in 1860 could envision "Immigrants arriving, fifteen or twenty
thousand in a week," could enclose in his lines "A million people," and,
on the verge of a bloody civil war, could tell the United States and all the
world that Mannahatta was "The free city! no slaves! no owners of slaves!"
(*WWA* 1860, 405).[34]

In another poem, "Yom Kippur 1984," also read at the Dickinson Centennial Conference, Rich models her lines after Whitman's long verse and
interweaves his words with her own:

I open a book searching for some lines I remember
about flowers, something to bind me to this coast as lilacs in the
    dooryard once
bound me back there— . . .
something that bloomed and faded and was written down
in the poet's book, forever.[35]

It is in this context of thought about poetry and the "tenuous, still unbirthed
democracy" (*WFT* 15) that Adrienne Rich writes "Beginners," choosing it

as the ground on which to build both her argument for Dickinson's and Whitman's importance for twenty-first-century Americans and her justi-fication of her own political choices.

Whitman's "Beginners"

> How they are provided for upon the earth, (appearing at intervals,)
> How dear and dreadful they are to the earth,
> How they inure to themselves as much as to any—What a paradox
>   appears, their age,
> How people respond to them, yet know them not,
> How there is something relentless in their fate, all times,
> How all times mischoose the objects of their adulation and reward,
> And how the same inexorable price must still be paid for the same
>   great purchase.
>
> (*WWA* 1860, 416)

Probably written between 1856 and 1857, and first published in the 1860 edition of his *Leaves*, "Beginners" makes one wonder why Whitman waited so long to present himself as a beginner and theorize about "beginners" in a universalizing poem.[36] I can detect two possible, and related, reasons. The first is that, by 1857, Whitman had become less interested in the reportorial truths the poet's eye could capture; the second is that the tensions within the nation made him less willing to delegate political action to politicians and more inclined to play a political role himself by making his poems perform the cultural and linguistic unity that politicians seemed unable to guarantee. Thus, he tried to imaginatively compose the vast, fragmented, geo-historical landscapes he had previously photographed, and the com-plexity and antagonisms of the nation's parts, into a coherent whole. And if in the first two editions of *Leaves* he had limited himself to assembling his poems in sequential order and building sense through repetitive patterns and additive accumulation, in the years that separate the second from the third edition he worked to integrate this quantitative process within a more unitary structure.

In "Proto-leaf," he clarifies that he "will thread a thread through [his]

217

poems," and "will not make poems with reference to parts, / But [he] will make leaves, poems, poemets, songs, says, thoughts, with reference to ensemble" (*WWA* 1860, 15–16). The third published edition bears formal evidence of his will to make a complex, articulated whole of his text (and nation). The unifying elements are both the organization of the 365 poems that comprise the volume into clusters, which brings to the fore the complexity of the work and the articulation of its parts into an organic whole symbolized by the number of days in one year; and the overt ideological web of words and references that makes Walt emerge as *the* poet of democracy and "America." Besides the cyclical symbolism of the year, what encompasses the poems and unifies them is, then, the persona of the political poet engaged in the building of democracy in his own country; a poet foreseeing the democratizing process expanding throughout the American continent with the United States at the forefront and—more imperialistically— as the hegemonic nation in a larger democratic continental unity. The thread connecting everything, from the personal to the public to the artistic, is the language of personal and political, emotionally charged feelings and relations. It plays down the emphasis on the birth of the poet; and the appearance of an original/new voice of the 1855 edition, and foregrounds growth and the relational process of love and cameraderie that would unite American to American. As a consequence, the image prevails of individuals connected in a community of people, and state cohering to state to build a single, whole, nation.

When read in relation to their pre-1860 versions, the poet's later revisions of the 1860 poems, in what is known as Whitman's *Blue Book,* show the poet's "evolving thinking," and, I would add, the evolving clarity and self-awareness in his thinking that led him to become an agent in the construction of the American democratic *civitas* and *civilitas.*[37] Between 1856 and 1857 Whitman had also been jotting down the poem "Premonition," entitled "Proto-leaf" in the 1860 edition and finally renamed "Starting from Paumanok," which included, in section 11, the line "*I,* now thirty-six years old, in perfect health, *begin.*"[38] One word, in that same poem, "*materials*" in the third line of stanza 29 ("These ostensible realities, *materials,* points?") was later replaced by the word "*politics,*" never to change again.[39]

That line that, slightly altered ("I, now thirty-seven years old"), would make its way into the opening section of "Song of Myself" in the deathbed edition of *Leaves*, manifests the determination that also bred "Beginners," and at the same time spells out Whitman's age and the chronological year: 1855. This might be an artistic ruse, to make it appear that *Leaves* was a political enterprise from its inception, but it might also be a way of stating that, although the idea had been there from the beginning, the will to pursue it and make a political career out of writing poems did not reach full fruition until the years when he was preparing the third edition, when his increasing number of readers and friends gave him enough confidence in himself.[40]

And there is evidence that this was the case. After, or with, the second edition of *Leaves,* Whitman had clearly become more self-confident and deemed it no longer necessary to rely on the authority of scholars like Emerson to support and promote his poems. Thayer & Eldridge's offer to publish the third edition of *Leaves* must also have boosted his self-confidence. In their letter of February 10, 1860, they told him that they considered the book "a true poem and writ by *a true man.*" They also pointed out that "when a man dares to speak his thought in this day of refinement, it is difficult to find his mates to act amen to it." For this reason, they wanted to be known as "the publishers of Walt. Whitman's books" and put their name as such "under his, on title-pages." Concluding their letter, they suggested that he try them, for "you can do us good. We can do you good—pecuniarily," adding fire to Whitman's desire to invest his life in poetry, and make it both a full-time job and a source of income.[41]

There are at least two aspects of the poem's text worth pointing out in the present context. The first is the significant differences between the manuscript and the printed text. The second is Whitman's use of economic terms to represent the cost or price of a beginner, an issue that Rich pointed out but did not investigate in her reading of the poem.

In the manuscript draft available on the *Walt Whitman Archive* website, the poem title was "Thought," and it began with the words "Of Originators," later changed to "Beginners." The two words are neither equivalent nor synonymous. As with Rich, Whitman's final choice may signify the difference between the innate power of the Romantic genius and the enacted power of the man who has chosen to make history out of poetry and become the poet as legislator.

As for the words "dear," "price," "purchase," unchanged in the manuscript and published texts, they gather in the poem within a single semantic system that runs through it like a backbone, pointing to an interpretation of the role of artists in economic terms. To fully understand Whitman's use of economic language, however, one must bear in mind Dickinson's economic imagery, not only to underscore, as Shira Wolosky does, "how far identity in America is established through ownership, possession, and inheritance," but to exemplify the Emersonian dictum: "Money . . . is . . . as beautiful as roses . . . Property . . . is always moral."[42] As a moral institution, money, like property, must be considered intrinsic to a people's culture, not only to its economy. Differently from his contemporary, Karl Marx, who represents the work of the artist as objectively part of a nation's superstructure, Whitman sees it as intrinsic to the economic system, whether the artist agrees or not. He was correct—especially in the light of contemporary soft American Power and the use of his lines to sell Levi's jeans[43]—even though to the hegemonic American frame of mind, in his time as in the present, the artist's work is still superstructural, and even utopian—or outright meaningless when more experimental and innovative.

Rich's "Beginners"

With Rich's own "Beginners," and for the first time in her criticism, Whitman and Dickinson meet on equal terms. As Rich puts it, the Puritan New England woman, "the very type and product of the mid-nineteenth-century's diagram for patriarchally protected middle-class femininity," and the New York man, "one paradigm of 'New World' masculinity" who "shared little beyond their white skin," move "together in a dialectic that the twentieth century has only begun to decipher" (*WFT* 92, 91, 90).

"Whitman and Dickinson shared the problematic status as white poets in a century of slavery, wars against the Indians, westward expansion, the Civil War, and the creation of the United States as an imperial power" (*WFT* 91), Rich writes, contextualizing their biographies, but also providing an important clue to her own essay. For indeed, her "Beginners" needs to be read within the frame of the dramatic transformation of the American social, political, and cultural scene in the last ten years of the twentieth century. The fall of the Berlin Wall in 1989, the American theorization, with Francis Fukuyama, of "the end of history,"[44] and a globalized financial and economic market would all be shaking the foundations of a nation-based world, which had found a polarized equilibrium during the Cold War years.

Anticipating that a new imperialist hubris in the United States would find widespread consensus, Rich tries once again to set the visionary truth of the poet and of poetry against the rhetoric of politics. In a movement of thought that seems to run parallel to that of history, she overcomes the duality and oppositional worldviews that had nourished gender, class, and ethnic polarization, and her own criticism. In this, however, she opens a path different from the one that would be taken by her country, by showing how the "two" could generate difference and the multiple rather than reverting to the Platonic truth of Godly unity. She also foregrounds the fact that criticism and distance from general consensus could, in the artist, breed vision, form, and unanticipated change, although she did not emphasize that, as history has taught us, even marginality and dissent could eventually be made subservient to the building of a nation's cultural economy and power politics.

Walt Whitman and Emily Dickinson, Rich writes in the opening of her essay, "are both 'beginners' in the sense of Whitman's poem," which is that they were both "openers of new paths" (*WFT* 90–91). Apparently fulfilling their prescribed roles, she argues, Whitman and Dickinson were not only "beginners" but true "misfits," for they were not what "'the times adulate and reward. Both the person and the times pay a price for this, yet the beginner is 'provided for'—part of the longer scheme of things" (*WFT* 91). Sharing Whitman's Hegelian dialectics, Rich underscores the two poets' programmatic, willful opening of new paths in the flow of time: their being historical agents, making their work the catalyst of change.

And it is within this complex vision of an American poetic tradition that, in the second part of the essay, she singles out Muriel Rukeyser as a third, twentieth-century, beginner. As a Jewish communist poet, Rukeyser is, in her view, not only the gatherer of Dickinson's and Whitman's poetic energy, but the representative of a non-Christian, Anglo-Saxon, tradition and the embodiment of an ethnic and political self she can identify with. Her presence in the essay also stands for the opening of the field of American poetry and the American canon that began with Dickinson and Whitman.

In Rich's interpretation, then, the two poets not only stand for the discontinuity of cultural and artistic processes, unanticipated explosions of new forms and language of the kind the Russian semiotitian Yuri Lotman has theorized in his *Culture and Explosion*, but mark the beginning of an antagonistic, inherently political, and culturally innovative line in American poetry to which she also belongs.[45] And if as "beginners" Whitman and Dickinson were "misfits," Rich claims, they were not the enraged "extremists" (*WFT* 94) that critics—including herself—have claimed. That of the extremist, she maintains, was only a mask they "created for themselves," and one of the masks that was "clapped on them by the times and customs" (*WFT* 95) and that is still filtering our appreciation of their work. Rather than "extremists," she continues, Dickinson and Whitman were a "paradox" in that they behaved in contradiction to good sense and common sense. Since they both unveiled the falsity that the *doxa* promotes to the function of abstract, universal, permanent "truth," the truths they offered, she argues, appeared incredible, contradictory, and illogical.

The "great purchase" so dearly obtained is not, however, for Whitman and Dickinson as for Rich, the reified work of art, the "good" to be either consumed or treasured and transformed into transcendental or universal value, to be sold in the market of power. It is rather the dissident work of art that is instrumental to the building of the self-awareness necessary to the subject in the polis, in its assumption of a cultural and political critical stance. It is instrumental, too, to the liberation of the imagination from the chains imposed on different desires and expectations by what the *doxa* presents as universal truths and values. It is, in sum, an instrument for the creation of the largest possible number of speakers and agents of culture as well as for the construction of democratic societies.

By pointing out how, by refusing to chime in with their own time, Dickinson and Whitman have become active agents of change in historical time; by calling our attention to the telos in their work, to their distilling "amazing sense / From Ordinary Meanings – " (Fr 446), Rich points out the movement their work set in motion in the culture. By separating their search for truth from the gendered and time-bound masks they wore to perform their lyric drama in the texture of their poems, Rich brings into play their paradoxical ability to destroy good sense as unique sense, and common sense as given identity.[46]

From the historical and cultural point of view then, Rich's beginner is, to adopt Alain Badiou's philosophical perspective, the individual who, through his/her body of work begins a truth procedure, producing a historical événement. Indeed, it is the people who "respond to" the beginners, who transform what could have been a mere happening in time into a historical/ cultural event. And even if they do not understand the beginners' slanted, indirect truths, those who respond to their words intuit the opening of new horizons. For an event/"événement" is, to quote Badiou, "quelque chose qui n'entre pas dans la loi immédiate des choses" (Éloge de l'amour, 38), something that lies outside the immediate laws that govern things.

Herself a beginner, starting in the 1960s and continuing, with an oxymoronic "wild patience," until her death in 2012, Rich had by 1993 begun to envision a cosmos of human beings whose differences are held together by necessary relations. By claiming Dickinson and Whitman as guides in the exploration of the not yet said, or indirectly said, she recognized that the two poets' work not only created a fracture in the continuity of poetry, in the English language, and in the U.S. historical context, but opened distinctive paths for future poets to follow.[47] By straddling both paths, she could turn to these nineteenth-century poets as to her poetic American home and pursue in her own poetry the individualizing expression *of her experience, aspirations, and ideology*, while concurrently striving for a poetic form that would *refract* social discourse and contribute to critically reorient her time's verbal consciousness.[48] In her poetry and criticism, Rich envisioned an American "home" that poets like Muriel Rukeyser and June Jordan could also inhabit, and that, at the turn of the twenty-first century, is starting to be inhabited by a wide range of poets of different ethnic and linguistic origins.[49] And even though, as Toni Morrison allegorically tells us, the gap that separates the Dreamed American Home and the one lived in is still very visible, the mental dwelling "in Possibility" (Fr 466) remains the way to bridge the gap.[50]

Contributors

ÉRIC ATHENOT is professor of American literature and translation at Université Paris-Est Créteil. He has published articles on Whitman and *Walt Whitman: Poète-cosmos* (2002). He also published the first French translation of the 1855 edition of *Leaves of Grass, Feuilles d'herbe (1855)* (2008), and translations of *Collect* and *An American Primer* (*Manuel d'Amérique*; 2016). In 2007 he launched the Transatlantic Walt Whitman Association with scholars from Europe and the Americas (http://transatlanticwhitman. org/), which brings together students and scholars from around the world for a week every year. His other research involves Emily Dickinson and contemporary American fiction writers such as Richard Powers, Rikki Ducornet, Mary Caponegro, and Gary Lutz.

MARINA CAMBONI is professor of American literature and director of the PhD program in comparative literature at the University of Macerata (Italy). Her publications include *Utopia in the Present Tense: Walt Whitman and the Language of the New World* (1992); *Walt Whitman e la lingua del mondo nuovo* (2004); *Networking Women: Subjects, Places, Links Europe-America: Towards a Rewriting of Cultural History, 1890–1839* (2004); *H. D.'s Poetry: "The Meanings That Words Hide"* (2003); and *H. D.: La donna che divenne il suo nome* (2007). She has translated H. D.'s *Trilogy* (1993). She coedited *Translating America: The Circulation of Narratives, Commodities, and Ideas across the Atlantic* (2011), served as president of the Italian Association of North American Studies, and she founded the Interdepartmental Center of Italian-American Studies at Macerata.

ANDREW DORKIN is a doctoral candidate in the English department at the University at Buffalo, SUNY, where he is completing a dissertation on humor, media theory, and American modernist poetry. He is a former managing editor of the *Emily Dickinson Journal*, and his research interests also extend to twenty-first-century aesthetics and poetics, with forthcoming essays about social media art and contemporary avant-garde children's literature.

VINCENT DUSSOL is an assistant professor at Université Paul-Valéry in Montpellier, France, and a member of EMMA (Etudes Montpelliéraines du Monde Anglophone). He has written about H. D., the Beats (Welch, Whalen), language poets (DiPalma, Gilfillan), Black Mountain (Dorn), Cormac McCarthy, and the epic, a genre on which he edited a collection of essays, *The Epic Expands* (2012). He is the editor of the Profils Américains series published by Presses Universitaires de la Méditerranée and has translated work by Charles Olson, Fanny Howe, Ray DiPalma, and Thomas McGrath, on whose *Letter to an Imaginary Friend* he wrote his dissertation.

BETSY ERKKILA is the Henry Sanborn Noyes Professor of Literature at Northwestern University (Evanston, Illinois). She is the author of *Walt Whitman among the French: Poet and Myth* (1980), *Whitman, the Political Poet* (1988), *The Wicked Sisters: Women Poets, Literary History, and Discord* (1992), and *Mixed Bloods and Other Crosses: Rethinking American Literature from the Revolution to the Culture Wars* (2005). She is currently working on a book entitled *Imagining the Revolution: Literature and Politics in Insurrectionary America*, and received a Guggenheim Fellowship and a National Endowment for the Humanities grant in 2015 to work on this study.

ED FOLSOM is the Roy J. Carver Professor of English at the University of Iowa. He is the editor of the *Walt Whitman Quarterly Review*, codirector of the online *Walt Whitman Archive*, and editor of the Whitman Series at the University of Iowa Press, where so far twenty-three Whitman books have been published. He has been awarded a Guggenheim Fellowship and six grants from the National Endowment for the Humanities. Folsom is the author or editor of twelve books, and his work has been chosen four times as a *Choice* Outstanding Academic Title. He has discussed Whitman on many national radio and television news programs and was featured in the 2008 PBS *American Experience* two-hour film documentary about Whitman.

CHRISTINE GERHARDT is a professor of American studies at the University of Bamberg, Germany. She is the author of *A Place for Humility: Whitman, Dickinson, and the Natural World* (2014) and a monograph on the reconstruction period in American novels, entitled *Rituale des Scheiterns: Die Reconstruction-Periode im amerikanischen Roman* (2002). She coedited *Religion in the United States* (2011), edited the *Handbook of the American Novel of the Nineteenth Century* (2017), and has published essays on Whitman, Dickinson, contemporary American poetry, and ecocriticism.

JAY GROSSMAN teaches eighteenth- and nineteenth-century American literature and culture, the history of the book, and the history of sexuality at Northwestern University (Evanston, Illinois). He is the author of *Reconstituting the American Renaissance: Emerson, Whitman, and the Politics of Representation*, and is at work on a cultural biography of the literary scholar and political activist F. O. Matthiessen.

JENNIFER LEADER is a professor of English at Mt. San Antonio College in Walnut, California, and the author of *Knowing, Seeing, Being: Jonathan Edwards, Emily Dickinson, Marianne Moore, and the American Typological Tradition* (2016).

CRISTANNE MILLER is SUNY Distinguished Professor and Edward H. Butler Professor at the University at Buffalo, SUNY. Her publications on Dickinson include *Emily Dickinson: A Poet's Grammar* (1987), *Comic Power in Emily Dickinson* (coauthored with Suzanne Juhasz and Martha Nell Smith, 1994), *Reading in Time: Dickinson in the Nineteenth Century* (2010), and most recently a new edition of the poems, *Emily Dickinson's Poems: As She Preserved Them* (2016). She now directs the *Marianne Moore Digital Archive* and is working on a project on Dickinson's letters.

MARIANNE NOBLE teaches at American University in Washington, DC. She is the author of *The Masochistic Pleasures of Sentimental Literature* and coeditor of *Emily Dickinson and Philosophy*. Currently, she is working on a book entitled *Sympathy and Human Contact in Antebellum Romantic Literature*, with chapters on Emerson, Whitman, Hawthorne, Douglass, Stowe, and Dickinson. She has served on the editorial boards of *American Literature* and *Legacy*, and the board of the Emily Dickinson International Society.

CÉCILE ROUDEAU is professor of American literature at Université Paris Diderot. She has published *La Nouvelle-Angleterre: Politique d'une écriture: Récits, genre, lieu* (2012), which revisits the notion of "place" in New England regionalist writing, and she has translated into French Jewett's *The Country of the Pointed Firs* (2004) and Melville's late poems (2010). Roudeau has also published numerous essays in French and American journals such as *Revue française d'études américaines,* ENS editions, and *ESQ*. She is currently working on a book provisionally entitled *Fictions of the Commons in 19th-Century American Literature.*

SHIRA WOLOSKY was associate professor of English at Yale University before moving to Hebrew University of Jerusalem, where she is professor of English. Her books include *Emily Dickinson: A Voice of War; Language Mysticism; The Art of Poetry; Feminist Theory across Disciplines: Feminist Community; Poetry and Public Discourse; The Riddles of Harry Potter; Major Voices in Nineteenth Century American Women Poets;* and *Defending Identity* with Natan Sharansky, as well as other writings on literary theory, religion, and poetics. She has been awarded Guggenheim, ACLS, and Fulbright fellowships, fellowships at the Institute for Advanced Studies in Princeton and Israel, a Tikvah fellowship at the New York University Law School, and Drue Heinz Visiting Professorships at Oxford University.

Notes

Introduction

1. Agnieszka Salska, *Whitman and Dickinson: Poetry of the Central Consciousness* (Philadelphia: University of Pennsylvania Press, 1985); and Christine Gerhardt, *A Place for Humility: Whitman, Dickinson, and the Natural World* (Iowa City: University of Iowa Press, 2014).

2. Emily Dickinson, letter to T. W. Higginson, April 25, 1862 (*L* 261).

3. The conference was held on March 12–13, 2015, two months after the terrorist attacks carried out against the French satirical magazine *Charlie Hebdo* (on January 7), ambushes against police officers outside Paris (January 7 and 8), and the hostage crisis at a kosher store near Porte de Vincennes (January 9). The death toll was twenty people—eight journalists, one visitor, one cleaning employee, and two policemen at *Charlie Hebdo*; one police officer near a synagogue outside Paris; four hostages at the kosher store; three ISIS-affiliated terrorists; and a dozen wounded. This wave of attacks led to expressions of global solidarity summed up in the catchword "Je suis Charlie" (I am Charlie) punctuating vigils around the world. On January 10–11, so-called republican marches saw over four million people and two dozen heads of state march in various French cities and Paris.

4. Walt Whitman, "Walt Whitman's Caution," in *Leaves of Grass* 1860, *WWA* 401.

5. There is one exception to this rule: Dorkin and Miller's essay was presented by Miller only as brief notes in a roundtable at the conference.

Rethinking the (Non)Convergence of Dickinson and Whitman

1. Ed Folsom, "Transcendental Poetics: Emerson, Higginson, and the Rise of Whitman and Dickinson," in *The Oxford Handbook of Transcendentalism*, ed. Joel Myerson, Sandra Harbert Petrulionis, and Laura Dassow Walls (New York: Oxford University Press, 2010), 263–90.

2. William Michael Rossetti, ed., *American Poems* (London: Ward, Lock, 187-).

3. Adrienne Rich, "Beginners," in the *Kenyon Review*, n.s. 15 (Summer 1993): 12–15,

and the essay was reprinted in her *What Is Found There: Notebooks on Poetry and Politics* (New York: Norton, 2003), 92–101.

4. Thomas Wentworth Higginson, "Letter to a Young Contributor," *Atlantic Monthly* 9 (April 1862): 401–11.

5. Ralph Waldo Emerson, "Letter to Walt Whitman," July 21, 1855, in Whitman, *Leaves of Grass* (New York: [Fowler and Wells], 1856), 345; *WWA*.

6. Thomas Wentworth Higginson, "Emily Dickinson's Letters," *Atlantic Monthly* 68 (October 1891); reprinted in Howard N. Meyer, ed., *The Magnificent Activist: The Writings of Thomas Wentworth Higginson* (Cambridge, MA: DaCapo, 2000), 545.

7. I am summarizing here my arguments in "Transcendental Poetics."

8. Emerson, "Letter to Whitman," 345.

9. Higginson, "Emily Dickinson's Letters," in *The Magnificent Activist*, 545.

10. Higginson's involvement in getting Dickinson into print is not a simple story, of course, and his role in encouraging or discouraging Dickinson is an ongoing source of contention in Dickinson criticism. Others tried getting Dickinson into print while Higginson was advising her against publication, including Susan Dickinson, who probably was responsible for sending her poems to Samuel Bowles at the *Springfield Daily Republican* (where five were published), and Helen Hunt Jackson, as we will see later in this essay. Dickinson's sister Lavinia pushed hard for publication after Emily's death, and she was the first to enlist Higginson's help. When Higginson was asked by Mabel Loomis Todd to aid her in editing the first volume of Dickinson's work, he at first resisted, though he did ultimately engage wholeheartedly in the editing, joining Todd in adding titles, altering lines, omitting stanzas, and arranging the poems in set categories. See Brenda Wineapple, *White Heat: The Friendship of Emily Dickinson & Thomas Wentworth Higginson* (New York: Knopf, 2008), 271–87, for a detailed investigation of Higginson's and Todd's work on the first volume of Dickinson's poems. While it is impossible now to determine which one of the editorial duo was responsible for the many alterations to Dickinson's poems, I agree with Wineapple that Todd's correspondence indicates that it was Higginson who initiated the major changes ("Higginson grouped the poems thematically under headings"; "Higginson wanted titles, and Mrs. Todd agreed" [280, 283]). Higginson's lifelong affinity with women's rights and with women authors made him a person that the group around Dickinson—including Susan, Lavinia, and particularly Mabel—were comfortable with, and they welcomed the influence he wielded in literary circles that helped to get her published and publicized. Right down to his insistence on including Todd as a coeditor, and indeed having her name appear first on the title page ("It is proper that yr name shld come first as you did the hardest part of the work," he wrote to her), Higginson demonstrated a positive collaborative spirit (see Wineapple, *White Heat*, 285).

11. Emerson to Higginson, May 16, 1849, in *The Selected Letters of Ralph Waldo Emerson*, ed. Joel Myerson (New York: Columbia University Press, 1997), 351.

12. Thomas Wentworth Higginson, "Sappho," *Atlantic Monthly* (July 1871); in *The Magnificent Activist*, ed. Meyer, 497.

13. For an extended treatment of Emerson's remarkable mentoring of mostly male poets, see David Dowling, *Emerson's Protégés: Mentoring and Marketing Transcendentalism's Future* (New Haven, CT: Yale University Press, 2014). Dowling examines in detail Emerson's mentoring of Margaret Fuller, Henry David Thoreau, Christopher Cranch, Samuel Gray Ward, Ellery Channing, Jones Very, and Charles King Newcomb.

14. Walt Whitman, *After All, Not to Create Only* (Boston: Roberts Brothers, 1871).

15. See Raymond L. Kilgour, *Messrs. Roberts Brothers* (Ann Arbor: University of Michigan Press, 1952), 107–8.

16. Niles knew when he took on the Whitman project just how controversial the poet was. "After All, Not to Create Only" was widely derided in the press coverage of Whitman's reading it to the American Institute Exhibition audience, and, when it became known the Roberts Brothers were going to publish it, the mockery continued. Ben Perley Poore wrote in the *Boston Journal* that the recent news that Tennyson had invited Whitman to England for a visit had led to a fear "that the latter intends to read aloud to the unfortunate Laureate that catalogue of American products and trades that he picked up in the American Institute and blindly labeled a poem," now to be published by Roberts Brothers "for the dementation of the American public." See "Waifs from Washington: Literary Notes," *Boston Journal* (October 7, 1871), supplement.

17. See Whitman's explanation of his plan for a new book in "Preface, 1872," in Walt Whitman, *Complete Poetry and Collected Prose*, ed. Justin Kaplan (New York: Library of America, 1982), 1000–1005.

18. See Edwin Haviland Miller, ed., *Walt Whitman: The Correspondence*, 6 vols. (New York: New York University Press, 1961–77), 2:244–45n, 345n. Whitman wrote to an unidentified correspondent in 1875 that "I publish & shall sell the volumes myself, for two good reasons. No established publisher in the country will print my books, & during the last three years of my illness & helplessness every one of the three successive book agents I have had in N. Y. has embezzled the proceeds" (*Correspondence*, 2:345).

19. Whitman wrote to Roberts Brothers in September 1871 that the publication of *After All* would be "plain sailing, if you have a careful printer & proof reader." Whitman went on to propose that "an ordinary 12 mo would be best," sent a sample page to give "my idea of size of page": "As to size of type for the poem, if English solid would not be too large, I would like to have that." No detail was overlooked: "In binding let the edges remain uncut, & bind in the kind of paper according to sample. See sample of title on cover. Send the revised proofs to me by mail." He even put a positive spin on the parodic and dismissive reviews the poem had received in numerous newspapers: "That the papers have freely printed & criticized the piece will much help, as it awakes interest & curiosity, & many will want to have it in good form to keep." See *Correspondence*, 2:139.

20. In 1889 Whitman's then-publisher David McKay had managed to purchase some unbound sheets of *After All* and had them bound up. He sent one over to Whitman for his signature, but Whitman demurred since he had already made sure his name was generously apparent: "I do not think I need to sign it: it does not need signing. There is the name on the title page—then here it is inside again. I do not like to triplicate it—then

triplicate the triplicate." As he examined the book, he expressed his admiration for it: "It is wonderful neat—wonderful! How healthy the print!—the big clean type! Why, yes, it is a revelation to me, also—a new book to me. . . . It did not sell—did not sell at all. Roberts must have issued about a thousand." And turning to the pictorial cover—"This is my design—I conceived it—it has a good familiar look, after a long absence. The whole book as it is here commends itself to me"; Horace Traubel, *With Walt Whitman in Camden*, 9 vols. (various publishers, 1906–96), 6:48.

21. One of the most illuminating discussions of Thomas Niles and the Roberts Brothers in relation to Dickinson is still Richard B. Sewall's chapter on Helen Hunt Jackson in his *The Life of Emily Dickinson* (New York: Farrar, Straus and Giroux, 1980), 577–92.

22. For background on the "No Name" series, see Kilgour, *Messrs. Roberts Brothers*, 137–50, 172–74, and 188–90; and for an incisive recent examination of the series, see Lara Langer Cohen and Meredith McGill, "The Perils of Authorship: Literary Property and Nineteenth-Century American Fiction," in the *Oxford History of the Novel in English*, vol. 5: *The American Novel to 1870*, ed. J. Gerald Kennedy and Leland Person (New York: Oxford University Press, 2014), 195–212.

23. Thomas Niles to Dickinson, March 1883, quoted in Sewall, *Life of Emily Dickinson*, 586. The previous year, in April 1882, Niles had written to Dickinson to tell her that Helen Hunt Jackson "once told me that she wished you could be induced to publish a volume of poems. . . . I wish also that you could" (Sewall, *Life of Emily Dickinson*, 585).

24. Helen Hunt Jackson wrote to Dickinson in April 1878 about the allure of the "No Name" series and offered to copy Dickinson's poems out in her own hand so that no one would know who wrote them; Jackson "promise[d] never to tell any one, not even the publishers, whose the poems are. Could you not bear this much of publicity? Only you and I would recognize the poems" (Sewall, *Life of Emily Dickinson*, 582). Sewall speculates that Dickinson's decision to continue sending poems to Niles after her single poem appeared in the "No Name" *Masque of Poets* "may have been" a "late bid for publication during the time of Mrs. Jackson's enthusiasm and the general interest in the No Name Series" (584).

25. In making this claim, I realize I am eliding a growing body of critical literature on Dickinson that argues in compelling ways that Dickinson actively sought to become a manuscript poet who might achieve immortality only in posthumous publication and thus wanted to defer publication of her work. See, for example, Mary Loeffelholz, "Really Indigenous Productions: Emily Dickinson, Josiah Holland, and Nineteenth-Century Popular Verse," in *A Companion to Emily Dickinson*, ed. Martha Nell Smith and Mary Loeffelholz (Malden, MA: Blackwell, 2008), 184–204, where Loeffelholz demonstrates just how pervasive the imagery of the (usually female) manuscript poet was in literature that Dickinson read: "Dickinson learned from print culture how to be an unpublished manuscript poet" (196). The whole question of whether or not Dickinson actually wanted her poems published in her lifetime remains a matter of active and illuminating debate.

26. Niles wrote to Dickinson in late 1878, thanking her for her "valuable contribution" to *Masque*, and told her that her poem, "for want of a known sponsor[,] Mr Emerson has

generally had to father" (Sewall, *Life of Emily Dickinson*, 583). "Success" was Dickinson's last published poem (1878) and her first in twelve years. It is worth nothing that the poem first appeared in the Brooklyn *Daily Union* in April 1864, where, interestingly, Whitman was regularly publishing his dispatches from the Civil War, one of them seven months before Dickinson's poem appeared, one seven months after. Just as we can be nearly sure that Dickinson read Whitman's poems in the *Atlantic*, so can we be almost as sure Whitman would have encountered her "Success" poem, anonymously, in the *Daily Union*. The Brooklyn *Daily Union*, then, becomes the earliest of a very select group of publishing enterprises (including Roberts Brothers, the *Atlantic*, *Harper's Monthly*, and the *Springfield Daily Republican*) to print work by both Whitman and Dickinson during their lifetimes.

27. Lathrop (1851–1898) edited the Boston *Courier* starting in 1879, lived in Concord, Massachusetts, until the mid-1880s, wrote poetry, fiction, and journalism, edited Rose Hawthorne's works, wrote a popular book about Nathaniel Hawthorne, and adapted *The Scarlet Letter* as an opera, produced in New York City in 1896. His novel *Afterglow* was the seventh book to appear in the No Name series (see Kilgour, *Messrs. Roberts Brothers*, 147).

28. Lathrop to Burroughs, May 19, 1877, in Traubel, *With Walt Whitman in Camden*, 1:16–17. Whitman was intrigued with this letter and commented that it was "touched with spiritual tragedy," demonstrating how "aristocratic" college education creates "difficulties" for those who go there, "crawl[ing] serpent-like out from college walls into the general world" and making it "impossible for such a man, fine as he is, fine as his letter is, to really build up and round out a capacious career" (1:15).

29. Lathrop to Whitman, April 20, 1878, in Traubel, *With Walt Whitman in Camden*, 2:315–16; also available in the "Letters" section of the *WWA*. Lathrop's suggestion that Whitman should submit something like "O Captain!" released in Whitman a kind of rage about how that poem was latched onto by the conventionally minded. Responding both to Lathrop's request and to a newspaper squib that had suggested that "if Walt Whitman had written a volume of My Captains instead of filling a scrapbasket with waste and calling it a book the world would be better off today and Walt Whitman would have some excuse for living," Whitman responded this way: "I'm honest when I say, damn My Captain and all the My Captains in my book! This is not the first time I have been irritated into saying I'm almost sorry I ever wrote the poem. It has reasons for being—it is a ballad—it sings, sings, in a certain strain with a certain motive—but as for being the best, the very best—God help me! what can the worst be like? A whole volume of My Captains instead of a scrap-basket! Well, that's funny, very funny: it don't leave me much room for escape. *I* say that if I'd written a whole volume of My Captains I'd deserve to be spanked and sent to bed with the world's compliments—which would be generous treatment, considering what a lame duck book such a book would have been!" (Traubel, *With Walt Whitman in Camden*, 2:304).

30. See Walt Whitman to Francis Fisher Browne, November 23, 1885, in Miller, *Walt Whitman: The Correspondence*, 6:31; and Ed Folsom, "The Mystical Ornithologist and

the Iowa Tufthunter: Two Unpublished Whitman Letters and Some Identifications," *Walt Whitman Quarterly Review* 1 (June 1983): 18–29.

31. Emily Dickinson to T. W. Higginson, April 25, 1862, *L* 404.

32. There has been some speculation about whether the editorials attacking Whitman reflect Bowles's view or Holland's view, with Holland generally considered the likely culprit, since he continued his attacks on Whitman when he left the *Republican* to start *Scribner's Monthly*. See Walter H. Eitner, "Emily Dickinson's Awareness of Whitman: A Reappraisal," *Walt Whitman Review* 22 (September 1976): 113.

33. "'Leaves of Grass'—Smut in Them," *Springfield Daily Republican* (June 16, 1860), 4. Available on the *WWA*.

34. "Literary Nonsense," *Springfield Daily Republican* (March 24, 1860), 4.

35. Adding to Dickinson's confusion when she read the *Daily Republican* review of "Bardic Symbols" would have been the newspaper's conflation of Whitman's "nonsense" with Emerson's poetic nonsense in a poem like "Brahma." For Lowell's role, see William Pannapacker, *Revised Lives: Walt Whitman and Nineteenth-Century Authorship* (New York: Routledge, 2004), 74–77. Pannapacker's third chapter, "'He Not Only Objected to My Book, He Objected to Me': Walt Whitman, James Russell Lowell, and the Rhetoric of Exclusion" (49–104), offers a detailed and nuanced reading of the Lowell-Whitman relationship.

36. See Whitman to Lowell, January 20, 1860, in Miller, *Correspondence*, 1:47–48, where Whitman reluctantly agrees to the omission of the lines "(See from my dead lips the ooze exuding at last! / See the prismatic colors glistening and rolling!)," lines that (so Whitman told Lowell) created "an effect in the piece which I clearly feel, but cannot clearly define." On Emerson's influence on Lowell's decision to publish "Bardic Symbols," see Pannapacker, *Revised Lives*, 75; and Gay Wilson Allen, *The Solitary Singer: A Critical Biography of Walt Whitman* (New York: New York University Press, 1967), 238.

37. See Traubel, *With Walt Whitman in Camden*, 2:21–23, for correspondence and commentary laying out Emerson's intervention.

38. Eitner, "Emily Dickinson's Awareness of Whitman," 111–15, offered in the mid-1970s a very full accounting of the number of places Dickinson likely encountered Whitman's poetry, from his two appearances in the *Atlantic* (1860 with "Bardic Symbols," then in 1869 with "Proud Music of the Storm") to Higginson's negative assessment of Whitman in the *Atlantic* in 1867, to the reviews in the *Springfield Daily Republican* (including a reprinted negative review that quoted extensive passages of "Song of Myself"), to the *Republican*'s reprinting of "After All, Not to Create Only" in 1871 (just before Roberts Brothers published the book version) and "Song of the Universal" in 1874, to five Whitman poems published in *Harper's* in the late 1870s and early 1880s.

39. Ruth Miller, *The Poetry of Emily Dickinson* (Middletown, CT: Wesleyan University Press, 1968), suggests that Dickinson's numerous occasions of encountering Whitman's poetry may have led to her being influenced by it; and Karl Keller, in *The Only Kangaroo among the Beauty: Emily Dickinson and America* (Baltimore: Johns Hopkins University

Press, 1979), with its ninth chapter, "The Sweet Wolf Within: Emily Dickinson and Walt Whitman," offers the most sustained suggestion of affinity and influence. Agnieska Salska, in *Walt Whitman and Emily Dickinson: Poetry of the Central Consciousness* (Philadelphia: University of Pennsylvania Press, 1985), considers the poets in relation to "the structure of each poet's imagination"; and recently Christine Gerhardt has put the poets in a dynamic relationship with each other by examining their responses to the nature writing of their time (*A Place for Humility: Whitman, Dickinson, and the Natural World* [Iowa City: University of Iowa Press, 2014]). Other critics have raised the issue in various more tentative ways; see, for example, Vivian R. Pollak, *The Erotic Whitman* (Berkeley: University of California Press, 2000), 188–89.

40. Thomas Wentworth Higginson, "Literature as an Art," in *Atlantic Essays* (Boston: J. R. Osgood, 1871), 44. Originally in the *Atlantic Monthly* 20 (December 1867).

41. The essay as reprinted in *Magnificent Activist* has been retitled "Emily Dickinson." The original essay appeared in *Atlantic Monthly* 68 (October 1891): 444–56.

42. The passage Traubel quotes is from *The Critic* 16 (September 19, 1891): 141, where it appeared as part of the popular column called "The Lounger" that commented on literary news and personalities, and was written by Jeanette Gilder, the coeditor, who was a great supporter of Whitman and published his work frequently. The passage was reprinted in *The Literary World* 22 (October 10, 1891): 360, where the writer suggests that "prosets" would be preferable to "proets" as the new "portmanteau" word to describe the likes of Whitman and Dickinson.

43. Remarkably, this moment has until now gone without comment, perhaps because Dickinson's name is not included in the otherwise comprehensive index for this volume of Traubel's memoirs of Whitman.

44. Howells's "The Strange *Poems of Emily Dickinson*" is reprinted in *The Recognition of Emily Dickinson,* ed. Caesar R. Blake and Carlton F. Wells (Ann Arbor: University of Michigan Press, 1968), 18–24. Higginson published an earlier article, "An Open Portfolio," in *The Christian Union*, September 25, 1890 (also reprinted in *Recognition*, 3–10), which was the first piece to introduce Dickinson's poetry to a wide national readership. It printed fourteen of her poems and characterized them in oddly Whitmanian imagery—as leaves of grass: "Her verses are in most cases like poetry plucked up by the roots; we have them with earth, stones, and dew adhering, and must accept them as they are" (*Recognition*, 10). Whitman had a kind of love/hate relationship with *The Christian Union*, and he certainly read and commented on articles that appeared there during his final years, expressing curiosity about the publication's religious affiliations (see Traubel, *With Walt Whitman in Camden*, 3:277). His disciple John Burroughs wrote pieces about Whitman for the *Union*, once telling the poet: "It is surprising how much heresy these papers can stand. I think they secretly like it" (*With Walt Whitman*, 8:20). It is possible, then, that as early as September 1890 Whitman had become aware of Dickinson's poetry by reading the Higginson *Christian Union* article.

45. Howells had sent a reminiscence of his original meeting with Whitman to Horace

Traubel just a few months after his Dickinson piece appeared (Traubel, *With Walt Whitman in Camden*, 8:386). Whitman followed Howells's career carefully and talked with Traubel about when Howells left *Harper's* at the end of 1891 (*With Walt Whitman*, 9:343), and Howells wrote a generous letter to Traubel in January 1892 in which he called Whitman "the great friend of human nature" (*With Walt Whitman*, 9:355); he was generally thought of as a good friend and supporter of Whitman (*With Walt Whitman*, 9:402), and he gave financial support to the poet in his final months (*With Walt Whitman*, 9:438, 565). Whitman and Traubel frequently mention him in the months following the publication of his Dickinson article.

46. Whitman's "Death's Valley" in fact did not appear until a few weeks after the poet's death, in the April 1892 issue of *Harper's*, nearly three years after it was accepted for publication; see Traubel, *With Walt Whitman in Camden*, 8:68–69.

47. Whitman's use of "lady's man" here is evocative. Both he and Higginson questioned the other's masculinity, but the term may also indicate his awareness that Higginson was very much a supporter of and mentor to women writers—and was especially, as Whitman was now finding out, the most vocal proponent of Dickinson.

48. For Whitman's one experience of rejection by the *Atlantic*, see Traubel, *With Walt Whitman in Camden*, 2:213–14.

49. "Whitman's Actual American Position," *West Jersey Press* (January 26, 1876), reprinted in *Walt Whitman's Workshop*, ed. Clifton J. Furness (Cambridge, MA: Harvard University Press, 1928), 245–46. Robert Scholnick, in "Whitman and the Magazines: Some Documentary Evidence," *American Literature* 44 (May 1972): 222–46, offers a full investigation of Whitman's surprisingly positive experience with the *Atlantic* and other magazines and analyzes the reasons for Whitman's negative characterizations of his relationship with what the poet called in the *West Jersey Press* article the "orthodox American authors, publishers and editors," with their "determined denial, disgust and scorn" that "have certainly wrecked the life of their author."

50. William Douglas O'Connor, *Three Tales* (Boston: Houghton Mifflin, 1892). Whitman's preface is on pp. iii–vii.

51. Horace E. Scudder, "Whitman," *Atlantic Monthly* 69 (June 1892): 831–35. Scudder (1838–1902), in addition to editing the *Atlantic*, was a noted children's author, wrote a biography of Lowell, and was the author of one of the earliest standard textbook histories of the United States (*A History of the United States* [1884]). Whitman was curious about Scudder, and when it was announced in 1890 that Scudder was to take over the editorship of the *Atlantic*, Traubel reports that Whitman asked him immediately "what did I know of Scudder &c?" (Traubel, *With Walt Whitman in Camden*, 6:483).

52. "Literary Affairs in Boston," *Book Buyer*, n.s. 8 (November 1891): 417; reprinted in *Emily Dickinson's Reception in the 1890s: A Documentary History*, ed. Willis J. Buckingham (Pittsburgh, PA: University of Pittsburgh Press, 1989), 221.

"Sickly Abstractions" and the Poetic Concrete

1. WPP 1855, Specimen Days, 950.

2. I freely translate Friedrich Hölderlin's question, "Wozu Dichter in dürftiger Zeit?" in his "Bread and Wine" ("Brot und Wein"), in *Odes and Elegies*, 1801, Projekt Gutenberg-DE, http://gutenberg.spiegel.de/buch/friedrich-h-262/168.

3. The Civil War was a war with no name, or more accurately, a war with more than one name. See, for example, Michael P. Musick, "Civil War Records: A War by Any Other Name," *Prologue Magazine* 27, no. 2 (Summer 1995): 149; and John M. Coski, "The War between the Names," *North and South* 8, no. 7 (2006): 62–71.

4. David Armitage, "What's the Big Idea? Intellectual History and the *Longue Durée*," *History of European Ideas* 38, no. 4 (2012): 493–507; 500.

5. Francis Lieber, *Instructions for the Government of Armies of the United States in the Field* (Washington: Government Printing Office, 1898), 42.

6. James MacPherson, *The War That Forged a Nation: Why the Civil War Still Matters* (Oxford: Oxford University Press, 2015), 10; emphasis in original unless otherwise noted.

7. Ibid., 6.

8. Jacques Rancière, "The Politics of Literature," *SubStance* 33, no. 1 (2004): 10–24; 10.

9. "The dream of humanity, the vaunted Union we thought so strong, so impregnable—lo! it seems already smash'd like a china plate" (*WPP* 734).

10. She wrote in a letter to Thomas Wentworth Higginson: "My Business is Circumference" (*L* 268).

11. In Alexander Gardner's sketchbook, he refers to the Battle of Gettysburg and, more particularly, to Timothy H. O'Sullivan's famous photograph captioned *A Harvest of Death*, from Gettysburg, Pennsylvania, in these terms: "Swept down without preparation, the shattered bodies fall in all conceivable positions. . . . Around is scattered *the litter of the battlefield*, accoutrements, ammunition, rags, cups, and canteens, crackers, haversacks &c., and letters that may tell the name of the owner although the majority will surely be buried unknown by strangers, and in a strange land" (Gardner, *Photographic Sketch Book of the War*, vol. 1 [Washington: Philip & Solomons, 1866], https://www.loc.gov/item/01021785/, 79; my emphasis). My understanding of the "Real," in this essay, is indebted to Lacanian theory. I capitalize the Real to signal that I am not referring to historical facts (what may loosely be referred to as "reality") so much as what eludes the Symbolic, what resists the symbolic order of discourse, the norms of representation. The "Real," as I understand it here, is what is left out of language as norm. Its very definition forbids its being captured within a form; it emerges as a remainder or supplement; what is left out of formalization, or what the poetic form can never contain. See Jacques *Lacan, Ecrits*, trans. Bruce Fink (1966, 1970, 1971; New York: Norton, 2006).

12. On Whitman's years in Washington and his role as a "nurse," see, for example, Peter Coviello's introduction to his edition of *Walt Whitman's "Memoranda During the War"* (Oxford: Oxford University Press, 2004); Roy Morris, Jr., *The Better Angel: Walt Whitman in the Civil War* (New York: Oxford University Press, 2000); Betsy Erkkila,

Whitman, the Political Poet (New York: Oxford University Press, 1989); and Ted Geno-
ways, "Memoranda of a Year (1863): Whitman in Washington, D.C." *Virginia Quarterly
Review* 23, no. 3 (2006): 155–73.

13. Cristanne Miller, *Reading in Time: Emily Dickinson in the Nineteenth Century*
(Amherst: University of Massachusetts Press, 2012), 147. See Miller's "Reading and Writing
the Civil War" in *Reading in Time*, 147–75; Shira Wolosky, *Emily Dickinson: A Voice of
War* (New Haven, CT: Yale University Press, 1984); and for a review of recent scholarship
on the subject, Faith Barrett, "Public Selves and Private Spheres: Studies of Emily Dickinson and the Civil War, 1984–2007," *Emily Dickinson Journal* 16, no. 1 (2007): 92–104.

14. See in particular Miller's chapter "Reading and Writing the Civil War" in *Reading
in Time* and Barrett's "Addresses to a Divided Nation...," in *To Fight Aloud Is Very Brave:
American Poetry and the Civil War* (Amherst: University of Massachusetts Press, 2012).

15. Miller, *Reading in Time*, 160.

16. "As in sleep – all Hue forgotten – / Tenets – put behind – / Death's large – Democratic fingers / Rub away the Brand – " ("Color – Caste – Denomination," Fr 836).

17. "The Soul has Bandaged moments –" (Fr 360). For a further analysis of Dickinson's
poems as thought experiments, see Jed Deppman, *Trying to Think with Emily Dickinson*
(Amherst: University of Massachusetts Press, 2008).

18. "Fall" is the other name of "autumn" in American English. As Éric Athenot has
aptly pointed out to me, the Fall (in the Christian meaning of the term) may be one of
the encrypted referents of "it" in the poem. Understood as the antitype of the Fall, i.e.,
that which condemns us to see through a glass darkly, the Civil War forbade any possible
adjustment of signifier and signified. Poetry itself was doomed to periphrasis, metaphors,
similes, that is, to writing *around* the thing never to attain it, never to put a name on "it."

19. Jacques Derrida, *Spectres of Marx: The State of the Debt, the Work of Mourning
and the New International*, trans. Peggy Kamuf (New York: Routledge, 1994); Derrida,
Spectres de Marx (Paris: Galilée, 1993), 5.

20. "The Figures I have seen / Set orderly, for Burial" (Fr 355).

21. "Le réel l'impasse de la formalisation" (Jacques Lacan), qtd. in Alain Badiou,
À la recherche du réel perdu (Paris: Fayard, 2015), 28.

22. See *Julie* Neveux, *John Donne: Le Sentiment dans la langue* (Paris: Éditions Rue
d'Ulm, 2013). Neveux's argument (from the English abstract of her dissertation, revised
for publication) is that "the 'concrete' is the result of indirect—implied, unsemiotized—
lyricism, a form of lyricism used by the poet when s/he is emotionally implicated in a
speech situation. The speaker's expressivity relies on a temporal decategorization enabling
him to (implicitly) claim that generalized (abstract) terms are insufficient to articulate
the specificity of his own sentimental experience" (http://www.paris-sorbonne.fr/article/
mme-julie-neveux-l-expression). See John Donne, *Devotions upon Emergent Occasions*
(Cambridge: Cambridge University Press, 1923).

23. Badiou's use of "diagonals" allows him to conceive of oppositions in a non-
dialectical way. Apropos Georgio Agamben's *The Coming Community*, for example,
Badiou explains how diagonalization enables one to go beyond, or between, dogmatic

oppositions without resorting to a dialectic resolution. A diagonal regime of thinking, therefore, allows us to actualize binaries anew, to reinvigorate them without losing them or having to frontally oppose them. See Badiou, "Intervention dans le cadre du Collège international de philosophie sur le livre de Giorgio Agamben: *La Communauté qui vient: Théorie de la singularité quelconque*" (transcribed by François Duvert, http://www.entretemps.asso.fr/Badiou/Agamben.htm).

24. "I felt my life with both my hands" (Fr 357).

25. For an analysis of this poem, see, for example, Faith Barrett, "Introduction," in *"Words for the Hour": A New Anthology of Civil War Poetry*, ed. Faith Barrett and Cristanne Miller (Amherst: University of Massachusetts Press, 2005).

26. I am referring here to the already quoted "staples, in the song" in stanza 4 of "The Soul has Bandaged moments – " (Fr 360).

27. This version of the poem is not included in Kaplan's edition. See the 1860 *Leaves of Grass* on *WWA* (Boston: Thayer and Eldridge, 1860–61), 185; my emphasis.

28. This passage was deleted when the bulk of the *Memoranda during the War* was inserted in *Specimen Days*. See Walt Whitman, *Memoranda during the War* (Camden, NJ: Author's publication, 1876), *WWA*.

29. "The Real War Will Never Get in the Books" is the title of the closing section of *Specimen Days* devoted to the Civil War and reproduced (with variants) from Whitman's *Memoranda during the War* (*WPP* 802).

30. Walt Whitman to Ralph Waldo Emerson, January 17, 1863 (*WWA*).

31. The 1855 version of these two lines reads, "All goes onward and onward . . . and nothing collapses, / And to die is different from what any one supposed, and luckier" (*WPP* 1855, 17).

32. To quote from J. K. Barnes, surgeon general of the U.S. Army in his preface to *The Medical and Surgical History of the War of the Rebellion*: "To facilitate the collection and preservation of all important information, medical officers serving with regiments in the field were furnished, in January 1864, with a compact and optable Register of Sick and Wounded" (Barnes, "Prefatory," *The Medical and Surgical History of the War of the Rebellion (1861–65)*, part I [Washington: Government Printing Office, 1870], iii–ix; iv).

33. One example among many is the table below, analyzed by the assistant surgeon general of the U.S. Army in his introduction to the above-quoted *Medical and Surgical History of the War of the Rebellion*:

	Present.	Absent.	Aggregate
July 1, 1861	169,480	849	170,329
January 1, 1862	507,333	46,159	553,492
" 1, 1863	676,175	212,859	889,034
" 1, 1864	540,643	237,650	778,293
" 1, 1865	523,536	309,395	832,931
March 31, 1865	554,720	294,351	849,071
Average mean strength†	544,704	196,803	741,507

"The *total number* of deaths of this class has been stated above at 265,265. Of this number, however, the death registers of the Surgeon General's Office show that 4,553 died subsequently to June 30, 1865, which would leave a *total* of 260,712 deaths from the outbreak of the War to that time, being at the rate of 65,178 deaths annually, or 88 per 1,000 of *average aggregate* mean strength" (J. J. Woodward, "Introduction," *The Medical and Surgical History of the War of the Rebellion (1861–65),* part 1 [Washington: Government Printing Office, 1870], xiii–xliii;xl–xli).

34. "What income he got came from working a few hours a day in the Corcoran Building as a copyist in the office of the army paymaster, Major Lyman Hapgood" (Coviello, "Introduction," xx). On Whitman and bureaucracy, see also Kenneth M. Price, "'Whitman, Walt, Clerk': The Poet Was a Seer of Democracy and Bureaucracy," *Prologue Magazine* 43, no. 4 (Winter 2011).

35. Christine Savinel, "La Pensée de la communauté chez Emily Dickinson," in *Littérature et politique en Nouvelle-Angleterre,* ed. T. Constantinesco and Antoine Traisnel, in *Actes de la Recherche à l'ENS* 7 (Paris: Éditions Rue d'Ulm, 2011), 134.

36. "What is it then between us?" the poetic persona famously asks in the poem "Crossing Brooklyn Ferry" (*WPP* 310). On this poem and the importance of the communality of experience in Whitman, see Peter Coviello's *Intimacy in America: Dreams of Affiliation in Antebellum Literature* (Minneapolis: University of Minnesota Press, 2005).

37. To give a few examples from Whitman's *Memoranda during the War* (Camden, NJ: Author's publication, 1876), *WWA:* "numbers of wounded" (7); "the dead and wounded" (9); "the scene of the wounded" (13); "a large lot of wounded" (19); "a train of wounded" (35).

38. That the war was fought for an abstraction can be found twice in Whitman's *Complete Prose:* "This war for a bare idea and abstraction" ("America's Bulk Average," in *WPP* 1323); "We have seen the alacrity with which the American born populace, the peaceablest and most good-natured race in the world . . . sprang, at the first tap of the drum, to arms—not for gain, nor even glory, nor to repel invasion—but for an emblem, a mere abstraction—for the life, *the safety of the flag*" (*Democratic Vistas, WPP* 968–69). As has already been suggested in the course of this essay, abstraction is a contested issue during the war—it is both what the war challenged and what it had no choice but to rely on. The negative connotations of both these later occurrences of the term in Whitman's collected prose may also be accounted for by the a posteriori reconsideration of the slaughter that the war produced.

Figural Mirrors in Biblical Traditions

1. Kenneth M. Price, ed., *Walt Whitman: The Contemporary Reviews* (New York: Cambridge University Press, 1996). See Betsy Erkkila, *Whitman the Political Poet* (New York: Oxford University Press, 1988), 238.

2. The classic elaboration of typology is Augustine's, in *On Christian Doctrine* (and, for example, *Confessions* 7.10.16). Modern discussion is reinitiated in Erich Auerbach, "Figura," in *Scenes from the Drama of European Literature* (New York: Meridian Books, 1958), 29–40.

3. Sacvan Bercovitch elaborated this American Puritan typology as historical and communal in *Puritan Origins of the American Self* (New Haven, CT: Yale University Press, 1975). There are of course many discussions of typology in America. My own can be found more fully in Shira Wolosky, *Poetry and Public Discourse* (New York: Palgrave Macmillan, 2012).

4. The term *manifest destiny* was introduced by John Thomas O'Sullivan concerning the annexation of Texas and other border disputes in the Northwest Territory; he claimed "the right of our manifest destiny to overspread and to possess the whole of the continent which Providence has given us for the development of the great experiment of liberty and federated self-government entrusted to us" (*New York Morning News*, December 27, 1845).

5. Classic discussions include Ernest Lee Tuveson, *Redeemer Nation* (Chicago: University of Chicago Press, 1968); and James Moorhead, *American Apocalypse: Yankee Protestants and the Civil War, 1860–1869* (New Haven, CT: Yale University Press, 1978).

6. The source of sacramental definition goes back to Augustine, for example in *On the Catechizing of the Uninstructed*, chapter 26:50 (http://www.newadvent.org/fathers/1303.htm). "On the subject of the sacrament, indeed, which he receives, it is first to be well impressed upon his notice that the signs of divine things are, it is true, things visible, but that the invisible things themselves are also honored in them, and that that species, which is then sanctified by the blessing, is therefore not to be regarded merely in the way in which it is regarded in any common use. And thereafter he ought to be told what is also signified by the form of words to which he has listened, and what in him is seasoned by that (spiritual grace) of which this material substance presents the emblem" (*De Catechizandis Rudibus*, 26.50). This became the basis for the definition of "outward visible sign" from the Council of Trent (1545–63), and was then adopted into the Thirty-Nine Articles of the Anglican Church Number 90, which the American pilgrims accepted.

7. Drew Faust, *This Republic of Suffering: Death and the American Civil War* (New York: Vintage, 2009), xiii, 188–89. See Shira Wolosky, *Emily Dickinson: A Voice of War* (New Haven, CT: Yale University Press, 1984), 44–45, 64–70.

8. Alice Fahs, *The Imagined Civil War* (Chapel Hill: University of North Carolina Press, 2003), 141, 95, 93–94, 146–48.

9. See "My life closed twice," where Dickinson writes: "Parting is all we know of heaven, / And all we need of hell" (*EDP* 686 [Fr 1773]).

10. I have discussed this text specifically as a war poem in *Emily Dickinson: A Voice of War*, 42; and again in "Formal, New and Relational Aesthetics: Dickinson's Multitexts," in *American Impersonal*, ed. Branka Arsic (New York: Bloomsbury, 2014), 254–80; 270–73. There the context is a broader aesthetic theory and the historicity within it. Note that this poem is listed as a war poem at http://courseweb.stthomas.edu/ajscheiber/ENGL%20214/Dickinson%20War%20Poems.htm.

11. Cristanne Miller, *Reading in Time: Emily Dickinson in the Nineteenth Century* (Amherst: University of Massachusetts Press, 2012), 169. See also Faith Barrett and Cristanne Miller, eds., *Words for the Hour: A New Anthology of Civil War Poetry* (Amherst: University of Massachusetts Press, 2005).

12. Eliza Richards, "'Death's Surprise, Stamped Visible': Emily Dickinson, Oliver Wendell Holmes, and Civil War Photography," *Amerikastudien* 54, no. 1 (2009): 13–33; 20. See also Richards's articles "Weathering the News in U.S. Civil War Poetry," in *Cambridge Companion to Nineteenth-Century American Poetry*, ed. Kerry Larson (New York: Cambridge University Press, 2011), 113–35, for imagery of weather in Dickinson and the surrounding rhetoric of the period; and "Correspondent Lines: Poetry, Journalism, and the U.S. Civil War," *ESQ* 54, nos. 1–4 (2008): 145–70, for rhetoric of the "line." In "'How News Must Feel When Traveling': Dickinson and Civil War Media," Richards focuses on the circulation of news; in *A Companion to Emily Dickinson*, ed. Martha Nell Smith and Mary Loeffelholz (Malden, MA: Blackwell, 2008), 157–80.

13. See especially Faith Barrett, "Addresses to a Divided Nation," *Arizona Quarterly* 61, no. 4 (2005): 67–99, and other writings by Barrett on Dickinson and war, including her book *To Fight Aloud Is Very Brave: American Poetry and the Civil War* (Amherst: University of Massachusetts Press, 2012), 3, 130.

14. See Shira Wolosky, "Public and Private in Emily Dickinson's War Poetry," in *A Historical Guide to Emily Dickinson*, ed. Vivian Pollack (New York: Oxford University Press, 2004), 103–32.

15. Sharon Cameron, *Lyric Time: Dickinson and the Limits of Genre* (Baltimore: Johns Hopkins University Press, 1981), 106–7.

16. Helen Vendler, *Dickinson: Selected Poems and Commentaries* (Cambridge, MA: Harvard University, Belknap Press, 2010), 84–85.

17. Jerome McGann, *Black Riders: The Visible Language of Modernism* (Princeton, NJ: Princeton University Press, 1993), 38.

18. Domhnall Mitchell, *Emily Dickinson: Monarch of Perceptions* (Amherst: University of Massachusetts Press), 205.

19. Vendler, *Dickinson: Selected Poems*, 85. Cameron sees the "Face of steel," "metallic grin" and "drill" as connecting "sexuality and death" (*Lyric Time*, 108).

20. The 150th anniversary of the end of the Civil War was widely marked by ringing of church bells, as reported on the internet. See also, for example, an entry, dated February 15, 1865, from the diary of Emma Florence LeConte, the daughter of scientist Joseph LeConte of Columbia, South Carolina. Emma writes about the impending destruction of Columbia: "The alarm bell is ringing . . . it is the Yankees" (http://blogs.lib.unc.edu/civilwar/index.php/2015/02/15/15-february-1865-the-alarm-bell-is-ringing-it-is-the-yankees).

21. See Wolosky, *Emily Dickinson: A Voice of War*, for a full argument on Dickinson's historical contexts of war.

22. Matthew 4:19: "And He said to them, 'Follow Me, and I will make you fishers of men.'"

23. Shira Wolosky, "Rhetoric or Not: Hymnal Tropes in Emily Dickinson and Isaac Watts," *The New England Quarterly* 61, no. 2 (June 1988): 214–32; 219–20.

24. Leigh-Ann Urbanovitcz Marcellin, "'Singing off Charnel Steps': Soldiers and Mourners in Emily Dickinson's War Poetry," *The Emily Dickinson Journal* 9, no. 2 (2000): 64–74, 73; Faith Barrett, "Slavery and the Civil War," in *Emily Dickinson in*

Context, ed. Eliza Richards (Cambridge: Cambridge University Press, 2013), 206–15, 207; Benjamin Friedlander, "Emily Dickinson and Battle of Ball's Bluff," *PMLA* 124, no. 5 (2009): 1582–99, 1591.

25. See Shira Wolosky, "Emily Dickinson: War and the Art of Writing," in *Cambridge History of American Civil War Literature,* ed. Coleman Hutchison (Cambridge: Cambridge University Press, 2015), 195–210.

26. Alicia Ostriker, "Re-playing the Bible: My Emily Dickinson," in *Emily Dickinson in Context,* ed. Eliza Richards (New York: Cambridge University Press, 2013), 462–70; 467. Pluralization of meaning, if not of figures, of course does not reflect every tradition of biblical hermeneutics, as she notes.

27. Betsy Erkkila, in *Whitman the Political Poet* (New York: Oxford University Press, 1996), 125–27, puts Whitman brilliantly into the political contexts of his personal life and public issues. Most readings of the poem, however, focus on its sexuality. For example, Huck Gutman notes that comparatively little has been written on "I Sing the Body Electric" (1855), which has often been regarded as "obvious and repetitive," as when Tenney Nathanson calls its concluding catalog "an obsessive enumeration" in *Whitman's Presence: Body, Voice, and Writing in "Leaves of Grass"* (New York: New York University Press, 1992), 288. But Gutman himself sees the poem as centrally about "Whitman's profound love of bodily flesh" (*WWA,* http://www.whitmanarchive.org/criticism/current /encyclopedia/entry_9.html). M. Jimmie Killingsworth, in "Whitman's Sexual Themes during a Decade of Revision: 1866–1876," *Walt Whitman Quarterly Review* 4, no. 1 (1986): 7–15, sees an evolution from the poem's 1855 untitled printing to its 1856 title as "Poem of the Body," to 1867 when "the poem's new title and opening lines made clear that the poet sang of not merely the body, but the 'discorrupted' body 'electrified' with 'the charge of the soul.' On the question of Emerson's reactions to Whitman's sexuality, see Jay Grossman, *Reconstituting the American Renaissance: Emerson, Whitman, and the Politics of Representation* (Durham, NC: Duke University Press, 2003), 79ff., 291n1, where he highlights the fact that Emerson never told his side of the story and that Whitman offered at least three distinct accounts of what happened.

28. Ludwig Wittgenstein, *Philosophical Investigations,* II.iv (New York: Macmillan, 1953), 178.

29. This change in the fundamental meanings and relations between dualistic terms is, I think, what Whitman meant when he wrote that "from another point of view 'Leaves of Grass' is avowedly the song of Sex and Amativeness, and even Animality—though meanings that do not usually go along with those words are behind all, and will duly emerge; and all are sought to be lifted into a different light and atmosphere. Of this feature, intentionally palpable in a few lines, I shall only say the espousing principle of those lines so gives breath of life to my whole scheme that the bulk of the pieces might as well have been left unwritten were those lines omitted"; "A Backward Glance O'er Travel'd Roads" (*WWA* 436).

30. Elizabeth Cady Stanton, *The Woman's Bible* (Boston: Northeastern University Press, 1993), 20–21.

31. Walt Whitman, *Notebooks and Unpublished Prose Manuscripts*, ed. Edward Grier (New York: New York University Press, 1984), 1:353. Whitman also calls *Leaves of Grass* "'Leaves of Grass'—Bible of the New Religion" as "the principal object—the main life work" (Whitman, *Notes and Fragments Left by Walt Whitman,* ed. Richard Maurice Bucke [London: A. Talbot, 1899], 55). See W. C. Harris, "Whitman's *Leaves of Grass* and the Writing of a New American Bible," *Walt Whitman Quarterly Review* 16 (Winter 1999): 172–90, for a discussion of Whitman in the context of contemporary Bible translations and secularization, M. C. Gardner, *Whitman's Code: A New Bible* (Patcheny, 2013) is a recent biographical/numerological rereading of *Leaves of Grass* as metaphorically a Bible.

32. For Whitman's philosophical engagements, see Shira Wolosky, "On Cavell on Whitman: Questions about Application," *Common Knowledge* 5, no. 2 (Fall 1996): 61–71.

"No Man Saw Awe" / "In the Talk of . . . God . . . He Is Silent"

1. Mircea Eliade, "Introduction to *The Sacred and the Profane,*" in *Mircea Eliade: A Critical Reader,* ed. Bryan Rennie (London: Equinox, 2006), 17–22; 20.

2. Rudolf Otto, *The Idea of the Holy: An Inquiry into the Non-Rational Factor in the Idea of the Divine and Its Relation to the Rational,* trans. John W. Harvey (London: Oxford University Press, 1924).

3. Eliade, "Introduction to *Sacred and the Profane,*" 18. I have chosen to use the more general term *hierophany* for this essay since it lacks the theological connotations of the more frequently used *theophany.* Hierophany, as Eliade explains, "is a fitting term because it does not imply anything further; it expresses no more than is implicit in its etymological content, i.e., that *something sacred shows itself* to us" (18–19).

4. Ibid.

5. There is a long critical history in the first half of the twentieth century examining Whitman's allusions to the Bible, as well as his interest in creating a new American Bible—see especially works by Gay Allen, including "Biblical Echoes in Whitman's Works," *American Literature* 6 (November 1934): 302–15. For helpful overviews of this critical tradition, see particularly Herbert J. Levine, "'Song of Myself' as Whitman's American Bible," *Modern Language Quarterly* 48 (June 1987): 145–61; and W. C. Harris, "Whitman's *Leaves of Grass* and the Writing of a New American Bible," *Walt Whitman Quarterly Review* 16, no. 3 (1999): 172–90. Although there has been relatively little scholarship considering Whitman and the Bible in the most recent two decades, as H. T. Kirby-Smith puts it, "in the end it seems best to take Whitman at his word, that he immersed himself in the Old and New Testaments, and see there his chief inspiration and model. There seems little need to provide supporting quotations from Whitman's work; the evidence is not only abundant, but almost inescapable" (Kirby-Smith, *The Origins of Free Verse* [Ann Arbor: University of Michigan Press, 1996], 154).

6. While much early Whitman scholarship takes the master-disciple relation between Ralph Waldo Emerson and Whitman as a given, scholars have increasingly troubled the

understanding of Whitman's debt to Emerson. See especially seminal works by Kenneth M. Price, *Whitman and Tradition: The Poet in His Century* (New Haven, CT: Yale University Press, 1990); and Jay Grossman, *Reconstituting the American Renaissance: Emerson, Whitman, and the Politics of Representation* (Durham, NC: Duke University Press, 2003).

7. Christina Davey, "Walt Whitman and the Quaker Woman," *Walt Whitman Quarterly Review* 16, no. 1 (1998): 1–22.

8. Susan Dean, "Seeds of Quakerism at the Roots of *Leaves of Grass*," *Walt Whitman Quarterly Review* 16, no. 3 (1999): 191–201; 194.

9. Horace Traubel, *With Walt Whitman in Camden*, vol. 7 (Carbondale: Southern Illinois University Press, 1992), 177.

10. The division occurred over questions of biblical authority and the divinity of Jesus, with the Hicksites maintaining that the Inner Light should hold the highest place in the individual Friend's spiritual hierarchies and the Orthodox maintaining the traditional Christian doctrine of submitting the inner witness to established biblical precepts.

11. Whitman's enumeration of the liberated poet's behaviors continues here with specific reference to the Quakers' practice of refusing to tip their hats to acknowledge social rank. The great poet should "have patience and indulgence toward the people, take off your hat to nothing known or unknown or to any man or number of men—go freely with powerful uneducated persons, and with the young, and with the mothers of families" (*WPP 1855*, 11).

12. Richard Bauman, *Let Your Words Be Few: Symbolism of Speaking and Silence among Seventeenth-Century Quakers* (Cambridge: Cambridge University Press, 1983), 23.

13. Lawrence Templin, "The Quaker Influence on Walt Whitman," *American Literature* 42, no. 2 (1970): 165–80.

14. David Kuebrich, *Minor Prophecy: Walt Whitman's New Religion* (Bloomington: Indiana University Press, 1989), 66. *Minor Prophecy*, one of the few full-length treatments of the impact of religious influences on Whitman's poetry, traces the roots of Whitman's religious cosmology not only to his avowed affinities with Quaker and Transcendentalist thought, but also to the poet's broad exposure to popular cultural elements of nineteenth-century American revival millennialism. Kuebrich finds evidence of Whitman's positive response to the movement's acceptance of perfectionism, a belief in the perfectibility of Christian believers through the indwelling of the Holy Spirit.

15. Ibid., 67.

16. V. K. Chari, *Whitman in the Light of Vedantic Mysticism: An Interpretation* (Lincoln: University of Nebraska Press, 1964), 27.

17. Eliade, "Introduction to *Sacred and Profane*," 19.

18. Mary Arensberg, introduction to *The American Sublime*, ed. Mary Arensberg (Albany: State University of New York Press, 1986), 1–21; 14.

19. Walt Whitman, from an 1872 fragment of an early draft of "Emerson's Books": "The sense of Deity is indispensable in grand poems—this is what puts [*inserted*: the book of Job & much of] the Old Hebrew Bible ~~with the Book of Job~~—and also the

plays of Eschuylus ahead of all poetry we know." This fragment was first published in Ed Folsom, "Whitman's Notes on Emerson: An Unpublished Manuscript," *Walt Whitman Quarterly Review* 18, no. 1 (2000): 60–62.

20. References to the Bible are to the King James Version.

21. Otto, *Idea of the Holy*, 81.

22. Ibid., 82–83.

23. After wrestling with Jacob, the Angel of God says, "Let me go, for the day breaketh. And he [Jacob] said, I will not let thee go, except thou bless me" (Gen. 32:26).

24. Robert M. Greenberg, *Splintered Worlds: Fragmentation and the Ideal of Diversity in the Work of Emerson, Melville, Whitman and Dickinson* (Boston: Northeastern University Press, 1993), 145.

25. Exodus 3:14 records what is known as the tetragrammaton, the Hebrew name of God written without vowels and considered too holy to be spoken out loud by the ancient Israelites.

26. There is some scholarly consensus today that while Dickinson rejected the formal teachings of the Christian Church, including doctrines concerning predestination, sin, and the need for redemption, she did retain a sense of affection for Jesus, a deep love for the powerful and mysterious language of the Bible, and a hard-won faith in the existence of God and the hope for an afterlife. On Dickinson and belief, see especially Jane Donahue Eberwein, *Dickinson: Strategies of Limitation* (Amherst: University of Amherst Press, 1985); Roger Lundin, *Emily Dickinson and the Art of Belief* (Grand Rapids, MI: William B. Eerdmans, 1998); and Alfred Habegger, *My Wars Are Laid Away in Books: The Life of Emily Dickinson* (New York: Modern Library, 2001).

27. Historical scholarship has shown that depictions of Dickinson as one who grew up in a harshly Calvinistic atmosphere have been overstated. On the moderate nature of Dickinson's religious environs and education, see especially Rowena Revis Jones, "The Preparation of a Poet: Puritan Directions in Emily Dickinson's Education," *Studies in the American Renaissance* (1982): 285–324; Jane Donahue Eberwein, "'Graphicer for Grace': Emily Dickinson's Calvinist Language," *Studies in Puritan Spirituality* 1 (1990): 170–201; Jane Donahue Eberwein, "Ministerial Interviews and Fathers in Faith," *The Emily Dickinson Journal* 9, no. 2 (2000): 285–324; and Jennifer Leader, *Knowing, Seeing, Being: Jonathan Edwards, Emily Dickinson, Marianne Moore, and the American Typological Tradition* (Amherst: University of Massachusetts Press, 2016).

28. Ralph Waldo Emerson, *Essays and Lectures*, ed. Joel Porte (New York: Library of America, 1983), 10.

29. Linda Freedman, *Emily Dickinson and the Religious Imagination* (Cambridge: Cambridge University Press, 2011), 191. For incisive critiques of Dickinson's literary relationship to Emerson, see especially Catherine Tufariello, "'The Remembering Wine': Emerson's Influence on Whitman and Dickinson," in *The Cambridge Companion to Ralph Waldo Emerson*, ed. Joel Porte and Saundra Morris (Cambridge: Cambridge University Press, 1999), 162–91; and Shira Wolosky, *Poetry and Public Discourse in Nineteenth-Century America* (London: Palgrave Macmillan, 2010).

30. William Dyrness, *Reformed Theology and Visual Culture: The Protestant Imagination from Calvin to Edwards* (Cambridge: Cambridge University Press, 2004), 92.

31. Horace Bushnell, *Sermons for the New Life,* 2nd ed. (New York: Scribner, 1858), 46. The mystical strains in nineteenth-century Christianity were not invented by Coleridge and the German idealists. Theologians such as Bushnell and Edward Amasa Park were informed as much by Jonathan Edwards's mystical impulses as they were by Emerson's call for "an original relation to the universe" (Emerson, *Essays and Lectures,* 7).

32. Dickinson uses the name Moses in five of her poems. In four of these poems— "Where bells no more affright the morn" (Fr 114; 1859), "If the foolish, call them '*flowers*'" (Fr 179; 1860), "It always felt to me – a wrong" (Fr 521; 1863), and "So I pull my Stockings off" (Fr 1271; 1871)—she commiserates with Moses at the end of his life. According to Deuteronomy 34, as a punishment for disobedience God allowed Moses to look into the Promised Land from Mount Nebo, but told him he would die without entering it himself.

33. Michelle Kohler, *Miles of Stare: Transcendentalism and the Problem of Literary Vision in Nineteenth-Century America* (Tuscaloosa: University of Alabama Press, 2014).

34. Ibid., 6–7.

35. Jed Deppman, *Trying to Think with Emily Dickinson* (Amherst: University of Massachusetts Press, 2008), 192–93.

36. Cristanne Miller, *Emily Dickinson: A Poet's Grammar* (Cambridge, MA: Harvard University Press, 1987), 127.

37. Sharon Cameron, *Lyric Time: Dickinson and the Limits of Genre* (Baltimore: Johns Hopkins University Press, 1979), 198.

38. Given Dickinson's use of the phrase "'am not consumed'" in "No man saw awe," it seems to me that the primary sense of "To pile like Thunder" calls for "consume" to be understood in the passive voice rather than the active. While Dickinson characteristically has no qualms about interrupting her meter, I would suggest that here she chose the iambic "consume" in order to set up the final line's dramatic iambic trimeter, "For none see God and live."

39. Agnieszka Salska, *Walt Whitman and Emily Dickinson: Poetry of the Central Consciousness* (Philadelphia: University of Pennsylvania Press, 1985), 93, 87.

Phenomenological Approaches to Human Contact in Whitman and Dickinson

1. Ralph Waldo Emerson, "Experience," in *Essays: Second Series* (1844), Emersoncentral.com, last modified March 9, 2009, http://www.emersoncentral.com/experience.htm.

2. Roger Joseph Boscovich, *A Theory of Natural Philosophy* (Venice, 1763), trans. J. M. Child (Chicago: Open Court, 1922), http://www.chemteam.info/Chem-History/Boscovich-1763.html.

3. Ralph Waldo Emerson, "Nature" (1836), Emersoncentral.com, last modified March 9, 2009, http://www.emersoncentral.com/nature.htm.

4. Roger Asselineau, *The Evolution of Walt Whitman* (Iowa City: University of Iowa

Press, 1962); Stephen John Mack, *Pragmatic Whitman: Reimagining American Democracy* (Iowa City: University of Iowa Press, 2002); Vincent J. Bertolini, "'Hinting' and 'Reminding': The Rhetoric of Performative Embodiment in *Leaves of Grass*," *ELH* 69, no. 4 (Winter 2002): 1047.

5. David Daiches, "Whitman as Innovator," in *The Young Rebel in American Literature*, ed. Carl Bode (London: Heinemann, 1959); qtd. in Edwin Haviland Miller, *Walt Whitman's "Song of Myself": A Mosaic of Interpretations* (Iowa City: University of Iowa Press, 1989), xviii.

6. Karen Sánchez-Eppler, *Abolition, Feminism, and the Politics of the Body* (Berkeley: University of California Press, 1993).

7. Jed Deppman, *Trying to Think with Emily Dickinson* (Amherst: University of Massachusetts Press, 2008), 7.

8. *Emily Dickinson and Philosophy*, ed. Jed Deppman, Marianne Noble, and Gary Lee Stonum (New York: Cambridge University Press, 2013).

9. All references are to the King James (Authorized Version) Bible.

10. Whitman's swerve from Emerson to his incipient phenomenology would appear to have occurred before 1855 and was part of the crucible out of which the first editions of *Leaves of Grass* emerged. According to Asselineau, after 1856, increasingly "Whitman passed from a materialism colored with spirituality to a spirituality tinged with materialism," a swerve he attributes to his "belated discovery of the German idealists whom Carlyle and the transcendentalists had brought into fashion long before." Asselineau implies, however, that materialism expresses Whitman's native thought and idealism results from external influence (Asselineau, *Evolution of Walt Whitman*, 31).

11. Allen Grossman notes that Whitman dislikes representation, which mediates and imposes hierarchy. Whitman "scrutinize[s] the logic of representation as he received it. This capacity takes the form of an extreme, interrogatory, phenomenological innocence: 'This then is life . . . How curious! How real!'" (116). Grossman emphasizes the problem of hierarchies, while I emphasize the problem of dualism, but we agree that Whitman turns to phenomenology to resolve these problems. Grossman, "Whitman's 'Whoever You Are Holding Me Now in Hand': Remarks on the Endlessly Repeated Rediscovery of the Incommensurability of the Person," in *Breaking Bounds: Whitman and American Cultural Studies*, ed. Betsy Erkkila and Jay Grossman (New York: Oxford University Press, 1996), 112–22.

12. Chris Frith, *Making Up the Mind: How the Brain Creates Our Mental World* (Malden, MA: Blackwell, 2007), 98.

13. Qtd. in Shaun Gallagher and Dan Zahavi, *The Phenomenological Mind: An Introduction to Philosophy of Mind and Cognitive Science* (New York: Routledge, 2008), 191.

14. Ibid.

15. Ibid., 182.

16. William James famously analyzes the corporeality of feeling in his 1884 "What Is an Emotion?" He says we falsely believe that emotions cause bodily actions (for example, fear causes us to run away). In fact, he claims "that *the bodily changes follow*

directly the PERCEPTION of the exciting fact, and that our feeling of the same changes as they occur IS the emotion" (189–90, emphasis in original). Though his hypothesis has been convincingly challenged, its basic claim has been experimentally documented. For example, when test subjects put a pencil between their lips, preventing the ability to smile, they registered lower measures of happiness than those whose mouths were not immobilized. Smiling is not simply the echo of a happy feeling; the very thing we feel is an impetus-to-smile, or a smile-producing-pleasure, and without a body to express it, the emotion is diminished. The bodily expression *is* the thought—if not entirely, at least more so than we tend to think (Frith, *Making Up the Mind*, 149; Gallagher and Zahavi, *The Phenomenological Mind*, 137–38). William James, "What Is an Emotion?" *Mind* 9, no. 34 (April 1884): 188–205. Published by Oxford University Press on behalf of the Mind Association, http://www.jstor.org/stable/2246769.

17. Qtd. in Marco Iacoboni, *Mirroring People: The Science of Empathy and How We Connect with Others* (New York: Picador, 2008), 22.

18. Gallagher and Zahavi, *The Phenomenological Mind*, 185.

19. Ibid.

20. Ibid., 183.

21. The idea of a self that is manifest in the things it does, and an ideal of contact that therefore implies no hidden reality, suggests a performative self, such as Vincent J. Bertolini identifies in Whitman. Bertolini suggests that "the other I am" might refer to something like "the abject," those aspects of consciousness that are repressed in the formation of the "I." Whitman's "hints" aim to restore their thinkability to the reader's consciousness (Bertolini, "'Hinting' and 'Reminding,'" 1056).

22. Gallagher and Zahavi, *The Phenomenological Mind*, 185.

23. Ibid., 187.

24. In *Studies in Classic American Literature*, D. H. Lawrence criticizes in Whitman a desire to feel "for" the other instead of "with" him or her, which is to say an aspiration to merge instead of an aspiration to care about and support the other *as other*. He criticizes martyrdom and calls instead for emancipatory activism and encouragement (Lawrence, *Studies in Classic American Literature* [New York: T. Selzer, 1923], http://xroads.virginia.edu/~hyper/LAWRENCE/dhltoc.htm). I agree with Eric Selinger, who in contrast to Lawrence argues that Whitman seeks neither to merge with nor to understand the other but instead affirms the role of the other in his own selfhood. Selinger, *What Is It Then between Us? Traditions of Love in American Poetry* (Ithaca, NY: Cornell University Press, 1998).

25. Walter Jacob Slatoff, *The Look of Distance: Reflections on Suffering and Sympathy in Modern Literature—Auden to Agee, Whitman to Woolf* (Columbus: Ohio State University Press, 1985), 136.

26. Leslie Jamison, "'A Thousand Willing Forms': The Evolution of Whitman's Wounded Bodies," *Studies in American Fiction* 35, no. 1 (Spring 2007): 22–23.

27. Ibid., 23.

28. Qtd. in Gallagher and Zahavi, *The Phenomenological Mind*, 190.

29. Jamison, "Thousand Willing Forms," 23.

30. Ibid.

31. Asselineau distinguishes the first two editions in their focus on "the poet in his relation with the universe" from the 1860 edition, which focuses on democracy and sex (*Evolution of Walt Whitman*, 120). *Drum-Taps* has a more other-oriented focus. On this, see also M. Wynn Thomas, who describes in *Drum-Taps* "a psychically healing process of bestowing a kind of identity on some poor unknown through a glance of sympathetic human recognition" and an effort to grasp the "hidden inner meaning of the war" (39). Such a poetics is different from the emphasis on self-creation and celebration of the reality of contact in the 1855 and 1856 editions (Thomas, "Fratricide and Brotherly Love: Whitman and the Civil War," in *The Cambridge Companion to Walt Whitman*, ed. Ezra Greenspan [Cambridge: Cambridge University Press, 1995]).

32. Maurice Lee, *Uncertain Chances: Science, Skepticism, and Belief in Nineteenth-Century American Literature* (Oxford: Oxford University Press, 2011).

33. Ibid., 161.

34. D. W. Winnicott, "Ego Distortion in Terms of True and False Self," in *The Maturational Process and the Facilitating Environment: Studies in the Theory of Emotional Development* (New York: International Universities Press, 1965), 140–57.

35. Robert Weisbuch, *Emily Dickinson's Poetry* (Chicago: University of Chicago Press, 1975), 134.

36. Recent work on Dickinson and phenomenology includes Marianne Noble, "Emily Dickinson on Perception and Consciousness: A Dialogue with Maurice Merleau-Ponty," in *Emily Dickinson and Philosophy*, ed. Jed Deppman, Marianne Noble, and Gary Lee Stonum (Cambridge: Cambridge University Press, 2013), 175–87; and, in the same volume, Farhang Erfani, "Dickinson and Sartre on Facing the Brutality of Brute Existence." See also Magdalena Zapécdowska, "The Event of Interiority: Dickinson and Emmanuel Levinas's Phenomenology of the Home," *American Studies* 20 (2003): 113–28; Joy Ladin, "'This Consciousness That Is Aware': The Consolation of Emily Dickinson's Phenomenology," in *Wider Than the Sky: Essays and Meditations on the Healing Power of Emily Dickinson*, ed. Cindy Mackenzie and Barbara Dana (Kent, OH: Kent State University Press, 2007).

37. A valuable resource for scholarship on Dickinson's letters is *Reading Emily Dickinson's Letters: Critical Essays*, ed. Jane Eberwein and Cindy MacKenzie (Amherst: University of Massachusetts Press, 2009). See also Ellen Louise Hart and Martha Nell Smith, *Open Me Carefully: Emily Dickinson's Intimate Letters to Susan Huntington Dickinson* (Ashfield, MA: Paris, 1998); Elizabeth Hewitt, "Dickinson's Lyrical Letters and Poetics of Correspondence," *Arizona Quarterly* 52, no. 1 (1996): 27–58, 202–8; Paula Bennett, "'By a Mouth That Cannot Speak': Spectral Presence in Emily Dickinson's Letters," *The Emily Dickinson Journal* 1, no. 2 (1992): 76–99; and Cristanne Miller, *Emily Dickinson: A Poet's Grammar* (Cambridge, MA: Harvard University Press, 1987).

38. Daniel M. Gross argues for the intentionality of emotion, rejecting the widespread misconception of emotions as transhistorical universals contained within the one feeling

them. In particular, he stresses the sociocultural determinants of the intentionality of thought, leveling a polemic against brain scientists like Antonio Damasio who, he argues, perniciously universalize the processes involved in the intentionality of consciousness. Gross, *The Secret History of Emotion: From Aristotle's "Rhetoric" to Modern Brain Science* (Chicago: University of Chicago Press, 2006). As Sara Ahmed argues in *Queer Phenomenology*, phenomenological theory calls for analysis of the cultural determinants of emotion in presenting people as necessarily situated in a culturally significant body in a particular time and place, yet its practitioners rarely heed that call (Ahmed, *Queer Phenomenology* [Durham, NC: Duke University Press, 2006]).

39. Qtd. in Gallagher and Zahavi, *The Phenomenological Mind*, 122.

"We Must Travel Abreast with Nature, if We Want to Understand Her"

1. Rachel Stein, *Shifting the Ground: American Women Writers' Revision of Nature, Gender, and Race* (Charlottesville: University Press of Virginia, 1997), 32, 43; Midori Asahina, "'Fascination' Is Absolute of Clime: Reading Dickinson's Correspondence with Higginson as Naturalist," *The Emily Dickinson Journal* 14, no. 2 (2005): 103–19; Christine Gerhardt, "'Often Seen–but Seldom Felt': Emily Dickinson's Reluctant Ecology of Place," *The Emily Dickinson Journal* 15, no. 1 (2006): 56–78.

2. M. Jimmie Killingsworth, *Walt Whitman and the Earth: A Study in Ecopoetics* (Iowa City: University of Iowa Press, 2004), 74, 100; M. Jimmie Killingsworth, "Nature," in *A Companion to Walt Whitman*, ed. Donald D. Kummings (Malden, MA: Blackwell, 2006), 322; and Maria Magdalena Farland, "Decomposing City: Walt Whitman's New York and the Science of Life and Death," *ELH* 74, no. 4 (Winter 2007): 802.

3. Daniel J. Philippon, "'I Only Seek to Put You in Rapport': Message and Method in Walt Whitman's Specimen Days," in *Reading the Earth: New Directions in the Study of Literature and Environment*, ed. Michael P. Branch, Rochelle Johnson, Daniel Patterson, and Scott Slovic (Moscow: University of Idaho Press, 1998), 188; Christine Gerhardt, "Managing the Wilderness: Walt Whitman's Southern Landscapes," *Forum for Modern Language Studies* 40, no. 2 (Spring 2004): 225–35; Christine Gerhardt, *A Place for Humility: Whitman, Dickinson, and the Natural World* (Iowa City: University of Iowa Press, 2014).

4. Walt Whitman, *Complete Poetry and Collected Prose*, ed. Justin Kaplan (New York: Library of America, 1982). Except where noted otherwise, all quotations from Whitman refer to Kaplan's *Whitman: Poetry and Prose* and will be cited in the text by the page numbers assigned in this edition, preceded by *WPP*. "*WPP 1855*" refers to the 1855 *Leaves of Grass*, and is followed by the page number in Kaplan's edition.

5. This is true, although Rosemary McTier, for instance, mentions insect migrations; see Rosemary Scanlon McTier, *"An Insect View of Its Plain": Insects, Nature and God in Thoreau, Dickinson and Muir* (Jefferson, NC: McFarland, 2013).

6. Killingsworth, "Nature," 322; Killingsworth, *Whitman and the Earth*, 101.

7. Lawrence Buell, *Writing for an Endangered World: Literature, Culture, and Envi-*

ronment in the U.S. and Beyond (Cambridge, MA: Harvard University, Belknap Press, 2001), 99–101.

8. George Handley, *New World Poetics: Nature and the Adamic Imagination of Whitman, Neruda, and Walcott* (Athens: University of Georgia Press, 2007), 13, 126.

9. Gerhardt, *Place for Humility*.

10. See Max Oelschlaeger, *The Idea of Wilderness: From Prehistory to the Age of Ecology* (New Haven, CT: Yale University Press, 1991), 4.

11. On Linnaean science, see Donald Worster, *Nature's Economy: The Roots of Ecology* (San Francisco: Sierra Club, 1988), 140.

12. George Perkins Marsh, *Man and Nature; or, Physical Geography as Modified by Human Action*, ed. David Lowenthal (1864; Cambridge, MA: Harvard University, Belknap Press, 1965), 36.

13. Worster, *Nature's Economy,* 140, 142, 144.

14. For discussions of the imperial entanglements of these scientific explorations, see especially Mary Louise Pratt, *Imperial Eyes: Travel Writing and Transculturation* (London: Routledge, 1992); and Richard H. Grove, *Green Imperialism: Colonial Expansion, Tropical Island Edens and the Origins of Environmentalism, 1600–1860* (Cambridge: Cambridge University Press, 1995). For a nuanced reappraisal of Humboldt's proto-ecological and proto-cosmopolitan vision and his influence on American writers from Emerson to Whitman, from Marsh to Muir, see Laura Dassow Walls, *The Passage to Cosmos: Alexander Von Humboldt and the Shaping of America* (Chicago: University of Chicago Press, 2009).

15. In a different article, which focuses on ecopoetics, ecocriticism, and mobility studies, I use a related reading of these four poems as a starting point to argue that Dickinson and Whitman point forward toward a modern ecopoetics of mobility; Christine Gerhardt, "Imagining a Mobile Sense of Place: Towards an Ecopoetics of Mobility," *American Studies/Amerikastudien* 61, no. 4 (2017): 421–43.

16. Dickinson poems are quoted from Ralph W. Franklin's edition *The Poems of Emily Dickinson*, ed. Ralph W. Franklin, 3 vols. (Cambridge, MA: Harvard University, Belknap Press, 1998). All subsequent references to Dickinson's poems will be cited in the text by the numbers Franklin assigns in this edition, preceded by Fr.

17. Allegorical readers include Albert Gelpi, *Emily Dickinson: The Mind of the Poet* (Cambridge, MA: Harvard University Press, 1965), 84; Eleanor Elson Heginbotham, *Reading the Fascicles of Emily Dickinson: Dwelling in Possibilities* (Columbus: Ohio State University Press, 2003), 143; and Judy Jo Small, *Positive as Sound: Emily Dickinson's Rhyme* (Athens: University of Georgia Press, 2010), 70. Historical readers include Carol Quinn, "Dickinson, Telegraphy, and the Aurora Borealis," *The Emily Dickinson Journal* 13, no. 2 (2004): 73–74; and Paul Muldoon, *The End of the Poem* (New York: Farrar, Straus and Giroux, 2007), 129–31.

18. Martha McDowell, *Emily Dickinson's Gardens* (New York: McGraw-Hill, 2005), 182.

19. Asa Gray, "Diagnostic Characters of New Species of Phaenogamous Plants, Collected in Japan by Charles Wright, Botanist of the U. S. North Pacific Exploring

Expedition. (Published by Request of Captain John Rodgers, Commander of the Expedition.) With Observations upon the Relations of the Japanese Flora to That of North America," *Memoirs of the American Academy of Arts and Sciences*, n.s., 6, no. 2 (1859): 447.

20. T. W. Higginson, "The Procession of the Flowers," *Atlantic Monthly* 10, no. 62 (1862): 652.

21. Ibid.; emphasis added.

22. John Muir, *A Thousand-Mile Walk to the Gulf*, ed. Peter Jenkins (1916; New York: Houghton Mifflin, 1998), 47; emphasis added.

23. See Peter J. Bowler, *The Earth Encompassed: A History of the Environmental Sciences* (New York: Norton, 2000), 273.

24. Lawrence Buell, *The Environmental Imagination: Thoreau, Nature Writing, and the Formation of American Culture* (Cambridge, MA: Harvard University Press, 1995), 7; Killingsworth, *Whitman and the Earth*, 107, 109; Handley, *New World Poetics*, 146; Gerhardt, *Place for Humility*, 120.

25. Wilson Flagg, "Birds of the Night," *Atlantic Monthly* 4, no. 22 (1859): 171–84; Olive Thorne Miller, "A Tricksy Spirit," *Atlantic Monthly* 56, no. 337 (1885): 676–85.

26. Edward A. Samuels, *The Birds of New England* (Boston: Noyes, Holmes, 1870), 168.

27. Midcentury publications mention how young mockingbirds were "sold in large numbers . . . for shipment North"; George H. Holden, *Canaries and Cage-Birds: The Food, Care, Breeding, Diseases, and Treatment of All House Birds* (Boston: Alfred Mudge, 1888), 161.

28. The fight against the songbird and millinery trade eventually led to the foundation of the American Ornithologists' Society in 1883 and the first Audubon society in 1886; see Leslie Kemp Poole, "The Women of the Early Florida Audubon Society: Agents of History in the Fight to Save State Birds," *The Florida Historical Quarterly* 85, no. 3 (2007): 300–301.

29. Flagg, "Birds of the Night," 179; Maurice Thompson, "In the Haunts of the Mockingbird," *Atlantic Monthly* 54, no. 325 (1884): 625.

30. Killingsworth, *Whitman and the Earth*, 74.

31. Killingsworth, "Nature," 322.

32. In "Imagining a Mobile Sense of Place: Towards an Ecopoetics of Mobility" (2017) I develop the concept of a "mobile sense of place" more broadly as a key manifestation of a mobile ecopoetics, which becomes tangible in poetic constructions of (1) places that are significantly shaped by the mobilities of nonhuman creatures and phenomena, (2) personas whose environmental insights are critically informed by their geographical movement, and (3) cultural frameworks characterized by the physical movements of people, materials, goods, and ideas.

33. Rebecca Patterson, *Emily Dickinson's Imagery* (Amherst: University of Massachusetts Press, 1979), 48; Timothy Morris, "The Development of Dickinson's Style," in *Emily Dickinson*, ed. Harold Bloom (New York: Chelsea House, 2008), 47.

34. Judith Farr and Louise Carter, *The Gardens of Emily Dickinson* (Cambridge, MA: Harvard University Press, 2004), 134–36; Gerhardt, *Place for Humility*, 42–43.

35. Ray Angelo, "Thoreau as Botanist: An Appreciation and a Critique," *Arnoldia* 45, no. 3 (Summer 1985): 15–16.

36. Ibid., 15–16, 16–17.

37. Ibid., 17.

38. Ibid., 16.

39. M. Wynn Thomas, *Transatlantic Connections: Whitman U.S., Whitman U.K.* (Iowa City : University of Iowa Press,2005), 185–87.

40. Muir, *A Thousand-Mile Walk*, 1, 14

41. Ibid., 31.

42. For a geographical discussion on how the rhythms of walking produce mobile place experience see Tim Edensor, "Walking in Rhythms: Place, Regulation, Style and the Flow of Experience," *Visual Studies* 25, no. 1 (April 2010): 69–79.

43. *L*, Prose Fragment 119.

Hyperbole and Humor in Whitman and Dickinson

1. The most important texts on Whitman, Dickinson, and humor are Ronald Wallace, *God Be with the Clown: Humor in American Poetry* (Columbia: University of Missouri Press, 1984); and Suzanne Juhasz, Cristanne Miller, and Martha Nell Smith, *Comic Power in Emily Dickinson* (Austin: University of Texas Press, 1993). Also of note are Richard Chase, *Walt Whitman Reconsidered* (New York: William Sloane Associates, 1955); and David S. Reynolds, "Whitman's Poetic Humor," in *Beneath the American Renaissance: The Subversive Imagination in the Age of Emerson and Melville* (New York: Alfred A. Knopf, 1988), 507–23. James T. F. Tanner surveys critical attention to Whitman's humor in "Four Comic Themes in Walt Whitman's *Leaves of Grass*," *Studies in American Humor* 5, no. 1 (Spring 1986): 62–71; see also Roger Asselineau's entry on "Humor" in *Walt Whitman: An Encyclopedia*, ed. J. R. LeMaster and Donald D. Kummings (New York: Garland, 1998), 289–90. John Wheatcroft surveys some early scholarship on Dickinson's humor in "'Holy Ghosts in Cages': A Serious View of Humor in Emily Dickinson's Poetry," *American Transcendental Quarterly* 22, no. 3 (1974): 95–104.

2. *WPP 1855* refers to the 1855 *Leaves of Grass* and is followed by the page number in Kaplan's edition.

3. Christopher D. Johnson, *Hyperboles: The Rhetoric of Excess in Baroque Literature and Thought* (Cambridge, MA: Harvard University Press, 2010), 9. Johnson posits a partial taxonomy of tropes and registers closely related to hyperbole that border on the comic—for example, excess, exaggeration, caricature, the grotesque, and other figures of emphasis or understatement. Hyperbole differs from bombast, he claims, as a matter of intention, self-awareness, and rhetorical craft: "As opposed to the mere purveyor of bombast, the Baroque hyperbolist, ever conscious of rhetorical precepts, and skillfully manipulating literary traditions and forms, solicits complicity rather than mockery. Shakespeare is a hyperbolist; Falstaff is not" (Johnson, *Hyperboles*, 2).

4. William Solomon, "Second Technologies: American Modernism and Silent Screen Comedy," *Interdisciplinary Literary Studies* 6, no. 2 (2005): 66–91; 75.

5. Jed Deppman, *Trying to Think with Emily Dickinson* (Amherst: University of Massachusetts Press, 2008), 62, 65.

6. Wallace, *God Be with the Clown*, 13. Wallace draws heavily on Constance Rourke's analysis of the "backwoodsman" and "Yankee" characters in her *American Humor: A Study of the American Character* (1931; reprint, Tallahassee: Florida State University Press, 1959), 174.

7. Wallace, *God Be with the Clown*, 17.

8. See, for example, Juhasz, Miller, and Smith, *Comic Power*; or more recently Shira Wolosky, "Gendered Poetics," in *Emily Dickinson in Context*, ed. Eliza Richards (Cambridge: Cambridge University Press, 2013), 169–78.

9. T. B. Thorpe, "The Big Bear of Arkansas," in *The Big Bear of Arkansas and Other Sketches Illustrative of Characters and Incidents of the South and Southwest*, ed. William T. Porter (Philadelphia: T. B. Peterson, 1843), 13–31; 17, 21.

10. Wallace writes that "prior to 1850 the backwoodsman was clearly a hero. The humorous tall tales associated with him were a way of coping with a threatening and large country, while asserting confidently that nothing was impossible for America or Americans"; as he asserts, Whitman was familiar with tall tales (*God Be with the Clown*, 14–15, 57–58).

11. Audrey Wasser, "Hyperbole in Proust," *MLN* 129 (2014): 829–54; 840.

12. Johnson, *Hyperboles*, 17.

13. Joshua R. Ritter, "Recovering Hyperbole: Rethinking the Limits of Rhetoric for an Age of Excess," *Philosophy and Rhetoric* 45 (2012): 406–28; 408. Ritter cites Paul Ricoeur, *Figuring the Sacred: Religion, Narrative, and Imagination*, trans. David Pellauer, ed. Mark I. Wallace (Minneapolis, MN: Fortress, 1995), 229.

14. Ritter, "Recovering Hyperbole," 407.

15. Ibid., 411.

16. Johnson, *Hyperboles*, 1, 8. Ritter summarizes hyperbole's relation to error as follows: "it presents a falsehood that is not intended to be deceptive and takes on the form of errancy, that is, possessing 'the *structure* of error without being an *error*' (Mileur 1990, 113), whereby one can move the audience toward alternate perceptions of truth(s) and reality through the paradox of 'erring' (Taylor 1984). Hyperbole is 'the language of detours, of errancy, extravagance, and even errantry' (Magnus, Stewart, and Mileur 1993, 139)" (Ritter, "Recovering Hyperbole," 421). Ritter's citations refer to Jean-Pierre Mileur, *The Critical Romance: The Critic as Reader, Writer, Hero* (Madison: University of Wisconsin Press, 1990); Mark C. Taylor, *Erring: A Postmodern A/Theology* (Chicago: University of Chicago Press, 1984); and Bernd Magnus, Stanley Stewart, and Jean-Pierre Mileur, *Nietzsche's Case* (New York: Routledge, 1993).

17. Harry Frankfurt defines bullshitting as distinct from both truth-telling and lying by virtue of its indifference to considerations of truth, in *On Bullshit* (Princeton, NJ: Princeton University Press, 2005), 30.

18. Deppman, *Trying to Think*, 148.

19. Johnson, *Hyperboles*, 8.

20. Ritter, "Recovering Hyperbole," 424.

21. See Andrew Dorkin, "'The Mind Sneezing': Humor, Media Theory, and Modernist Poetry" (PhD diss., University at Buffalo, SUNY). Gregg Camfield writes that "humor takes pleasure in the chaotic exuberance of life" in *Necessary Madness: The Humor of Domesticity in Nineteenth-Century American Literature* (New York: Oxford University Press, 1997), 5.

22. Matthew M. Hurley, Daniel C. Dennett, and Reginald B. Adams, Jr., *Inside Jokes: Using Humor to Reverse-Engineer the Mind* (Cambridge, MA: MIT Press, 2011), 5. The pleasure of mirth, Hurley, Dennett, and Adams argue, is our reward and motivation for the "data-integrity checking"—or debugging—process, "a trick to get our brains to do all the tedious debugging that they must do if they are to live dangerously with the unruly piles of discoveries and mistakes that we generate in our incessant heuristic search" (*Inside Jokes*, 292, xi).

23. Camfield, *Necessary Madness*, 164.

24. Deppman, *Trying to Think*, 10. Because humor monitors the integrity of one's own mental spaces, first-person humor (when one laughs at one's own suddenly faulty assumption) is its fundamental form (Hurley, Dennett, and Adams, *Inside Jokes,* 133). Following Hurley, Dennett, and Adams, Camfield, and others, we understand humor differently from the long theoretical tradition that equates laughter with ridicule and deems most humor to be predicated on overt or concealed malice, superiority, or critique. In Hurley, Dennett, and Adams's model, laughter is a response to a flaw or error, but this does not foreclose the possibility of empathy. In most jokes, it is the listener—the one who laughs—that is fooled: "Either you are laughing at something in your own mind, or you are laughing at something that has a mind or to which we might counterfactually attribute a mind" (ibid., 293). When we laugh at others, we do so by projecting an erroneous mental state on to them, that is, we "identify at a distance with the object of laughter" (Camfield, *Necessary Madness,* 171).

25. Juhasz, Miller, and Smith, *Comic Power*, 10. As Regina Barreca documents, generations of readers have misunderstood women's (especially feminists') comic texts or failed to perceive their texts as humorous because the readers either did not understand the writer's indications of humor as possible or did not accept a humorous—or subversively critical—intention as likely for that writer (ibid., 11). See Barreca, *They Used to Call Me Snow White . . . but I Drifted: Women's Strategic Use of Humor* (New York: Viking Penguin, 1991).

26. Johnson, *Hyperboles*, 11.

27. Chase, *Walt Whitman Reconsidered,* 58, 59; Wallace, *God Be with the Clown,* 73–75. Wheatcroft similarly argues that Dickinson's poetry "is a continuous, episodic lyrical adventure of the soul. Such structure is, of course, traditional in comedy" ("'Holy Ghosts in Cages,'" 99). Such claims may themselves be understood as critical hyperboles,

for although we may doubt whether their claims are literally true, their disorienting propositions may lead to new insights.

28. According to Wasser, hyperbole is "situated somewhere between metaphor and irony, a figure of self-differentiation in excess of metaphor but lacking with respect to self-conscious irony" ("Hyperbole in Proust," 845).

29. The hyperbolic grandeur of Whitman's poetic project and voice makes it an easy target for parody, as in F. C. Goldsborough's "The Personified Walt Whitmanesque" (1912), which begins, "I, Walt Whitman, as large as my size and no larger (neither larger by a jot or a tittle, nor smaller by a jot or a tittle,— / O know you, all men such as I am, that this is equally true of you and of all else in the universe)—" (in *Parodies of Walt Whitman*, ed. Henry S. Saunders [New York: American Library Service, 1923]; 127). In fact, the number of parodies of Whitman's poems suggests the always potentially humorous edge in his early verse.

30. Whitman's visions of equality and liberty were of course hampered by many mid-nineteenth-century assumptions about gender and race. See, for example, Betsy Erkkila (*Whitman: The Political Poet* [Oxford: Oxford University Press, 1996]) and Vivian Pollak (*The Erotic Whitman* [Berkeley: University of California Press, 2000]). This does not change the hyperbolic grandeur of the ideal he wanted to enable and claim. In fact, it suggests that many of his equations would have seemed even more hyperbolic to nineteenth-century ears.

31. Camfield, *Necessary Madness*, 176. Emerson praised Whitman's "wit and wisdom" in his famous first letter to the poet, but he also preferred a moderating sense of humor over a biting wit: "A perception of the Comic seems to be a balance-wheel in our metaphysical structure" ("The Comic," qtd. in Camfield, *Necessary Madness*, 176).

32. Daniel Wickberg, *The Senses of Humor: Self and Laughter in Modern America* (Ithaca, NY: Cornell University Press, 1998), 63. "The exaggeration characteristic of American humor," Wickberg posits, "seems to reside in the accumulation of concrete details, as if to make reality even more real than it initially seems; such would be the case with the grotesqueries of southwestern humor, the tradition of tall tales, and other characteristically American forms" (ibid., 63). See also John Bryant's description of "The Grand American Humor Skirmish of 1844–45" in *Melville and Repose: The Rhetoric of Humor in the American Renaissance* (New York: Oxford University Press, 1993), 43–51.

33. Johnson, *Hyperboles*, 17.

34. Walt Whitman, "After All, Not to Create Only," *New York Commercial Advertiser*, September 7, 1871: [3]; *WWA*.

35. Wallace, *God Be with the Clown*, 21. Wallace draws this formulation from Whitman's essay "Slang in America": "Considering Language then as some mighty potentate, into the majestic audience-hall of the monarch ever enters a personage like one of Shakspere's clowns, and takes position there, and plays a part in even the stateliest ceremonies" (*WPP* 1165–66).

36. On this revision, see Karen Wolfe, "'Song of the Exposition' [1871]," in *Walt*

Whitman: An Encyclopedia, ed. LeMaster and Kummings, 661–62. We would like to thank Éric Athenot for drawing our attention to this poem.

37. What Dickinson hears in the bird's note, Whitman sees in the eyes of cattle: "Oxen that rattle the yoke or halt in the shade, what is that you express in your eyes? / It seems to me more than all the print I have read in my life" (*WPP 1855,* 37).

38. Dickinson's use of the gnat to epitomize smallness, limited perspective, or both appears repeatedly in *Emily Dickinson and Philosophy,* ed. Jed Deppman, Marianne Noble, and Gary Lee Stonum (New York: Cambridge University Press, 2013). In "Astonished Thinking: Dickinson and Heidegger" (227–48), Deppman looks at "Wonder – is not precisely knowing," in which Dickinson describes the question of "Whether Adult Delight is Pain / Or of itself a new misgiving – " as "the Gnat that mangles men – ," hyperbolizing the gnat's annoyance as something that "mangles" creatures much larger and, theoretically, higher in the chain of being than itself (Deppman, "Astonished Thinking," 236; *EDP* 585 [Fr 1347]). In "Truth and Lie in Emily Dickinson and Friedrich Nietzsche" (131–50), Shira Wolosky probes the echo between Nietzsche's assertion that "the gnat . . . feels within itself the flying center of the world" and Dickinson's "Who Giants know, with lesser Men," which ends with the gnat "Unconscious that his single Fleet / Do not comprise the skies – " (Wolosky, "Truth and Lie," 135; *EDP* 390 [Fr 848]). Evoking another gnat poem, Wolosky writes, "Just as Nietzsche intuits the power of perspective to frame understanding, Dickinson devotes many poems to how 'We see – Comparatively'"—a poem that concludes by describing "Some Morning of Chagrin – / The waking in a Gnat's – embrace – / Our Giants – further on – " (*EDP* 265 [Fr 580]). Renée Tursi analyses this same poem in "Emily Dickinson, Pragmatism, and the Conquests of Mind," 151–74; 158. Whitman uses the gnat for his own hyperbolic purposes when he writes, "If you would understand me go to the heights or water-shore, / The nearest gnat is an explanation" (*WPP 1855,* 84).

39. Wolosky, "Truth and Lie," 135.

40. Jane Eberwein, Stephanie Farrar, and Cristanne Miller, eds., *Dickinson in Her Own Time* (Iowa City: University of Iowa Press, 2015), 82, 105–6, 110, 111.

41. Horace Traubel, *With Walt Whitman in Camden,* vol. 4, ed. Sculley Bradley (Philadelphia: University of Pennsylvania Press, 1953), 49; Richard Maurice Bucke, *Walt Whitman* (Philadelphia: David McKay, 1883), 28. Harold Jaffe attributes "more than half" of Bucke's biography to Whitman himself, including the passage we quote here, in "Bucke's *Walt Whitman*: A Collaboration," *Walt Whitman Review* 15 (1969): 190–94; 191, 192. Jaffe notes that many of Whitman's revisions to Bucke's text involve removing, inserting, or modifying hyperboles; for example, "Bucke quoted an acquaintance as saying that 'almost everybody knew' Walt; Whitman excised the 'almost'" (Jaffe, "Bucke's *Walt Whitman*," 192).

42. John Phoenix [George Horatio Derby], "A New System of English Grammar," in *Phoenixiana; or, Sketches and Burlesques* (New York: D. Appleton, 1855). Camfield reprints this story as an appendix in *Necessary Madness*; page numbers refer to Camfield.

43. Walt Whitman, "Slang in America," in *WPP* 1170.

Radical Imaginaries

1. See, for example, my early essays, "Walt Whitman: The Politics of Language," *American Studies* 24, no. 2 (Fall 1983): 21–34; and "Emily Dickinson and Adrienne Rich: Toward a Theory of Female Influence," *American Literature* 56, no. 4 (December 1984): 541–59. After completing *Whitman the Political Poet* (New York: Oxford University Press, 1989), it was my realization that I was speaking in two very different critical voices in my work on Dickinson and Whitman—one feminist and celebratory, the other political and against the grain—that led me to write "Emily Dickinson and Class" (*American Literary History* 4 [Spring 1992]: 1–27), an essay that was described as "notorious" in the annual review *American Literary Scholarship* in 1992.

2. Mabel Loomis Todd, ed., *Letters of Emily Dickinson* (New York: Harper, 1931), 132; "I'm Nobody! Who are you?" [Fr 260]).

3. See Betsy Erkkila, "Dickinson and the Art of Politics," in *A Historical Guide to Emily Dickinson*, ed. Vivian Pollak (Oxford: Oxford University Press, 2004), 138–44.

4. Erkkila, "Dickinson and Class," 1–27.

5. Charles Sumner, "Report on the War with Mexico" (April 1847); reprinted in *Old South Leaflets*, vol. 6 (Boston: Old South Work, 1902), 30.

6. Walt Whitman, *Prose Works 1892,* ed. Floyd Stovall, 2 vols. (New York: New York University Press, 1964), 1:288. According to "Emily Dickinson's Schooling: Mount Holyoke Female Seminary," "Dickinson was among eighty without hope when she entered and was among twenty-nine who remained so by the end of the year"; see https://www.emilydickinsonmuseum.org/mount_holyoke.

7. Walt Whitman, "Resurgemus," June 21, 1850, in Walt Whitman, *Early American Poems and Fiction*, ed. Thomas L. Brasher (New York: New York University Press, 1968), 38.

8. Walt Whitman (unsigned in original), "Walt Whitman and His Poems," *United States Review* 5 (September 1855): 205–12; *WWA*.

9. Betsy Erkkila, *The Wicked Sisters*: *Women Poets, Literary History, and Discord* (New York: Oxford University Press, 1992), 38–39; see also Martha Nell Smith, *Rowing in Eden*: *Re-Reading Emily Dickinson* (Austin: University of Texas Press, 1992).

10. In *The Poems of Emily Dickinson: Variorum Edition* (Cambridge, MA: Harvard University, Belknap Press, 1998), R. W. Franklin identifies 557 poems that Dickinson sent to family and friends, but there may have been many more poems sent and many other unidentified recipients (see Appendix 7: "Recipients," 1547). According to Mabel Loomis Todd, Lavinia told her that while she preserved Dickinson's poems, "she had burned without examination hundreds of manuscripts, and letters to Emily, many of them from nationally known persons," in "Emily Dickinson's Literary Début," *Harper's Monthly Magazine* (March 1930): 463.

11. For classic readings of Whitman as a mystical poet, see James E. Miller, Jr., "'Song of Myself' as Inverted Mystical Experience," *PMLA* 70 (September 1955): 636–61; and Malcolm Cowley, "Introduction," in Walt Whitman, *Leaves of Grass: His Original Edition*, ed. Malcolm Cowley (New York: Viking, 1959), xii. For readings that challenge

this more transcendental Whitman, see Robert K. Martin's pioneering essay, "Walt Whitman's *Song of Myself:* Homosexual Dream and Vision," *Partisan Review* 42 (1975): 80–96; Jay Grossman, "'The Evangel-Poem of Comrades and Love': Revising Whitman's Republicanism," *American Transcendental Quarterly* 4 (September 1990): 201–18; Michael Moon, *Disseminating Whitman: Revision and Corporeality in Leaves of Grass* (Cambridge, MA: Harvard University Press, 1991); and Betsy Erkkila, "Whitman and the Homosexual Republic," in *Walt Whitman: The Centennial Essays*, ed. Ed Folsom (Iowa City: University of Iowa Press, 1994), 153–71.

12. On Dickinson's love relationship with Susan Gilbert, see Lillian Faderman, "Emily Dickinson's Letters to Susan Gilbert," *Massachusetts Review* 18 (1978): 197–225; on the formative presence of this love relationship in Dickinson's life and work, see Erkkila, *Wicked Sisters*, 27–42; and Smith, *Rowing in Eden*, which also includes a discussion of Austin's "work" in attempting to erase the specifically lesbian dimensions of this relationship.

13. For a discussion of the more negative, guilt-ridden homosexual dimension of Dickinson's love relationships with women, especially Susan Gilbert, see Vivian Pollak, *Dickinson: The Anxiety of Gender* (Ithaca, NY: Cornell University Press, 1984).

14. Charley Shively was the first to identify Fred Vaughan as the inspiration of the "Calamus" poems, in *Calamus Lovers: Walt Whitman's Working Class Camerados*, ed. Charley Shively (San Francisco: Gay Sunshine, 1987), 114, 36–50. See also Gary Schmidgall, *Walt Whitman: A Gay Life* (New York: Dutton, 1997); Jonathan Ned Katz, *Love Stories: Sex between Men before Homosexuality* (Chicago: University of Chicago Press, 2001); and Betsy Erkkila, "Songs of Male Intimacy and Love: An Afterword," in *Walt Whitman's Songs of Male Intimacy and Love: "Live Oak, with Moss" and "Calamus,"* ed. Betsy Erkkila (Iowa City: University of Iowa Press, 2011), 99–162.

15. Walt Whitman, "A Word Out of the Sea," in *Leaves of Grass*, facsimile edition of the 1860 text, ed. Roy Harvey Pearce (Ithaca, N.Y.: Cornell University Press, 1961), 276.

16. It was not until after the Civil War, in the 1871 edition of *Leaves of Grass*, that Whitman first used the title "Out of the Cradle Endlessly Rocking."

17. Of the eleven poems that Dickinson is known to have published during her lifetime, seven were published during the Civil War, including her manifesto poem "I taste a liquor never brewed – " (Fr 207), which was published as "The May-Wine" in the *Republican* a few weeks after the war began. In 1864 she published four poems, three of which appeared in *Drum Beat,* a fund-raising magazine for the United States Sanitary Commission, which was founded in 1861 to provide medical supplies and help for the Union Army. Karen Dandurand has argued importantly that these poems "must be seen as [Dickinson's] contribution to the Union cause," in "New Dickinson Civil War Publications," *American Literature* 56 (1984): 17–27; 17. However, if she did contribute these poems voluntarily, and there is no evidence for this, they were more likely sent to support the sick, wounded, and dying who were sacrificing their lives in support of a cause that was—in Dickinson's view—at best questionable. For a detailed discussion of Dickinson's poems in relation to the Civil War, see Thomas Ford, "Emily Dickinson and the Civil War," *University of Kansas City Review* 31 (Spring 1965): 199–203; and especially

Shira Wolosky, *Emily Dickinson: A Voice of War* (New Haven, CT: Yale University Press, 1984); and Shira Wolosky, "Public and Private in Dickinson's War Poetry," in *Historical Guide*, ed. Pollak, 103–32.

18. Abraham Lincoln, *The Collected Works of Abraham Lincoln,* ed. Roy P. Basler (New Brunswick, NJ: Rutgers University Press, 1953–55), 7:23, 8:333.

19. Henry Adams, *The Education of Henry Adams* (Boston: Houghton Mifflin, 1961), 34.

20. On Dickinson as an admirer of George Washington and a witty and articulate spokesperson for a conservative tradition, which has not been legible within the primarily textual and/or national democratic frames of American literary studies, see Erkkila, "Dickinson and the Art of Politics," 134–38. See also Lionel Trilling, who at the very moment American literary studies was being constituted as a distinct national field, observed: "In the United States at this time liberalism is not only the only dominant but even the sole intellectual tradition. For it is a plain fact that nowadays there are no conservative or reactionary ideas in general circulation" ("Preface," in *The Liberal Imagination: Essays on Literature and Society* [New York: Harcourt Brace Jovanovich, 1950], n.p.). For an approach to Dickinson's poetry and lyric reading more generally that resists modern and contemporary idealizations of the lyric, see Virginia Jackson, *Dickinson's Misery: A Theory of Reading Lyric* (Princeton, NJ: Princeton University Press, 2005).

Queer Contingencies of Canonicity

1. Dana Nelson provides a pointed summary: "F. O. Matthiessen's magisterial New Critical approach to nineteenth-century literature . . . would definitively orient critical interest away from nineteenth-century women's writing for the next twenty-some years. . . . The most notable effect of his approach was to delineate a separate literary sphere not so much for *women*, but for (select) male writers, a rarified sphere where we could witness the production not of 'fiction' but of *art*. In subsequent years, women writers like Emily Dickinson—who refused to publish her poetry—might become honorary members of this sphere, but the 'mass' of 'scribbling women' became literally invisible, except as a caricature against which to balance the underappreciated artistic productions of elite writers" (43). (Dana Nelson, "Women in Public," in *The Cambridge Companion to Nineteenth-Century American Women's Writing,* ed. Dale M. Bauer and Philip Gould [New York: Cambridge University Press, 2001], 38–67.)

2. Letter 1084, March 9, 1931; unless otherwise noted, quotations from Matthiessen's letters are cited from the Matthiessen Correspondence held in Yale's Beinecke Library.

3. On Whitman-as-Emerson, see my "The Canon in the Closet: Matthiessen's Whitman, Whitman's Matthiessen." *American Literature* 70, no. 4 (1998); and "'Profession of the Calamus': Whitman, Eliot, Matthiessen," in *"Leaves of Grass": The 150th Anniversary Conference,* ed. Ed Folsom, Kenneth M. Price, and Susan Belasco (Lincoln: University of Nebraska Press, 2008), 321–42.

4. F. O. Matthiessen, *American Renaissance: Art and Expression in the Age of Emerson and Whitman* (1941; New York: Oxford University Press, 1968), 229n1. Hereafter *AR*.

5. Anna Mary Wells, "Early Criticism of Emily Dickinson," *American Literature* 1, no. 3 (1929): 259.

6. F. O. Matthiessen, *Sarah Orne Jewett* (Boston: Houghton Mifflin, 1929), 151. Hereafter *SOJ*.

7. Ann Douglas, *The Feminization of American Culture*, 1st ed. (New York: Knopf, 1977); Jane P. Tompkins, *Sensational Designs: The Cultural Work of American Fiction, 1790–1860* (New York: Oxford University Press, 1985).

8. Letter 65, December 2, 1924, quoted from *Rat and the Devil: Journal Letters of F. O. Matthiessen and Russell Cheney*, ed. Louis Hyde (Boston: Alyson Publications, 1988), 63. Hereafter *R&D*. A recently discovered letter from Matthiessen to his close Yale friend Louis Hyde casts additional light on Matthiessen's early reading of both Whitman and Dickinson: "Have you ever really attacked Whitman? If you haven't, you must. I am absolutely convinced that he is the one great American literary figure. Now don't shake your Thoreau locks at me. For Whitman makes articulate everything that Thoreau just hints in Walden. And a great deal more. And then how about Emily Dickinson? I read her solidly for the first time just before leaving Oxford. The praise that she has been getting this autumn in England—"the greatest woman who ever wrote in the English language"[—]is extravagant. But there is a terseness of line and a clarity of spirit that gives her a note all her own. And except for Edna Millay she is the whale among the tadpoles of American poetesses. Hardly an apt metaphor, since she was the diminutive, delicate New England lady. But then . . ." (F. O. Matthiessen to Louis K. Hyde, Jr., December 17, 1924 [postmark], letter in the possession of the author).

9. F. O. Matthiessen, ed., *The Oxford Book of American Verse* (New York: Oxford University Press, 1950), xiv–xv.

10. F. O. Matthiessen, "The Problem of the Private Poet," *Kenyon Review* 7, no. 4 (Autumn 1945): 584–97; this quotation on 590. Hereafter "P.P." Matthiessen has a different second line: "Than a rising sun."

11. Matthiessen's 1945 account of Dickinson in relation to the metaphysical poets not only reflects the persistence of Eliot's literary criticism, but also shares its angle of vision with his Harvard colleague and friend Theodore Spencer's 1929 understanding of her work in his review of *Further Poems of Emily Dickinson*: "her genius went deeper, and by its very isolation blossomed from the roots of the New England mind; she is mentally related, not to Tennyson, but to the metaphysical poets of two centuries before" ("Concentration and Intensity," rpt. in Caesar R. Blake and Carlton F. Wells, *The Recognition of Emily Dickinson* [Ann Arbor: University of Michigan Press, 1964], 131). We have barely begun to excavate the genealogies and collaborations—tacit and otherwise—that lay behind Matthiessen's pronouncements in *American Renaissance*. Eliot's review essay is of course legendary: "The Metaphysical Poets," *Times Literary Supplement* (October 20, 1921): 669+. *Times Literary Supplement Historical Archive*, Web.

12. For more on Whitman's role in the constitution of the Matthiessen/Cheney relationship, see my "The Canon in the Closet."

13. Emily Dickinson, *Open Me Carefully: Emily Dickinson's Intimate Letters to Susan*

Huntington Dickinson, ed. Ellen Louise Hart and Martha Nell Smith (Ashfield, MA: Paris, 1998). Richard B. Sewall's *The Life of Emily Dickinson* (Cambridge, MA: Harvard University Press, 1997) was first published in 1974; "Homosexuality" has four brief mentions in the index. Thomas H. Johnson's edition of *The Poems of Emily Dickinson* was first published in 1955 (Cambridge, MA: Harvard University, Belknap Press).

14. Matthiessen's mother, Lucy Orne Matthiessen, was Sarah Orne Jewett's sixth cousin, once removed.

15. Marjorie Pryse gestures toward a Jewett/Rich connection in the introduction to her edition of *The Country of the Pointed Firs, and Other Stories* (New York: Norton, 1994), p. xx n.12. This edition also includes an additional introduction, first published in 1968, by Mary Ellen Chase, who taught at Smith College, lived much of her life in the intimate company of another female professor, and for both of whom two adjoining student residences at Smith are now named. Taken together these preliminary texts especially celebrate Jewett's emphasis on female nurturance and continuity, "the kind of vision 'mother' possesses [that] gives her daughter the wisdom of her ancestral and mythical mothers" (xv). Both David Bergman in "F. O. Matthiessen: The Critic as Homosexual" (*Raritan* 9, no. 4 [1990]), and Travis M. Foster, in "Matthiessen's Public Privates: Homosexual Expression and the Aesthetics of Sexual Inversion" (*American Literature* 78, no. 2 [2006]), also discuss the alignments between Jewett's sexuality and Matthiessen's.

16. Adrienne Rich, "Blood, Bread, and Poetry: The Location of the Poet," in *Arts of the Possible: Essays and Conversations* (New York: Norton, 2001), 41–61. This quotation on 45–46.

17. See William Wright, *Harvard's Secret Court: The Savage 1920 Purge of Campus Homosexuals* (New York: St. Martin's, 2005).

18. Adrienne Rich, "Not How to Write Poetry, but Wherefore," in *What Is Found There: Notebooks on Poetry and Politics* (New York: Norton, 1993), 190–96. This quotation on 195.

19. Adrienne Rich, "Vesuvius at Home: The Power of Emily Dickinson (1975)," in *On Lies, Secrets, and Silence: Selected Prose, 1966–1978* (New York: Norton, 1979), 157–83. This quotation on 158.

20. Adrienne Rich, personal correspondence with the author, March 22, 2003.

21. Rich carefully credits Sewall by name for altering the trends in Dickinson biography by opening out the possibility of reading Dickinson's attachments to women with fewer preconceptions in his 1974 biography, published the year before Rich's essay ("Vesuvius," 162).

Whitman, Dickinson, and Their Legacy of Lists and "It"s

1. From "Knows how to forget!" (Fr 391).

2. Walt Whitman, *Daybooks and Notebooks*, ed. William White, vol. 3 (New York: New York University Press, 1978), 816. Subsequent references will be cited in the text with the abbreviation *Daybooks*.

3. Georges Perros, *Papiers collés II* [*Glued Papers II*] (Paris: Gallimard, 1973), 97–100; unless otherwise noted, all translations are my own and Ray DiPalma's. A collection of fragments, *Papiers collés II* was published in 1971, nine years before Jean-Luc Nancy and Philippe Lacoue-Labarthe's work on the German Romantics, *The Literary Absolute*, sparked fresh interest in the short broken form. Perros's work was never translated into English. There is little doubt that the narrative and relatively accessible nature of his two collections of poetry made him virtually invisible in the days of rarefied words on the page, *la modernité blanche*. His fragments, on the other hand, often verge on the aphoristic, more Dickinson's letters than *Specimen Days*. Perros died in 1981.

4. To the best of my knowledge, there is little critical writing bringing out the epic features in Dickinson's work. Susan Howe's *My Emily Dickinson* (Berkeley, CA: North Atlantic Books, 1985) does. Howe calls Fr 764, "My Life had stood – a Loaded Gun – ," "a pioneer's terse epic" (35). "My-Life is a woman and a weapon," she writes (103). *Her* Emily Dickinson is emphatically not the "Spider-Artist" expert at patching and mending as she is made out to be in Sandra M. Gilbert and Susan Gubar's *The Madwoman in the Attic: The Woman Writer and the Nineteenth-Century Literary Imagination* (New Haven, CT: Yale University Press, 1979), 639, that dedicated seamstress already satirized by Elizabeth Barrett Browning in *Aurora Leigh*, ed. Margaret Reynolds (New York: W. W. Norton, 1996), 1:455–64. The title of the third part of *My Emily Dickinson*—"Trumpets Sing to Battle"—makes it clear that Howe sees Dickinson as a heroine engaged in a battle with her poems to be received as so many battle cries.

In "Brave Columbus, Brave Columba: Emily Dickinson's Search for Land," Cynthia Hallen concludes from her analysis of Dickinson's metaphors related to Christopher Columbus that the poems as a whole constitute a *Columbiad*, that is, a literary work inspired by the discovery of the American continent (*The Emily Dickinson Journal* 5, no. 2 [Fall 1996]: 169–75). She shows how "Dickinson adapted images from Washington Irving's 1828 *Life and Voyages of Columbus* in her epic portrayal of the poet's voyage." More generally, she argues that "Dickinson's epic work is a circuit, a circumference, a circumlocution, and a circumnavigation of language, love, and life as the poet searches for promised lands." John Shoptaw also implies Dickinson's link to epic: "My goal in this paper is to explore what the war meant for Dickinson *in her capacity as a poet*," he writes in "Dickinson's Civil War Poetics: From the Enrollment Act to the Lincoln Assassination," *The Emily Dickinson Journal* 19, no. 2 (2010): 1–19; 1.

5. Revelation: 19:13 and 19:21, and 1:16, Authorized King James Version.

6. Revelation is itself a clear reference in Browning's poem. The characters' words often echo that book of the New Testament. For instance, Aurora's final words, about "the first foundations of that new, near Day" (312), are directly inspired by Rev. 21:19–21.

7. Christine and the Queens, performance of "iT," on *Chaleur Humaine*, Because Music, compact disc, 2014. The lyrics (in English) tell the story of the female speaker who seems to have reached a high degree of psychological gender fluidity, which involved going through the death of her original identity: "With iT / I become the death Dickinson feared / . . . / Wet infans for my coronation / I'll rule over all my dead impersonations

/ I've got iT / I'm a man now / And I won't let you steal iT!" The opening track on the CD, the song is clearly inspired by Dickinson's "I'm ceded – I've stopped being Their's – " (Fr 353). Christine's "wet infans" and "my coronation" respectively echo the baptism and new coronation scenes in stanzas 1 and 3 of the poem. Like Dickinson, she is no longer "A half unconscious Queen – ." No doubt the gender-neutral "it" held special appeal for Christine. And the songwriter's choice to have each letter of the pronoun printed in a different typeface—a lowercase "i" followed by a capital "T"—may well be meant to materialize the gender fluidity celebrated in the song. However, the shifting references of the pronoun in the song testify to a deeper knowledge of Dickinson.

8. Cristanne Miller, *Emily Dickinson: A Poet's Grammar* (Cambridge, MA: Harvard University Press, 1987).

9. Ibid., 81.

10. *The Holy Bible, Containing the Old and New Testaments* (Authorized Version) (Philadelphia: J. B. Lippincott, 1843), http://nrs.harvard.edu/urn-3:FHCL.Hough:4906292.

11. It was part of the translators' rules to highlight in some manner the words added to the text of the original manuscripts: "Whereas the necessity of the sentence required anything to be added (for such is the grace and propriety of the Hebrew and Greek tongues, that it cannot but either by circumlocution, or by adding the verb, or some word, be understood of them that are not well-practised therein) we have put it in the text with another kind of letter" (quoted from the Geneva edition of the Bible of 1578 in Frederick Henry Ambrose Scrivener, *A Supplement to the Authorized English Version of the New Testament: Being a Critical Illustration of Its More Difficult Passages from the Syriac, Latin, and Earlier English Versions, with an Introduction* [London: William Pickering, 1845], 60–61, https://archive.org/details/cu31924090851779). The 1611 Bible was in fancy black letter type. Originally, the added words were in smaller Roman type and not in italics (Gordon Campbell, *Bible: The Story of the King James Version 1611–2011* [Oxford: Oxford University Press, 2011], 42).

12. Jack L. Capps, *Emily Dickinson's Reading* (Cambridge, MA: Harvard University Press, 1966), 30.

13. Eccles. 8:17.

14. Miller's pages on this provide all the documentation needed (*Emily Dickinson: A Poet's Grammar*, 75–82).

15. In "It dont sound so terrible – quite – as it did – " (Fr 384), Dickinson lists a few strategies that can be implemented to attenuate the dread elicited by the word "dead." One is precisely to substitute "it" for the dreaded word ("it" is used five times in the first four lines). But that is not enough. The more effective method exemplified by the poem consists in altering "it" itself by "[s]hift[ing] it," disguising it, concealing it under the mask of other words: "Shift," "Habit," "'a fit.'" Doing so may muffle the "shriek" the word "[d]ead" initially provokes. The equation of death with "Murder" introduced in the poem's last line brings God back into the picture although he is not named. Who else might the murderer be? In this case, too, the path of the inexpressible links death to God through "it" and the list.

16. Miller, *Emily Dickinson: A Poet's Grammar*, 24.

17. From "Under the Light, yet under" (Fr 1068).

18. Lawrence Buell, "Transcendental Catalog Rhetoric: Vision versus Form," *American Literature* 40, no. 3 (1968): 325–39; 334.

19. *Ralph Waldo Emerson to Walt Whitman*, July 21, 1855, Charles E. Feinberg–Walt Whitman Collection, Library of Congress, hdl.loc.gov/loc.mss/mcc.012.

20. Bernard Sève, *De haut en bas: Philosophie des listes* (Paris: Le Seuil, 2010), 48.

21. Except for the quotations from the *Daybooks* and where otherwise noted, all quotations from Whitman refer to Justin Kaplan's *Whitman: Poetry and Prose* (New York: Literary Classics of the United States, 1996) and will be cited in the text with "*WPP*" and the page number.

22. A third example in Whitman's writings of a list based on the reiteration of indefinites is found in a notebook that illustrates Whitman's more complementary than contradictory attitudes toward completion: the entry on "the greatest and truest knowledge [that] can never be taught" consists of half a dozen anaphoric sentences starting with "It" which, were they not prose, could be fitted into "Song for the Occupations"; it is followed by notes for "Who Learns My Lesson Complete?" (*Daybooks*, 774).

23. Jed Deppman, *Trying to Think with Emily Dickinson* (Amherst: University of Massachusetts Press, 2008), 119.

24. Ibid., 122, 124.

25. Daniel Madelénat, "Présence paradoxale de l'épopée: Hors d'âge et sur le retour," in *Désirs & débris d'épopée au XXe siècle*, ed. Saulo Neiva (Bern: Peter Lang, 2009), 379–91, 379; my translation.

26. Umberto Eco, *The Infinity of Lists: From Homer to Joyce*, trans. Alastair McEwen (London: MacLehose, 2009), 49.

27. Ibid., 49.

28. F. O. Matthiessen, *American Renaissance: Art and Expression in the Age of Emerson and Whitman* (Oxford: Oxford University Press, 1941), 521, 796–97.

29. Ibid., 575.

30. I omit the dedication and the final poem from this count.

31. Stevens leaves room for humor: "They will get it straight one day at the Sorbonne." Wallace Stevens, *Collected Poems* (London: Faber and Faber, 1954), 406.

32. Hilda Doolittle (H. D.), *Trilogy* (New York: New Directions, 1973).

33. This speaker, rendered powerless by fascination, seems consistent with H. D.'s less ironic personality.

34. Susan Stanford Friedman, *Psyche Reborn: The Emergence of H. D.* (Bloomington: Indiana University Press, 1981), 253.

35. Ibid.

36. J. W. Walkington, "Mystical Experience in H. D. and Walt Whitman: An Intertextual Reading of 'Tribute to the Angels' and 'Song of Myself,'" *Walt Whitman Quarterly Review* 11 (Winter 1994): 123–36.

37. Ibid., 133.

38. The word "triangulation" is borrowed from Gary Schmidgall's "Triangulating Blake, Whitman, and Ginsberg," *Walt Whitman Quarterly Review* 32 (2015): 131–43.

39. "Draft 1" was first published in *Temblor* 5 (1987).

40. As in "Make it new" or "I cannot make it cohere." Jean-Paul Auxeméry, "Note sur le 'poème long,'" in Rachel Blau DuPlessis, *Brouillons*, trans. Jean-Paul Auxeméry (Paris: Corti, 2013), 266–72; 267, 269.

41. Rachel Blau DuPlessis, *Drafts 1–38, Toll* (Middletown, CT: Wesleyan University Press, 2001), 4.

42. See also "Not hero, not polis, not story, but it" (DuPlessis, *Drafts 1–38*, 102).

43. Whitman seems to have intuited the theory of language which Saussure would later advocate, that is, as "only a system of pure values" and value itself as "purely negative and differential." Ferdinand de Saussure, *Course in General Linguistics*, trans. Wade Baskin (New York: Philosophical Library, 1959), 11, 111. In "A Song for Occupations," Whitman introduces the "it" lines by saying "I . . . offer no representative of value / but offer the value itself" (*WPP* 357). Put another way, as he is about to tackle the absolute indefinite in terms of content, he chooses to offer the form that makes any content possible, that is, the concept of value itself. As Dickinson puts it, "internal difference – / Where the Meanings, are – " (Fr 320).

44. "Yes—there is LOTS of 'it' in all of the *Drafts*. The word IT is a definite motivic element. (I won't say motivic center, because I am 'acting as if [or 'so'] there is no use in a center' as Stein says." Rachel Blau DuPlessis's e-mail message to the author, August 1, 2015.

45. Emphasis mine. Marina Camboni made this remark in response to a presentation of this material at the "Walt Whitman & Emily Dickinson: A Colloquy" conference, Université Paris-Est Créteil on March 12–13, 2015. See Lew Welch, *How I Read Gertrude Stein*, ed. Eric Paul Shaffer (San Francisco: Grey Fox, 1996), 84.

46. Gertrude Stein, *How to Write* (Mineola, NY: Dover, 1975), 339. The "A Vocabulary of Thinking" chapter is a gold mine for examples.

47. Written in 1995. Ann Lauterbach, *The Night Sky: Writings on the Poetics of Experience* (New York: Viking Penguin, 2005). For lack of space, I will just mention Kerouac's inflamed descriptions of bebop performances chasing and reaching the transcendental "it," in which the pronoun becomes shorthand for a musician's most inspired moments. The best example is probably found in *On the Road* (1957; Harmondsworth, Eng.: Viking, Penguin Books, 1972), 194–96. About the influence of Transcendentalism on Beat writers, see the first seven pages of Robert Faggen, "The Beats and the 1960s," in *The Cambridge History of the American Novel,* ed. Leonard Cassuto, Clare Virginia Eby, and Benjamin Reiss (Cambridge: Cambridge University Press, 2011), 909–24.

48. Lauterbach, *The Night Sky*, 44–45.

49. Ibid., 152–53.

50. Bill Berkson, "Tarps," in *Walt Whitman hom(m)age 2005/1855,* by Éric Athenot and Olivier Brossard (Éditions joca seria & Turtle Point, 2005), 25.

51. From Dickinson's "Their Hight in Heaven comforts not – " (Fr 725) and "If What we could – were what we would – " (Fr 540).

52. Agnieszka Salska, *Walt Whitman and Emily Dickinson: Poetry of the Central Consciousness* (Philadelphia: University of Pennsylvania Press, 1985), 157.

53. Ibid., 156.

54. Éric Athenot, "'Of Hard-Fought Engagements or Sieges Tremendous What Deepest Remains?' A Few Questions around Walt Whitman's Epic of Democracy," in *Elle s'étend l'épopée/ The Epic Expands*, ed. V. Dussol (Brussels: P.I.E. Peter Lang, 2012), 383–92. The first two pages address the question of unnecessary labeling.

55. Trace Peterson, "Drones," in *Devouring the Green: Fear of a Human Planet: Anthology of New Writing*, ed. Sam Witt (Seattle, WA: Jaded Ibis, 2015), 198.

56. Sam Truitt, "Zone," in *Devouring the Green*, 424.

"Beginners"

1. Adrienne Rich, interview at *ChilePoesía* 2001, https://www.youtube.com/watch?v=ogWSt7zBErk. June Jordan's words are taken from an exerga in Adrienne Rich's essay "History Stops for No One," in *What Is Found There: Notebooks on Poetry and Politics* (New York: Norton, 1993), 128.

2. Whitman's "Beginners" in 1860 was part of the "Thoughts" cluster of poems, one of the last in the volume, but in the 1891–92 edition it was included, unchanged, in "Inscriptions," the opening cluster. Both editions can be consulted in *The Walt Whitman Archive*. Rich's "Beginners" was published in the *Kenyon Review* 15, no. 3 (Summer 1993): 12–19, and reprinted in *What Is Found There*, 90–101 (my source). All quotations from "Beginners" are cited as *WFT*, followed by the page number. The essay is included in *Walt Whitman: The Measure of His Song*, ed. Jim Perlman, Ed Folsom, and Dan Campion (Duluth, MN: Holy Cow, 1998), 447–51.

3. Adrienne Rich, *A Human Eye: Essays 1997–2008* (New York: Norton, 2009), 96. All other quotations from this text appear as *HE*, followed by page number.

4. Martha Nussbaum, *Poetic Justice: The Literary Imagination and Public Life* (Boston: Beacon, 1995).

5. Hannah Arendt, *The Life of the Mind* (San Diego, CA: Harcourt, 1978), 19. On her conception of politics, see "Concern with Politics in Recent European Philosophical Thought," in her *Essays in Understanding 1930–1954* (New York: Shocken Books, 1994), particularly p. 429.

6. Adrienne Rich, "Heroines," in *A Wild Patience Has Taken Me This Far* (New York: Norton, 1981), 35, 36.

7. See in particular Pierre Bourdieu, "The Field of Cultural Production; or, The Economic World Reversed," *Poetics* 12 (1983): 311–56; Alain Badiou (with Nicolas Truong), *Éloge de l'amour* (Paris: Flammarion, 2009); Yuri Lotman, *Culture and Explosion: Semiotics, Communication and Cognition 1*, ed. Marina Grishakova, trans. Wilma Clark (Berlin: De Gruyter Mouton, 2009).

8. John Lyons, *Semantics*, vol. 1 (Cambridge: Cambridge University Press, 1977), 280.

9. This quotation from Audre Lorde's "Power" is one of the many that introduce her

own 1978 essay, "Disloyal to Civilization: Feminism, Racism, Gynephobia," in *On Lies, Secrets, and Silences* (New York: Norton, 1979), 278. Rich's "Vesuvius at Home: The Power of Emily Dickinson" was also included in the volume. All quotations from the essay, and the volume, are cited in the text as *LSS* followed by the page number.

10. Adrienne Rich, *Poems: Selected and New 1950–1974* (New York: Norton, 1975), 56. Quotations from poems in the volume are cited in the text as *Poems* followed by the page number.

11. Jean-Claude Milner, *L'Universel en éclats: Court traité politique 3* (Lagrasse: Verdier, 2014), 15; my translation.

12. I quote Dickinson's text here as Rich presents it, as I do elsewhere in the essay (as indicated through bibliographic reference).

13. Although in many ways it opens the path to an essentialist criticism, Rich's essay does not simply anticipate what later feminist critics theorized, that is, that Dickinson's metaphors and cryptic texts were a version of the duplicitous language used by socially and verbally chastised nineteenth-century women poets. See Cheryl Walker, "Dickinson in Context: Nineteenth-Century Women Poets," in *A Historical Guide to Emily Dickinson*, ed. Vivian R. Pollak (Oxford: Oxford University Press, 2004), 175–200. For Rich, Dickinson's metaphors and slanted language were also the very place that allowed her to stand her ground and explore the unsaid.

14. James McIntosh, *Nimble Believing: Dickinson and the Unknown* (Ann Arbor: University of Michigan Press, 2000), 1.

15. For Crumbley, Dickinson had a totally different attitude toward history than Emerson and Whitman. Where Emerson could construct a collective present and Whitman placed his I on the apex that was the present, Dickinson, he states, "issues a cautionary note . . . Rather than trusting in the ultimate union of poetic truth and history, Dickinson's language calls for a personality courageous enough to promote changes that will shock those whose vision of the future is founded on past precedent." Crumbley, *Winds of Will: Emily Dickinson and the Sovereignty of Democratic Thought* (Tuscaloosa: University of Alabama Press, 2010), 81.

16. Crumbley, *Winds of Will*, 81; Shira Wolosky, "Truth and Lie in Emily Dickinson and Friedrich Nietzsche," in *Emily Dickinson and Philosophy*, ed. Jed Deppman, Gary Lee Stonum, and Marianne Noble (Cambridge: Cambridge University Press, 2013), 131–50.

17. Roger Lundin, *Emily Dickinson and the Art of Belief* (Grand Rapids, MI: W.B. Eerdmans, 1998), 45. On Dickinson's personae or masks, see Fred D. White, "Emily Dickinson's Existential Dramas," in *The Cambridge Companion to Emily Dickinson*, ed. Wendy Martin (Cambridge: Cambridge University Press, 2002), 91–106. For "outer configurations" and gender identity performances, see Suzanne Juhasz and Cristanne Miller, "Performances of Gender in Dickinson's Poetry," in *The Cambridge Companion to Emily Dickinson*, 107–41.

18. Rich refers to William Luce's play, first performed in 1976, in the note that introduces her 1975 essay in the collection *On Lies*, published four years later.

19. Rich quotes from Toni McMaron.

20. Pierre Bourdieu has given a specific sense to the "field of art" in "The Field of Cultural Production."

21. For an overall analysis of Rich's reading of Dickinson, see Betsy Erkkila's *The Wicked Sisters: Women Poets, Literary History and Discord* (New York: Oxford University Press, 1992). On Rich's interpretation of a "wild" Dickinson, the influence of John Berryman and the New Critics must also be taken into consideration, as Christopher Benfey has pointed out in "Emily Dickinson and the American South," in *The Cambridge Companion to Emily Dickinson*, ed. Wendy Martin (Cambridge: Cambridge University Press, 2002), 30–50. Shira Wolosky, on the other hand, calls attention not only to "her poetry of anger, dissatisfaction, and critique" but to the ways God incarnates both a closed and an open frontier; see "Emily Dickinson: Being in the Body," in *The Cambridge Companion to Emily Dickinson,* ed. Wendy Martin (Cambridge: Cambridge University Press, 2002), 129–42; 133, 131.

22. Adrienne Rich, "In the Wake of Home," in *The Fact of a Doorframe: Poems Selected and New 1950–1984* (New York: Norton, 1984), 322.

23. For a Jungian reading of Dickinson and Rich, see Albert J. Gelpi's "Adrienne Rich: The Poetics of Change," in *American Poetry since 1960: Some Critical Perspectives,* ed. Robert Shaw (Chaedle, UK: Carcanet, 1973), 130–48; and Gelpi, "Emily Dickinson and the Deerslayer: The Dilemma of the Woman Poet in America," in *Jungian Literary Criticism,* ed. Richard P. Sugg (Evanston, Ill.: Northwestern University Press, 1992), 103–17.

24. Domhnall Mitchell devotes two chapters of his book to addressing the issue of "house" and "home." He considers the home in which Dickinson lived "a trope for a site of refuge," linked to notions of subjectivity, culture, and protection, and "a literal and literary ownership over which there are conflicting claims of ownership." Mitchell, *Emily Dickinson: Monarch of Perception* (Amherst: University of Massachusetts Press, 2000), 44. However, it must be pointed out that in her letters, Dickinson usually associates "home" with her father and with male authorities. To Higginson, for instance, she wrote: "I often go Home in thought to you" (*L* 450); and, after her father's death, she repeatedly lamented, "home is so far from home, since my father died" (*L* 433 and *L* 441).

25. The emphasis on "*last year's flies*" is mine.

26. *De Vulgari Eloquentia* (1303–04) is a treatise, written in Latin, where Dante illustrates the need for an illustrious vernacular to be created by poets out of the common Italian dialects of the time and used in literature in place of Latin.

27. At the beginning of what became "Song of Myself," Walt listens to the "sounds of the belched words of my voice," while in the very last section of the poem, he says: "I sound my barbaric yawp over the roofs of the world" (*WPP* 27, 87).

28. The two quotations in the paragraph are from Rich's *The Dream of a Common Language: Poems 1974–1977* (New York: Norton, 1978), 7, 5.

29. See the essays gathered in *A Human Eye.*

30. See, in particular, the chapter "Architecture of Meaning," in Howe's *My Emily Dickinson,* with a preface by Eliot Weinberger (New York: New Directions, 2007).

31. Adrienne Rich, *Blood, Bread, and Poetry: Selected Prose 1979–1985* (New York: Norton, 1986), 224.

32. In "This Is My Third and Last Address to You" (Mp3 file, http://www.emilydickinson.org/titanic-operas/folio-one/adrienne-rich), Rich addresses herself to Dickinson and reads her poem "Spirit of Place," where she quotes Dickinson's *L* 203 (Rich, *The Fact of a Doorframe*, 300). Smith makes her comment in "Poet as Cartoonist," 71; qtd. in Cristanne Miller, *Reading in Time* (Amherst: University of Massachusetts Press, 2012), 5.

33. Rich, *The Fact of a Doorframe*, 323.

34. "Mannahatta" was first published in Whitman's 1860 *Leaves*. The line referring to slaves was later deleted. Quotations refer to *Leaves of Grass*, 1860, in the *Walt Whitman Archive*, and are cited in the text as *WWA* 1860, followed by the page number, http://www.whitmanarchive.org/published/LG/1860/whole.html.

35. Adrienne Rich, *Your Native Land, Your Life: Poems* (New York: Norton, 1986), 75.

36. In the book he devotes to the genesis of the 1860 edition of *Leaves*, Fredson Bowers prints the July 20, 1857 letter Whitman sent to an unknown correspondent saying that, having a hundred poems ready ("Beginners" was the 49th) he considered publishing a third and "*true Leaves of Grass*," with "an aspect of completeness." Bowers, ed., *Whitman's Manuscripts: Leaves of Grass (1860), A Parallel Text* (Chicago: University of Chicago Press, 1955, Web), xxxv–xxxvi. In a notebook entry of June 1857, however, Whitman reveals that rather than simply adding more poems, he plans the "Great Construction of a New Bible," composed of "three hundred and sixty-five" poems, which would be his main "life work." Walt Whitman, *Notebooks and Unpublished Prose Manuscripts*, vol. 1, ed. Edward F. Grier (New York: New York University Press, 1984), 353. For an articulate and comprehensive study of Whitman and politics, see Erkkila's *Whitman the Political Poet* (New York: Oxford University Press, 1989).

37. Kenneth M. Price, "Love, War, and Revision in Whitman's Blue Book," *Huntington Library Quarterly* 73, no. 4 (2010): 679.

38. Bowers, *Whitman's Manuscripts*, 7; my emphasis.

39. Walt Whitman, *Blue Book Copy of Leaves of Grass*. (Whitman's annotated copy of the 1860 edition, Rare Book Division, New York Public Library, 12. Digitized version: http://digitalcollections.nypl.org/items/510d47db-c76d-a3d9-e040-e00a18064a99.)

40. See chapter 4 in Ed Folsom and Kenneth M. Price, eds., *Re-Scripting Walt Whitman: An Introduction to his Life and Work* (Malden, MA: Blackwell, 2005); also available in the *WWA*.

41. All quotations are from Bowers, *Whitman's Manuscripts*, xxxii and xxx.

42. Wolosky, "Being in the Body," 135; Ralph Waldo Emerson, *Emerson's Essays*, "Introduction" by Sherman Paul (London: Dent, 1971), 328.

43. Levi's Go Forth commercials commodify Whitman's "O Pioneers" and "America," using them to sell jeans. "Levi's—OPioneers! (Go Forth) Commercial," YouTube video, 1:02, posted by "Homotography," July 5, 2009, https://www.youtube.com/watch?v=HG8tqEUTlvs.

44. In the aftermath of the fall of the Berlin Wall, Francis Fukuyama published an article entitled "The End of History?" (*The National Interest* 16 [Summer 1989]: 3–18, later expanded in the book *The End of History and the Last Man* [1992]) where he proclaimed that the victory of capitalist liberal democracy as a system of government would bring about the end of history in the Hegelian sense, and that it was time to shape the world in the image of U.S. democracy. For a critique of his theory, see chapter 1 of Charles A. Kupchan, *The End of the American Era: U.S. Foreign Policy and the Geopolitics of the Twenty-First Century* (New York: Knopf, 2002); Robert D. Kaplan, *The Revenge of Geography: What the Map Tells Us about Coming Conflicts and the Battle against Fate* (New York: Random House, 2012), particularly p. 4; and Fukuyama's own *The End of History and the Last Man* (New York: Free, 1992).

45. There is a wide debate over Dickinson's political and social stance. See in particular Betsy Erkkila, "Dickinson and the Art of Politics," in *A Historical Guide to Emily Dickinson*, ed. Vivian R. Pollak (Oxford: Oxford University Press, 2004), 133–74; Alfred Habegger, *My Wars Are Laid Away in Books: The Life of Emily Dickinson* (New York: Morn Library, 2002), 504ff.; and Crumbley who, closer to Rich's position, maintains that "for Dickinson, resistance to the status quo is crucial to the emergence of democratic sovereignity" (*Winds of Will*, 81).

46. On the sense effect of paradox, see the brief definition given by Gilles Deleuze in *Logique du sens* (Paris: Les Éditions de Minuit, 1969); Deleuze, *The Logic of Sense*, trans. Mark Lester with Charles Stivale, ed. Constantin V. Boundas (London: Athlone, 1990), 12, and in the chapter on paradox.

47. "The expression of the American poet is to be transcendent and new . . . indirect and not direct or descriptive" (*WPP* 8).

48. On social linguistic consciousness and conflict, see chapter 1 of Valentin Nikolaevich Volosinov, *Marxism and the Philosophy of Language* (1929), trans. Ladislav Matejka and I. R. Titunik (New York: Seminar, 1973).

49. See Rich's introduction to Jordan's *Directed by Desire: The Collected Poems of June Jordan*, "Foreword" by Adrienne Rich (Port Townsend, WA: Copper Canyon, 2005); and Marina Camboni, "What the Times Require: American Poetry at the Turn of the Twenty-First Century," *RSA Journal* 23 (2012): 27–55.

50. See the Exerga in Morrison's *Home* (New York: Knopf, 2012).

Index

Melville, Herman, 55, 184
Merleau-Ponty, Maurice, 87–88, 90, 93, 95, 109
Milner, Claude, 210
Mitchell, Domhnall, 54, 270n24
Morrison, Toni, 223
Mount Holyoke Female Seminary, 75, 152–53
Muir, John, 113, 117–18, 125–27

naming, 27–45, lexicography, 27. *See also* language
nature, 31, 33, 37–38, 58, 180; ecology, 111–28; ethics, 113, 123, 140; evolution, 64, 69, 72, 75, 78, 88; plant and animal migration, 116–20, 124. *See also* Darwin
Nietzsche, Friedrich, 180, 211, 215
Niles, Thomas, 15–16, 18, 157, 231n16. *See also* Roberts Brothers

Osgood, James, 14–15
Ostriker, Alicia, 57
Otto, Rudolf, 66, 73, 77

Perros, Georges, 187, 204
phenomenology, 52–55, 66–67, 85–110. *See also* Husserl, Edmund; Merleau-Ponty, Maurice
Phoenix, John, 146–47
Plato, 62, 86, 221
poetic form; in Dickinson's poetry, 22–23, 34–36, 38, 43, 45–46, 54, 64, 109; meter, 31, 36–37, 161; poetic address, 51, 69–70, 157; in Whitman's poetry, 36–40, 43, 45–46, 161
politics, 68, 118–19, 121, 125, 207, 220–21; Democratic Party, 151, 153; gender, 13, 157, 173, 183–84, 210; humor and, 136–37, 147; Republican Party, 157, 165; U.S. expansionist, 48–49, 113, 128, 152–53, 220; Whig party, 151–53. *See*

also Civil War; Dickinson, politics of; feminism; Whitman, politics of
pronouns, indefinite, 33–34, 38, 43, 188–205, 215

Real, the, 29, 31–38, 40–43, 45–46. *See also* reality
reality, 29, 65, 83, 85–110, 167–68, 207, 218, 237n11. *See also* the Real
religion, 65–82, 104, 154, 164, 179–80, 211, 221; American civil, 50; Congregationalism, 75–76, 154; immortality, 168–69; Protestantism, 48, 50, 59, 75–76, 88, 154; Quakerism, 67–70, 82. *See also* Bible, the; God/YHWH
Rich, Adrienne, 10, 183–85, 207–23; "Beginners," 207–09, 216, 220–21, 223; "Vesuvius at Home," 184–85, 208, 212–13, 215
Richards, Eliza, 52
Ricoeur, Paul, 133
Ritter, Joshua R., 133–34
Roberts Brothers, 14–16, 19, 25, 157, 231n16. *See also* Niles, Thomas
Romanticism, 36, 86, 213, 219; sublime, 79
Rukeyser, Muriel, 215, 221, 223

Salska, Agnieszka, 83, 204
sexuality, 150, 153–54, 163, 176; homosexuality, 9, 63, 67, 150–51, 158–62, 181–83
Slatoff, Walter J., 99
slavery, 57–60, 152–53, 155–56, 165–66, 216, 220; abolition, 58, 152–53, 155–57, 166. *See also* Civil War
Smith, Martha Nell, 216. *See also* Juhasz
Solomon, William, 130
Springfield Daily Republican, 19, 132, 157
Stein, Gertrude, 202
Stevens, Wallace, 198

The Iowa Whitman Series

The Afterlives of Specimens: Science, Mourning, and Whitman's Civil War,
by Lindsay Tuggle

*Conserving Walt Whitman's Fame: Selections from Horace Traubel's
"Conservator," 1890–1919*, edited by Gary Schmidgall

Democratic Vistas: The Original Edition in Facsimile,
by Walt Whitman, edited by Ed Folsom

*Intimate with Walt: Selections from Whitman's Conversations with Horace
Traubel, 1888–1892*, edited by Gary Schmidgall

Leaves of Grass, 1860: The 150th Anniversary Edition,
by Walt Whitman, edited by Jason Stacy

Life and Adventures of Jack Engle: An Auto-Biography,
by Walt Whitman, introduction by Zachary Turpin

A Place for Humility: Whitman, Dickinson, and the Natural World,
by Christine Gerhardt

The Pragmatic Whitman: Reimagining American Democracy,
by Stephen John Mack

Song of Myself: With a Complete Commentary, by Walt Whitman,
introduction and commentary by Ed Folsom and Christopher Merrill

Supplement to "Walt Whitman: A Descriptive Bibliography,"
by Joel Myerson

Transatlantic Connections: Whitman U.S., Whitman U.K.,
by M. Wynn Thomas